Mixed Martial Arts and the Quest for Legitimacy

# Mixed Martial Arts and the Quest for Legitimacy

*The Sport vs. Spectacle Divide*

MARK S. WILLIAMS

McFarland & Company, Inc., Publishers
*Jefferson, North Carolina*

LIBRARY OF CONGRESS CATALOGUING-IN-PUBLICATION DATA

Names: Williams, Mark S., 1981– author.
Title: Mixed martial arts and the quest for legitimacy : the sport vs. spectacle divide / Mark S. Williams.
Description: Jefferson : McFarland & Company, Inc., Publishers, 2018 | Includes bibliographical references and index.
Identifiers: LCCN 2018009176 | ISBN 9781476671291 (softcover : acid free paper) ∞
Subjects: LCSH: Mixed martial arts—History. | Mixed martial arts—Social aspects.
Classification: LCC GV1102.7.M59 W583 2018 | DDC 796.815—dc23
LC record available at https://lccn.loc.gov/2018009176

BRITISH LIBRARY CATALOGUING DATA ARE AVAILABLE

ISBN (print) 978-1-4766-7129-1
ISBN (ebook) 978-1-4766-3055-7

© 2018 Mark S. Williams. All rights reserved

*No part of this book may be reproduced or transmitted in any form or by any means, electronic or mechanical, including photocopying or recording, or by any information storage and retrieval system, without permission in writing from the publisher.*

Front cover images © 2018 iStock

Printed in the United States of America

*McFarland & Company, Inc., Publishers*
  *Box 611, Jefferson, North Carolina 28640*
  *www.mcfarlandpub.com*

# Table of Contents

*Preface* 1

1. The Aspirations of MMA: Sport and Spectacle 11
2. National Pride and Prejudice 33
3. The Rise and Fall of TRT 55
4. The Spectacle of Violence 73
5. Feminization, Fighting for Recognition and Octagon "Girls": Spectacle and Patriarchy 93
6. The Needle and the Locker Room Bonus 114
7. "There is no other guy" 133
8. The Epitome of MMA: The Sport and the Spectacle of Conor McGregor 149

*Conclusion* 182
*Chapter Notes* 187
*Bibliography* 190
*Index* 193

# Preface

When U.S. Senator John McCain labeled mixed martial arts (MMA) as "human cockfighting" in the mid–1990s, he attached a label that has since haunted the aspirations of MMA to achieve mainstream acceptance as a legitimate sport. This idea of MMA as human cockfighting has persisted in the imaginations of many, many people, and was even indirectly invoked at the 2017 Academy Awards show.

The cockfighting label is a remnant from a different era in the history of a spectacle that had branded itself alternatively as "no-holds-barred" fighting and "ultimate fighting." Groin shots, hair pulling, kicking the head of a downed opponent, head butts—all these tactics were once legal. The only two attacks that were banned from the contests of the early years were eye gouging and biting. Calling it "human cockfighting" was semi-rhetorical when John McCain said it two decades ago, but the characterization was not entirely facetious.

Today, bouts are contested between consenting adults who receive financial compensation, potentially quite lucrative for a select handful. Contestants are certainly not abused cocks with hot pepper jammed into their anuses to make them feisty. Another difference pertains to the lethality of cockfighting, which is accentuated by the attachment of spurs to the legs of cocks. MMA only allows for unarmed conflict, though the introduction of hand-wraps with 4-ounce gloves was originally mandated to protect fists, not faces and brains, and opened competition up for much more forceful blows. Most importantly, MMA today, unlike cockfighting, dreads the prospect of in-competition death. The UFC has not yet experienced a death in the octagon, or in the direct aftermath of a contest, but other smaller organizations certainly have, or come very close, such as in Bellator in 2016 at the end of a bout contested by two YouTube brawlers well past their athletic primes. While the possibility of an in-cage fatality

# Preface

likely kept Zuffa management awake at night during their ownership of the UFC between 2001 and 2016, the early days of the UFC were much different. Long before Zuffa purchased the brand and vaulted it into the mainstream, the UFC marketed itself as a place where "anything" could happen, not so subtly promoting the possibility of an in-cage death.

MMA is not cockfighting. It has evolved beyond its gruesome freakshow early years into a modern and sophisticated sport, dominated by highly trained technicians of grappling and striking. Yet there persists a powerful resonance between cage-fighting and cockfighting in the minds of many in society, one that serves to limit its appeal to the public and restricts its acceptance.

Meryl Streep's Oscar speech from early 2017 is only the most recent public condemnation of MMA. After surveying the theatre to give a selectively multinational composite portrayal of Hollywood, Streep breathlessly warned that if America were to "kick" out the "outsiders and foreigners ... you will have nothing left to watch but football and mixed-martial arts." To dig the knife in a bit further, Streep admonished the choir she was preaching to that mixed-martial arts is "not the arts."

Meryl Streep was practicing her right to political expression as an American, and furthermore I sympathize with her political views. America is once again caught in a polarizing era, and I share her concerns regarding the threat to openness and inclusivity the republic is facing. I cringe when I hear my own Canadian politicians, such as Kellie Leitch, play the demagogue in Donald Trump-inspired orations of racially based populism.

While Streep's speech elicited rancorous applause from the millionaire plutocrats of the film industry, half of the MMA community rolled its collective eyes. Once again, MMA is derided on spurious grounds. If Streep ever bothers to descend from her gated community to watch an MMA event with the "common people," possibly even to eat some nachos with friends who double-dip into the salsa, and to wash down the taste of other people's fingers with the best of the worst of American swill, she would likely be struck by how many "outsiders and foreigners" are to be found on your average UFC card, which must be at least as diverse as "#OscarsSoWhite."

Even the promotion of fighters and cards calls attention to the similarities that exist between MMA and the arts. I challenge Meryl Streep to watch a Conor McGregor press conference and deny the artistry involved.

*Preface*

Though one-half of the MMA community rolled its eyes, the other half of the MMA community exuberantly widened its eyes to Streep's comments. Rather than perceiving a denunciation of their sport, Streep had elevated MMA to the lofty status of American football! For a moment, and wholly unintentionally, Streep made MMA fans feel as if they had made it. Not only does Meryl Streep of all people know that MMA exists, but she associated it with football!

MMA is not cockfighting, but there are perhaps parallels between the two. There might even be parallels between cockfighting and Streep's beloved arts, if you look closely enough. The most thoughtful commentary on the cockfight, "Deep Play: Notes on the Balinese Cockfight," from the anthropologist Clifford Geertz's *The Interpretation of Cultures*, a canonical work on ethnography, provides a startling point of departure for reflecting on cage-fighting. It is startling because of how closely the themes explored by Geertz are reflected in MMA today.

Based on his 1950s field notes from visiting Bali, a small island in the Republic of Indonesia only 3.5 kilometers east of Java but strikingly different culturally and politically, Geertz attempted not to interpret the salience of cockfighting to the Balinese, but to understand how the Balinese themselves interpret the social significance of the cockfight. His commentary on gender, inter-village conflict, status, and money evoked many of the contemporary themes that we find in cage-fighting. MMA, like cockfighting, is a sport of masculine virtues, of nationalistic antagonisms, a narrative on evil and the nature of man, and of course, cockfighting and MMA are both intimately connected to gambling. MMA exists in a state of tension between spectacle and sport, and like the cockfight, it is violence as entertainment, but it represents a violence that is not only entertaining, but for many in society, like John McCain and Meryl Streep, quite horrifying.

Geertz was both captivated and horrified by the barbarism of the cockfight, on what makes it so, in his words, "disquietful."[1]

> The reason it is disquietful is not that it has material effects (it has some, but they are minor); the reason that it is disquietful is that, joining pride to selfhood, selfhood to cocks, and cocks to destruction, it brings to imaginative realization a dimension of Balinese experience well-obscured from view. The transfer of a sense of gravity into what is in itself a rather blank and unvarious spectacle, a commotion of beating wings and throbbing legs, is effected by interpreting it as expressive of something unsettling in the way its authors and audience live, or, even more ominously, what they are.

# Preface

He wondered if "the slaughter in the cock ring is not a depiction of how things literally are among men, but, what is almost worse, of how, from a particular angle, they imaginatively are."[2] Perhaps the most "disquietful" dimension of cage-fighting is what it says about our society, and what exists in the realm of our imaginations. It is a sport where violence is not simply a means to an end, such as stopping a touchdown by the opposing team, or preventing the other team from shooting a puck into a net, but where violence is the purpose of the competition. Forcing a tapout, winning a judges' decision, or bludgeoning an opponent into a state of near unconsciousness, or even well past such a state, is the point of it all.

Cage-fighting is so controversial, so disquietful, so *political*, because of what its popularity might be revealing about ourselves and what we imagine ourselves fundamentally to be. To many in society, the octagons, circles, and rings of MMA present expressions of the dimensions of ourselves that are incompatible with civilization. It is disquietful because it may represent what we fear exists in a Hobbesian state of nature, a prehistoric phase in human history that is pre-political, before hierarchical authority and before society, and likely a realm that never existed. The cockfight was disquietful to the Balinese, according to Geertz, because it represented an animal spirit of man, and the base instincts that must be repressed for civilization to flourish. Perhaps, MMA might represent those same fears, of man stripped of civilization, as another beast struggling to survive in a natural state. MMA might represent our fears, our enmities, and our hatreds. The egoism of man and his cruelty in a state of nature.

The most significant obstacle for the UFC, as the largest organization in the sport by far and the one most responsible for launching it into the mainstream, is not the literal violence in the octagon, but how the sport is imagined by society. This is the dilemma of the sport; it is neither wholly MMA nor is it wholly ultimate fighting. It is pulled by these two opposing poles. Ultimate fighting, the promise of extreme violence for the sole purpose of entertainment where winning is not as relevant as "putting on a show," and "hyping a fight" is valued over personal humility and respect for opponents, will foster a public imagination where the sport will forever be likened as "human cockfighting," and distinctly not the arts. Building the sport as MMA, of self-disciplined athletes, competing for the purposes of achieving an honorable victory, will be the most important device for extricating human cockfighting from the public imagination, and abolishing

## Preface

the social meaning of MMA that makes it, much like the cockfight, so disquietful. However, I have my doubts that many will ever view it as one of the arts.

Mixed Martial Arts, or MMA, is often cited as the fastest-growing sport in the world. The UFC has planted itself amongst the mainstream sports organizations of North America, having completed a transition from Spike TV to the Fox-owned channels, and even airing high-profile cards on the Fox flagship channel itself, much like the NFL. The sale of the UFC, from Zuffa to WME-IMG, for approximately $4 billion in 2016, represents the largest financial transaction in the history of professional sports in North America. However, this presence of MMA on network television has not been accompanied by a proportionate presence of MMA on the shelves of major bookstores. There are a few history books that chronicle the early years of MMA, such as Clyde Gentry's *No Holds Barred*, and Jonathan Snowden's *Total MMA: Inside Ultimate Fighting*. These books are indispensable for people wanting to learn more about the history of the sport, especially for the sport during the 1990s, but are light on providing a more political analysis of the tensions that are defining it today. A handful of former UFC champions have had their autobiography ghostwritten, such as Georges St-Pierre's *The Way of the Fight*, B.J. Penn's *Why I Fight*, Chuck Liddell's *Iceman: My Fighting Life*, Ronda Rousey's *My Fight/Your Fight*, and a slew of others. The extent to which any of these autobiographies delve into the controversial politics of MMA is generally quite limited. These books are primarily written by men (and one important woman) who have become fantastically wealthy while fighting for the UFC and are reluctant to question the prevailing norms of the sport. The only one that deliberately drifts into challenging the politics of the sport is B.J. Penn's. Another group of books on the market are those that try to understand the psychology of fighters. Sam Sheridan has written a couple of excellent books on this subject, such as *The Fighter's Mind* and *A Fighter's Heart*.

The present work is not intended to serve as a call to ban MMA, nor do I accept some of the naïve norms that the UFC have been pushing regarding the "safeness" of the sport. The point of this book is to argue that the spectacle of ultimate fighting undermines MMA as a legitimate sport. There is tension between MMA and ultimate fighting that is pulling it in two different directions. MMA represents a pull toward sport, whereas ultimate fighting represents the pull toward spectacle. The normative

## Preface

argument of the book is that MMA will never truly emerge as a legitimate mainstream sport if the spectacle of ultimate fighting is dominant.

The rise of MMA to mainstream sports has not been fully realized, as it continues to be hindered by the spectacle of ultimate fighting that undermines the martial virtues of MMA. The characteristics that define martial arts—such as discipline, humility, and respect—are often compromised by the spectacle that characterizes ultimate fighting. Rather than expressing humility, fighters are often characterized by a preening vanity. Instead of demonstrating respect, many of the most financially successful fighters in the UFC hype a fight by hurling personal attacks against their opponents, such as by questioning their sexuality or making racist attacks against entire groups of people. It is a spectacle where unconscious fighters are subjected to extra wallops to the head from an opponent who seems less like a professional athlete, let alone a martial artist, and more of an undisciplined brawler who is barely able to control his actions, speaking to Clifford Geertz's comments on what makes the violence of the cockfight so disquietful.

When I first revealed to my colleagues in academia that I was writing a collection of reflections on the politics relating to MMA, their response typically struck me as the meeting ground of bemusement, incredulity, and a barely restrained sense of disgust. "Why would you write a book about cage-fighting? I don't think that the kind of person who watches fights reads many books a year," was but one notable reaction. Perhaps for now, the stereotypical MMA fan is James Ladner, a shirtless man in the crowd at UFC 15 back in 1997. While the name is unfamiliar to most people, the gif of him is forever a part of MMA culture. With "UFC" painted in green across his forehead, and "JUST BLEED" in white across his chest, Ladner flexed for the camera with as much gusto as he could muster, sporting what looked to be a grimace of anguish as another man behind him leaned into the camera while taking a toke off a joint. Ladner became the archetypal face in the crowd of the UFC and its fan-base. A young male, bursting with energy and fanaticism, desperate for a blood sacrifice to the Just Bleed gods of violence, and possibly drunk.[3]

Crowd shots at UFC events today offer continuity with the past. As the camera pans across the arena, we see a seething mass of humanity, flexing and shouting incoherently into the camera. We hear the cat-calls to the sexy women who are there to remind you which round is about to start. You might even see someone with JUST BLEED ironically scrawled

## Preface

across his torso, as UFC fighter Tom Lawlor did for one of his memorable weigh-ins. It is an energy, born out of the anticipation of the spilling of blood, that ripples in the arenas and casinos where events are held, as well as in the bars, and possibly even in the hearts, of some of those watching at home. It is a sport that celebrates greatness, but one that also revels in violence.

I was at a bar in Hamilton, Ontario, on the 6th of July when Chris Weidman knocked out long-time middleweight champion, and one of the young sport's debatable GOAT (Greatest of All Time) frontrunners, Anderson "The Spider" Silva. The bar I was in seemed to erupt with a spiteful exuberance when Weidman's left hook separated Silva from consciousness. I would like to believe that the jubilation of the crowd must have been partly created by the perception that Silva's taunting of Weidman went too far. Silva often employed the dangerous tactic of drawing a fighter into his counter-striking, dropping his hands, standing against the fence, waiving his opponent into a foolhardy exchange, relying on a once-iron chin and the reflexes of an apex predator. On that fateful night against Weidman, Silva instead crossed into some rather unsportsmanlike conduct, unbecoming of his iconic status. Hamiltonians, denizens of a blue-collar, working-class city still known as "steel-city," regardless of how dead the steel industry is in North America, are not typically the kind of people who root for immodest displays of ostentation by millionaires.

However, there are too many other examples of audience indignation in the octagons of the UFC. Another notable example occurred during the post-fight interview after the rematch of Cain Velasquez and Junior dos Santos in December of 2012. Following a five round beat-down where dos Santos lost his heavyweight championship to a merciless and unrelenting Velasquez, dos Santos, who had left everything he had in the cage, perhaps even leaving some years of his life in there too, was viciously booed by the crowd. The Brazilian former champion, battered, but still lucid enough to respond in English, his second language, asked the crowd why they were booing him. Fighting in Vegas, the reason for the booing was probably related to gambling. The very people who wanted dos Santos to win were booing him because he lost them money.

The fan base of MMA has, to an extent, evolved along with the sport, and is as complex and diverse as the feelings generated from watching the sport itself. A large number of websites sporting names like "Sherdog," "MMA Fighting," "Bloody Elbow," and "MMA Junkie" have proliferated, featuring

## Preface

highly literate and thoughtful journalists who sincerely want the best for this sport they cover, such as Ben Folkes, Luke Thomas, Chuck Mindenhall, Dave Doyle, Ben Popper, John Tucker, and many others. The online forums are outlets for fan and public expression. These places are often petty, polarized, and abusive places, but also full of reflective people who genuinely seem to care about the legitimacy of a sport they love, but who know all too well the skepticism in mainstream society regarding the limits of MMA as a mainstream contact sport like football or hockey.

Through the UFC, MMA has entered into the global media landscape and the *milieu* of entertainment options competing for the public's attention. Is it sport or spectacle? It is both of these things. Tell me which sport on network television that is packaged for commodification is not spectacle on some levels? Furthermore, tell me which movies and television shows are not also partially spectacle. The relative youthfulness of MMA means that it is evolving quite rapidly. Public discourse becomes that much more meaningful in such an environment, that much more impactful, as the sport has not crystallized to the extent that others, such as baseball, basketball, soccer (apologies to my European reader!), and football have. It is a sport that is *becoming*, and so it is inherently political, as opinions and perspectives will oppose each other, and seek to project their vision of what MMA should look like. The direction of the sport, its aesthetics and rules, are being pushed and shoved by these multiple tensions and controversies, with an industry worth billions at stake.

We are embarking on what could possibly be a new era for MMA in 2016 with Zuffa's sale of the UFC to WME-IMG (William Morris Endeavor–International Management Group) for approximately $4 billion. The sale of the UFC to a massive talent agency involved in sports as diverse as football and tennis, along with, as Meryl Streep should be reminded, notable stakes in film and television, may prove to catapult the UFC, and by default, MMA, into the mainstream like never before. Zuffa has brought the UFC to venues beyond the U.S., such as Canada, Brazil, the UK, Japan, and even to Macau, but the joint ventures of WME-IMG augur a global reach for the UFC beyond even what Zuffa accomplished, such as hosting events in mainland China as the proportion of Chinese ascending into the middle class continues to grow at an incredible rate.

However, one should not assume that the sale of the UFC to WME-IMG will inevitably boost the credibility of the sport. The new owners, after spending an unfathomable amount of capital on the UFC, are likely having to service annual debt payments of around $100 million. This crushing debt load, largely due to the WME-IMG merger itself, places discernable pressure on the conglomerate to maximize profitability and to squeeze out a high rate of return on their investments. The question is whether this will be attempted through a prudent and long-term strategy that helps the UFC gain recognition and legitimacy from mainstream society, or if short-term gains will determine promotional efforts. The new owners must resist the men in black who would pressure the company simply to pander to the lowest common denominator. WME-IMG must be wary of trumpeting the spectacle, the aggression, and the promotion of a package that will forever remain "disquietful" to society. Such an approach will undermine the long-term potential of the sport, and instead reify MMA as a throwback to a pre-social state of nature, and that of a cultural wasteland. The unwillingness of the new owners of the UFC to effectively manage the tension between sport and spectacle of MMA will prevent the breakthrough into the mainstream that the new owners envision, keeping it restricted to a niche market of angry young men and gamblers.

    I thank my brother, Paul Williams, a doctoral candidate in interdisciplinary humanities at Brock University, who influenced the manuscript. When I first mentioned to him back in 2005 that I had returned to watching MMA again, after a hiatus from the sport, he was truly appalled, looking at me like I just told him I was gambling on dog fighting or heading off for a sex tourism trip to Southeast Asia. After reluctantly giving it a shot himself, he came to appreciate why I had taken an interest in the sport, and I think he quickly came to surpass my knowledge of the history of the sport and its fighters. I would also like to thank Sohaib Khan, and his brother Zohaib, for our countless hours spent at the bar watching pay-per-views together, being entertained by this sport, as well as sometimes disgusted, embarrassed, and often bored. I must also thank Linda Brooymans, who did more than endure stories about fighting, and watching broadcasts on TV, but also offered profound insight based on her experiences teaching a course on violence at McMaster University while I was working on this project. I'd like to thank both the Political Studies department and the Global Studies department at Vancouver Island University for providing me with the opportunity to discuss politics each week with our wonderful students, and for providing me with the academic freedom to take a brief departure from the study of the international political economy

## Preface

to allow me to offer my thoughts on the dynamics shaping the fastest-growing sport in the world.

Quotes found within, if not accompanied by a citation, come from press conferences and conference calls, promotional events or tours, interviews conducted for television or over video online, as well as from social media posting on Facebook or Twitter. Additional unattributed quotes are from actual MMA broadcasts, made by either commentators, corners, or the fighters themselves. Transcription of video and audio interviews and commentaries was conducted by the author and any errors in the transcription process are the responsibility of the author.

# 1

# The Aspirations of MMA
## *Sport and Spectacle*

Sport has that rare ability to transcend its individual parts and generate social meanings for people. Sport is not just a closed system, directed by its rules, organization, and action, but one that is capable of powerfully interacting with society. Sport is shaped by our values, for good and for ill, but it even has the ability to influence social values and norms. Baseball, for instance, has its legions of fans, eager to wax poetically on the symbolism of the game.[1] How it captures the spirit of America, of a pastoral society in open green fields, the impossibility of the game without community, and the reverential reflections on pioneers like Jackie Robinson, who did not simply change the sport of baseball for the better, but also helped a society to confront the social and political injustices that permeated the U.S.

Hockey resonates in much the same way in Canada as baseball does for Americans. In 2004, the CBC (Canadian Broadcasting Corporation) polled Canadians on the "Greatest Canadian." The top ten included one former NHL player, Wayne Gretzky, a soft-spoken gentleman who completely obliterated the previous points records of the league, and one controversial NHL commentator and former coach, Don Cherry. The 1972 Summit Series against the Soviet Union endures in the Canadian consciousness as a defining event, not just in hockey history but in Canadian national history, with Paul Henderson's goal a collective act of redemption, proving to the world, but most importantly to themselves, that Canada's professional hockey players could compete at the international level with the best that a Cold War superpower could put on the ice. Canadians wouldn't be able to stop Soviet advances on West Berlin, but they sure could beat them man-to-man on the ice.

## Mixed Martial Arts and the Quest for Legitimacy

During the 2014 Olympic Games in Sochi, the women's gold medal game between Canada and the U.S. was headed into overtime just as a class I was teaching at Vancouver Island University, *Identities and Communities: An Introduction to Politics*, was getting started. I started playing hockey when I was four years old and continued to do so until I was 18. During the fall, winter, and early spring, I would have practice between two and five times a week, and play in games two or three times a week, a lot more often than that when we were playing in a tournament. Hockey even dominated many of my summer vacations, as the hot and humid weather of the Great Lakes brought with it the grueling all-day hockey camps. I played on the high school varsity team in my hockey-obsessed city, Hamilton, a city whose ambitions to host a NHL team have been forever thwarted by the Toronto Maple Leafs, terrified of how a second hockey team in the region might impact their ability to charge outrageous prices for tickets to one of the worst teams in the league. Hockey was this enormous presence in my life, but I have a complicated relationship to hockey, which I will explain in other places in the book. However, as in many classrooms around the country, I turned on the game at the start of the class to watch the OT drama, celebrating Marie-Philip Poulin, a new addition to the Canadian athletic pantheon, who scored both the goal to tie the game and then the OT winner. After the game concluded, we discussed the ways in which sport is given meaning in society, and the reasons behind hockey's powerful resonance in Canadian identity.

The transcendence of sport beyond its immediate circumstances to a place in the social consciousness is facilitated by an identification with the game and its participants. Putting a son or daughter into ice hockey is expensive, even in countries that experience colder winters, such as Canada. I'm sure that my middle-class parents must have made sacrifices to their plans to pay for my brother and me to play hockey every year. But even these formidable class restraints are shattered in Canadian streets through neighborhood participation in road hockey. The identities of Sydney Crosby, Jonathan Toews, Hayley Wickenheiser, and P. K. Subban are assumed by kids with sticks and a tennis ball in the street, just as the names of Wayne Gretzky, Mario Lemieux, Gordie Howe, and Bobby Orr were long before them. Sport, a children's game played by adults, remains linked to one's own childhood, for better or for worse, and is revisited through our children and grandchildren.

It is not only this identification with the past that gives sports its

## 1. The Aspirations of MMA

social significance. It is also something primal and intuitive. Sport is conflict. It is competition with others and competition with yourself. It is a realm where excellence is a product of self-improvement, which demands discipline and dedication. Kick a ball between three posts. Throw a ball into a hoop. Whack a puck into a net. Carry a ball across a field. It is this conflict that generates the drama of sport. It is sometimes a conflict of one against all, but it is also conflict that requires cooperation, where working together is the only hope for achieving victory. Even in sports where the competition is at an individual level, like tennis or boxing, success of that individual is dependent on having a strong support group of sparring partners, coaches, nutritionists, and genuine friends.

We can appreciate the beauty of sport and the way in which community can be strengthened by it, but we must not be naïve about it either. So-called "national pastimes," whether official or unofficial, like hockey, can be highly alienating for those who have no such bond with the game, either as a participant or as one who is not entertained by its drama. Most sports that are aired on major networks are played at the professional level by exceptionally wealthy athletes, living in enclosed communities, far removed from the societies that are on some level identifying with them. Athletes are all too often held up as "heroes" and "idols," especially to kids, only to have these virtuous facades unraveled when the whoring and blow-filled personal lives are exposed. Another reason to avoid being too naïve about the relationship between society and sport relates to the substantial level of physical violence in many professional sports, such as the NHL and NFL. Abuse and punishment are marketed as adding excitement to the product, dehumanizing those athletes at the wrong end of a highlight reel. And there are histories of racism and exclusion in all professional sports, not just in baseball. Of course, even the Olympic Games, which supposedly celebrate the unity of humanity and progressive social politics, providing states the opportunity to perform what Liam Stockdale refers to as a "virtuous identity," are plagued by cheating and corruption.[2]

Sport creates a drama that, for some, involves the highest of stakes, even though it is abstract. In "Deep Play: Notes on the Balinese Cockfight," Clifford Geertz provided a commentary that spoke not just to the cockfighting he was observing in Indonesia, but to all sport, and a commentary that is especially pertinent for MMA and maybe even Hollywood.[3]

> Like any art form—for that, finally, is what we are dealing with—the cockfight renders ordinary, everyday experience comprehensible by presenting it in terms of acts

## Mixed Martial Arts and the Quest for Legitimacy

and objects which have had their practical consequences removed and been reduced (or, if you prefer, raised) to the level of sheer appearances, where their meaning can be more powerfully articulated and more exactly perceived. The cockfight is "really real" only to the cocks—it does not kill anyone, castrate anyone, reduce anyone to animal status, alter the hierarchical relations among people, or refashion hierarchy; it does not even redistribute income in any significant way. What it does is what, for other peoples with other temperaments and other conventions, *Lear* and *Crime and Punishment* do; it catches up these themes—death, masculinity, rage, pride, loss, beneficence, chance—and, ordering them into an encompassing structure, presents them in such a way as to throw into relief a particular view of their essential nature.

Fans of MMA bristle at the comparison to cockfighting that has often been made by prominent politicians, such as John McCain's comparison in the 1990s, and I can only imagine the indignation that these comments would draw from Meryl Streep, but what Geertz is offering here does find expression in the sport. MMA and cockfighting are not the same, but Geertz is helping us to understand the grand importance that sport plays in the lives of so many. The conflict in the ballpark, on the gridiron, in arenas, and in the octagon is only really "real" to the athletes, coaches, teammates, and loved ones of the participants. However, it speaks to society, and society interacts with it. Fans of the sport are figuratively transfixed to the competitors, and their drama becomes our own, despite our passive relationship to it.

I grew up in Hamilton, Ontario, and my American and European readers may laugh, but the season of the CFL's (Canadian Football League) Ti-Cats represents a drama of sorts for me, even now that I live on the Pacific coast of the country (see, I told you that you would laugh). I also dislike the Leafs, as anyone from southern Ontario, but outside of the Greater Toronto Area, with a shred of self-respect should. I also have now come to identify with the Seattle Seahawks to an extent. I don't hold these attachments to sport at the same level as I do my work as a professor of Political Studies, nor do I enjoy sports more than reading a good book, or even playing a well-crafted video game, but sport represents something a great deal more important to me than a television show or a movie. Sport is live, it is unscripted, and it transcends itself, it enters into our imagination, and it interacts with our ethics, our morality, and our very *politics*.

The eminent Greg Jackson, trainer, corner-man, and the tactician *par excellence* of the sport, has often described the appeal of MMA as comparable

## 1. The Aspirations of MMA

to a morality play. Fans and curious audiences are drawn to the octagon to watch high drama unfold, but also to witness the victory of discipline and the personal triumph of the work-ethic. Spend some time following MMA and you will come to think of Greg Jackson as a pretty brilliant guy. I think that there is a lot of truth to Jackson's interpretation of the allure of MMA, and it also helps us to understand why Geertz thought that sport can be as meaningful to some as watching Shakespeare or reading translated Russian literature might be for others.

While MMA can be interpreted as a morality play for casual audiences, this metaphor starts to look less convincing the more we learn about the sport. Machiavelli, the Italian Renaissance thinker who is often described as founding modern Political Philosophy, argued that success in politics, as in life, is the result of both *virtù* as well as *fortuna*. *Virtù* represents your actions and the totality of the decisions you make. When Greg Jackson refers to MMA as a morality play, he is communicating this Machiavellian idea on the correlation between hard work and success, with a clear lesson to all of us. Success is dependent on *virtù*. Conversely, MMA, like all sport, is also shaped by *fortuna*, what Machiavelli has also described as the "bitch goddess of luck." The greatest politicians down to the most ordinary people living paycheck to paycheck understand the power of unmovable structures and the force of what former Secretary of Defense Donald Rumsfeld ominously described as "known unknowns" and "unknown unknowns" that threaten to undo the most carefully laid plans, and often decimating the more reckless plans, as Rumsfeld would know more than most. *Fortuna*, and luck, can be empowering, but it can also be crushing. Success is often dependent on one's ability, or *virtù*, to overcome *fortuna*, possibly even to shape it.

I'll boldly suggest that MMA is impacted more by *fortuna* more than most sports. As MMA promoters love to shout at us, anything can happen in four-ounce gloves. Unlike boxing, where fights will typically go to decision or end by TKO only in later rounds, a MMA fight can, and often will, end in seconds. The small gloves not only mean that fists have little surrounding cushioning, but also make it very difficult to retreat behind the gloves and fight defensively while in the pocket. Furthermore, the submission threat of elite grapplers has also been described as comparable to one-punch KO power, as MMA and jiu-jitsu coach John Danaher has noted.

Perhaps the presence of *fortuna* is another big reason why MMA represents such an attraction and garners so much fanfare. It is an unpredictable

## Mixed Martial Arts and the Quest for Legitimacy

sport. Sure, heavy favorites often win, but they still lose, sometimes spectacularly. However, the role of *fortuna* is what contributes to MMA being understood as a morality play. The *Book of Job*, one of the oldest books of the Old Testament, chronicles the continuous tragedies that befall a largely faultless man. Life, like MMA, isn't always fair, and it certainly isn't always moral. Perhaps this too is part of any morality play.

Machiavelli is not only often regarded as the founder of modern Political Philosophy, but to International Relations he is also a founder of political realism. *Virtù* does not necessarily mean virtue. If one can't be both feared and loved, as Machiavelli famously noted, it is better to be feared. Though Machiavelli occasionally expressed his contempt of leaders who are dishonest and lie, he also acknowledged how duplicity and conniving behavior might also be components of *virtù*. The concept of MMA as a morality play is also undermined due to the prevalence of performance enhancing drugs (PEDs), and the lingering questions of just how clean anyone really is. Can a sport that is as defined by steroids, synthetic testosterone, diuretics, estrogen-blockers, and more, to the extent to which MMA is, truly emerge as a legitimate sport to the mainstream? Or is it a spectacle, intended only for misanthropic, angry men, those worshiping at the "Just Bleed" altar of depravity whose cheers for violence speak of the egoistic bleakness that characterizes an imaginary state of nature?

What was your first experience watching MMA? Was it something monstrous? An expression of bloody violence and cruelty, compelling you to pontificate to those around you that we are experiencing the moral disintegration of civilization that always precedes political and economic collapse? Instead, maybe you witnessed a slick "submission" on the mat, as one man coaxed another to admit defeat and "tap-out" of a hold that you were trying to understand the mechanics of, well, you know, just in case. Alternatively, your first experience of watching MMA might have been something much more prosaic. Two fighters, circling, pawing each other, trying to gauge distance with leg kicks, warning the opponent back with feints and front kicks to the body. You might have instead watched something that resembled a low-level wrestling match. The fighters clinched together, leaning on each other to escape the cage, to get their opponent to the canvas and smother them in a dominating embrace. Maybe this left you thinking that MMA isn't just cage-fighting, or at least perhaps it is something with a degree of complexity. A sport, perhaps. Or maybe you just found it boring.

## 1. The Aspirations of MMA

Many North Americans first encountered MMA when *The Ultimate Fighter* (*TUF*) aired on Spike TV in 2005, which culminated in an epic fight waged between finalists Forrest Griffin and Stephan Bonnar. The fight was a technical brawl, endearing viewers with its display of heart, determination, and chin. In 2013, the fight earned Griffin and Bonnar entry to the entirely partial Ultimate Fighting Championship (UFC) Hall of Fame.

Your first encounter with cage-fighting might have been the debut of the UFC on Fox, when the sport once derided as human cockfighting entered into the big time, landing on the most-watched network in America. The stakes of this first fight were no less than the heavyweight championship title between Cain Velasquez and Junior dos Santos. Countless others must have first viewed MMA while surfing the internet to satisfy some pressing curiosity. A few might have first come across the Japanese organization "Pancrase" during the 1990s, a name inspired by the Olympic event of "Pankration" ("all powers, or strengths") that originated about 2,600 years ago. Some of you, like myself, might even have had their initiation into the world of cage-fighting in the early 1990s with the first of the UFC one-night, last-man-standing tournaments.

As a boy growing up in Hamilton, Ontario, I was a consumer of violence. I thought that fighting was morally wrong, and I never fought at school or on the street. In middle school, I threw one hard punch at another boy during recess, after the boy spat in my friend's face, and I regret it to this day. The only fights I ever got into were during hockey games, and I always hated it when a fight broke out, believing that fighting had no place in the game. My complicated feelings toward hockey are in a small way still shaped by the derision I felt regarding fighting in hockey. You were never sure when you would receive a sucker-punch to the head in front of the net, or a shot to the back of the head after a game was over, not to mention the many hooks with a stick to the groin, which I had received more times than I'd care to admit in polite conversation. Hockey fighting apologists will say that fighting is fine when there is consent between participants. This may be true of professional leagues and amateur ones involving players that are at least 18 years old, but do kids give consent the same way adults do? I am highly suspicious of such claims. I played hockey to *play hockey*, not to fight. So many kids, influenced by watching NHL games, by angry hockey moms and dads, and by each other, were looking for any opportunity to drop the gloves and pretend that this is how the adult world solves disputes.

## Mixed Martial Arts and the Quest for Legitimacy

Despite my distaste for fighting, I still consumed violence through my entertainment. I was part of the generation that came of age as the comic book industry boomed during the late 1980s and the early 1990s (before its bust for a decade), and I loved superhero comics. The once-sharp line that divided heroes from villains became a much finer one during the 1980s with books such as Alan Moore's *Watchmen* and Frank Miller's *The Dark Knight Returns*. Even established heroes, such as Wolverine, might, in a certain context, kill people. I suppose, as a 12-year-old, I accepted these moral ambiguities, only vaguely aware of the critique of violence in superhero comics being communicated in *Watchmen*.[4] It was pure entertainment for me, mythic stories, a rich world with an immense cast of colorfully dressed characters, an impossibly convoluted continuity, and kick-ass women fighting in bathing suits. It contained all the necessary ingredients to convince me to sink what allowance I could get from my working class family into the fantastical, often sexist, and consistently violent world of sequential artwork.

Video gaming was another hobby of my childhood that was increasingly captured by violence. It started off so innocently though. My favorite games on the Nintendo Entertainment System (NES) involved Italian plumbers jumping on the heads of "goombas" and "koopa troopas."[5] Looking for a change of games for the next generation of consoles, I was able to convince my parents to get my brother and me the Sega Genesis (I know, I should have gone SNES, but I wanted a change). Once again, these games were wondrously innocent (though fiendishly difficult), featuring a super-fast hedgehog destroying evil robots to protect a forest. While such games did little to feature violent behavior in its gameplay, the home-market industry began to experience some changes by the early-to-mid-1990s, when ports of arcade fighters arrived, such as Street Fighter II and, in particular, Mortal Kombat, with the latter game featuring an opportunity to actually *kill* a completely defenseless opponent at the menacing prompt of "Finish Him!"[6] The video game industry was undergoing a transformation at the time to a greater emphasis on violence, which I suppose seems almost quaint compared to the games that have been on the market for the last ten years.

As mentioned, I also played a lot of hockey growing up. For a time, an annual Christmas present I received was the latest installment of CBC commentator Don Cherry's *Rock-em, Sock-em Hockey*. The videos were a collection of highlights from the NHL's previous season, but the selling

## 1. The Aspirations of MMA

point was the violence. These videos featured an endless parade of crushing hits, with Cherry extolling the masculine virtues of the mostly Canadian players who were dishing out the punishment. The video climaxed with a couple of Cherry's favorite "enforcers" squaring off for some hockey fights. For a time at least, I loved the violence in these videos. I didn't know what to make of the fighting in the NHL as I had come to loathe its presence in my house league, and Cherry's right-wing Canadian nationalism mostly went over my head, but the hits, the hits were pure excitement. Of course, the physical toll taken on these men was never a part of the narrative.

In December 2016, Steve Downie, an NHL journeyman who has bounced between the NHL and AHL and is best known for his vicious hit on Dean McAmmond, went to Twitter to condemn *Rock-em, Sock-em Hockey*. Accompanying a gif of the hit, Downie tweeted, "That hit is what happens when you watch don cherry [sic] rock em sock em videos from age 5 to 18. Nothing good comes from those vids." He quickly followed that tweet with another, explaining, "I just did what I had to do to play. I still think about what I did to Dean Macomond [sic] and what I caused him to go through with his family." Referencing Don Cherry's constant presence on the CBC broadcast of *Hockey Night in Canada*, a more revered broadcast for many Canadians than the nightly news show *The National*, Downie tweeted, "But again, I did what don cherry [sic] said to do every Saturday night. Just fucking disgusted when I look back. Wish I never played."

This trinity of violence—comic books, video games, and hockey—constituted a big part of my patterns of consuming entertainment between the ages of seven and 12. This was approximately where my mind was when I ventured into the neighborhood video rental store[7] in early 1994. The VHS packaging of *The Ultimate Fighting Championship I: The Beginning*, boasted of a sport that was "Unedited! Uncensored! Unleashed!" The cartoon strongman straddling the globe as a colossus was enough to make me pick up the box to look it over. I didn't ask my dad to rent it for us the first time it caught my notice, or even the second time. Eventually, though, my curiosity got the better of me, and I brought it over to him and said I'd like to see this. He was a little unsure about how to respond, but, after a brief reservation, agreed.

I didn't know what to expect, but what I watched wasn't it. On some levels, I understood very well that the violence in the NHL I was watching

## Mixed Martial Arts and the Quest for Legitimacy

was very different from playing video games with names like "Streets of Rage," or reading a comic where Doomsday beat Superman to death. And yet, the violence in hockey was still not entirely real to me at the time. I knew that these were real people I was watching, but they were wrapped up in equipment and uniforms, with their bodies and their faces largely obscured. The physical punishment experienced by hits along the boards was lost as cameras switched, following the puck up the ice. The fights Cherry generally aired in *Rock-em, Sock-em Hockey* were evenly contested fights, leaving out the worst beatings from the season, unless the guy getting the beating was a despised "pest" or "instigator" of the NHL, when it became less a beating than a narrative of justice. As I sat before the TV, the UFC effectively shattered whatever illusions I had about the realities of violence in sport. Garbed in a gi, or little more than pajamas, or even what could have been a speedo, there was no mistaking the violence, the broken faces of beaten men, and the pain.

I think it was in the first fight of UFC I, when the Dutch karateka, Gerard Gourdeau, literally kicked the teeth out of the head of a sumo wrestler, Teila Tuli, that I became horrified. This was not the world of imaginary characters drawn on the printed page. This was what violence really looked like. Marvel's *X-Men* stories were metaphors for civil rights, protecting a world that hated and feared them. Sonic was trying to rescue small, cute woodland creatures from robots controlled by a deranged psychopath! At least in Street Fighter and Mortal Kombat, you had the sense that you were defeating evil in M. Bison and Shang Tsung. For my 12-year-old self, there was nothing to fight for in this tournament. The purpose of violence in the UFC was money, ego, and, at the time, disciplinary bragging rights. Even hockey was different. The point was to put the puck in the net of the other team. Body checks facilitate this objective but earn a team no points. In the UFC, violence was the goal, to force another person to quit, the objective. I didn't reveal to anyone what I thought, certainly not to my father, partly because I didn't want to reveal how traumatized I felt, but mostly because what I was feeling was too complex for me to express as a child.

The positive story line in the UFC I that I could identify with, and the silver lining for me, was the tournament winner, Royce Gracie. Here was an intense, yet unassuming young Brazilian, weighing a modest 175–180 lbs but taking on guys far bigger. In such a strange and unknown world, I searched for ways to make sense and relate to what I was watching.

## 1. The Aspirations of MMA

In some ways, Royce Gracie was a little like Bruce Lee to me, having watched *Enter the Dragon* a few weeks before that first UFC event. Lee epitomized the smaller man, being triumphant not because of size and physical advantages, but because of a dedication to his craft and a technical superiority. Gracie grabbed hold of his opponents, tripped them, and squeezed their throats closed. There was even something less violent about it than the searing images of disfigured faces, the casualties of bare-knuckle punches and soccer kicks. Bruce Lee was a symbol of grace, composure and a spirit of utilizing martial arts to subdue the aggressor.

Royce Gracie represented these virtues to an extent, but let's face it, for all the deferential praise heaped on him, the man is not and has never been Bruce Lee. Gracie was the kind of guy who wasn't above some vicious hair-pulling or setting up his trips with a wicked kick to the balls. In the championship fight of that first UFC one-night tournament, up against the hard-kicking Gordeau, Gracie caught Gordeau with a rear-naked choke, and instead of letting go of the choke after the tap-out, he held on, seemingly intent on separating Gordeau from consciousness. Only after the tentative referee, who seemed like he was afraid to intervene at all, finally remembered that he was probably the one person who could best prevent someone from being murdered in the cage, more forcefully tugged at Gracie's arms to break the choke.

There are even stories out of Brazil of how the Gracie Jiu-Jitsu practitioners would "invade" gyms, dojos, and academies. A Gracie invasion force would enter another gym and challenge the teachers and masters to combat, Gracie rules of course, which allowed the Gracie to wear their gi (to help them stick to their opponent better during grappling exchanges and even to use the gi to strangle their opponent), but denied advantages, such as hand-wraps for strikers, to their foes. By defeating the instructors in combat, the Gracies would humiliate the gym, driving away students who wanted to learn skills that are perceived to be better suited to street fighting, and shattering the confidence of the instructors. From these gym invasions, the Gracie name, and jiu-jitsu itself, would grow.

In some ways Royce Gracie *is* MMA, for better or worse. MMA is both martial arts, that ideal that technique and self-discipline triumphs over size and brute strength, and it is the spectacle of a well-placed kick to the balls in a tournament of questionable legitimacy that was largely organized by members of your own family.

To be fair to Royce Gracie, in his fight prior to the championship one

## Mixed Martial Arts and the Quest for Legitimacy

against Gordeau, he caught Ken Shamrock in the same choke. After forcefully tapping out, Shamrock acted like he hadn't just quit on the mat. This must have played in Gracie's mind when he refused to relinquish the choke against Gordeau. It is hard to tell, but the story is that Gordeau might have intentionally bit Gracie on the ear when he got caught in the jiu-jitsu black-belt's guard. Gordeau would go on to ever greater notoriety after illegally eye-gouging his opponent so badly in a Vale Tudo fight against Yuki Nakai that the Japanese fighter permanently lost vision in his eye, though he would submit Gordeau to win the fight. I didn't want to talk about what I had just watched in UFC I, and I was never going to ask my dad to rent another one of those horrifying videos again.

    I was only vaguely aware of the continued existence of the UFC, and the Japanese rival organization, Pride Fighting Championship (Pride FC, commonly known as Pride), throughout the rest of the 1990s and into the first four years of the twenty-first century. And then, the first season of *The Ultimate Fighter* (*TUF*) debuted. I was, like many, profoundly touched by the difficult lives of some of its contestants, such as Chris Leben, who confided his story of growing up without a father. I was also horrified at the level of inhumanity displayed by some of the contestants, such as Bobby Southworth, who derided Leben as a "fatherless bastard," as well as even Leben himself, who "spritzed" (if you don't know, don't ask) the pillow of the woefully inexperienced Canadian, Jason Thacker, whom he mercilessly bullied. Most of all, I was struck by how normal many of the fighters were, guys like Griffin and Bonnar, as well as Kenny Florian and Nate Quarry. I did not consider myself a fan of the show, but watching it on a weekly basis intrigued me enough to catch myself up with the sport. It didn't brush away the reservations I had as an adolescent, but as a graduate student in political science at the time, I felt much more capable of dealing with ethical complexity than a 12-year-old comic book fan who watched Don Cherry videos.

    I started looking up records, watching old matches online from the UFC and the soon-to-be-defunct Pride, trying to get myself caught up on the lineages of belts and careers. It was confusing, but also quite exciting. For me it was the drama of sport and the rise and fall of modern gladiators. It wasn't *Crime and Punishment* or *King Lear* to me, perhaps like cockfighting is to the Balinese in the eyes of Geertz, but it was still pretty exciting to learn about. Fighters like Mark Coleman, winner of the first UFC heavyweight championship title fight, who exited the UFC after suffering

## 1. The Aspirations of MMA

a head-kick KO loss to Pete Williams, but then went on to capture the 2000 Pride Grand Prix, an open-weight tournament that included notables like Royce Gracie, Kazushi Sakuraba, and Igor Vovchanchyn. Or B.J. Penn, not content to remain the lightweight (155-lb) champion of the UFC, but went up in weight to also take the welterweight title (170-lb) from another champion and legend in the sport, Matt Hughes. And of course, a soft-spoken Russian who fought at heavyweight even though he was likely capable of making light-heavyweight and went a decade without losing a single fight in a weight class where anyone can knock anyone else out.

For Dana White, the UFC's fiery president since 2001, the expansion of the UFC is easy to understand. Impossibly easy, even. As the UFC was banned in most states and denied a presence on U.S. PPVs during the mid to late 1990s, the organization appeared to be destined to remain an esoteric footnote in the annals of sport in North America. White saw a much different destiny. Managing Tito Ortiz and Chuck Liddell, two of the more recognizable fighters of the era, White convinced casino magnates Frank and Lorenzo Fertitta to purchase the floundering organization. White's justification for the investment, stated in a television interview, was based on the most parsimonious interpretation of sport ever given: Fighting is in our genes.

> I think we're going to be the biggest sport in the world. Bigger than the NFL. Bigger than soccer. Bigger than anybody. This thing crosses borders so well that, like, for instance, soccer's huge all over the world. It's never really become big here in the United States. NFL is huge here in the U.S. Isn't big anywhere else. I put two guys in an octagon. They can use any martial art they want. It transcends all cultural barriers, all language barriers, because I don't care what color you are, what country you come from or what language you speak, we're all human beings. And fighting's in our DNA. We get it and we like it.

I'm always uneasy when human behavior is essentialized to human nature, as clearly not everyone gets fighting, nor does everyone like it. In fact, fighting is something that most people are uncomfortable with. Imagine a world where fighting was a common occurrence in the street, the marketplace, the workforce, the home, or the school? The presence of fighting in society would quickly erode our public institutions and turn the adjudication of justice into a Thrasymachus-ordered, "might makes right" world. A culture that truly embraced fighting and accepted it as a norm would be a barbaric wasteland of death and suffering. In place of justice through a predictable and reliable rule of law, society would be at the mercy of the physically powerful.

Furthermore, if fighting were truly in our genes, then I doubt boxers would have to get their hands wrapped to prevent their hand bones from shattering when they punched their opponent. And it does not follow that something that exists throughout human history should be mindlessly entertained or accepted. Yes, violence is deeply rooted in the evolutionary history of humanity, but that does not mean it is inherently something to be indulged. Stealing, sexual assault, hating people who look different from you, and murder are also deeply connected to the human condition, but that does not make such practices anything less than morally repugnant and the perpetrators deserving of punishment to protect the common good.

The violence of MMA might forever prevent it from gaining acceptance from mainstream audiences and prevent a fan from acknowledging her familiarity with the sport at a cocktail party. My biggest fear for the sport is that the new ownership will simply back away from any pretentions to elevate the UFC to a more legitimate stationing in sports and instead cater to "just bleed" freak-shows, granting the promotional push only to the talented athletes who are also notorious trash-talkers and the occasional sexy female athlete.

It is very possible that the violence of MMA will quite easily facilitate this movement toward spectacle and that even attempts to legitimize will be unsuccessful. We are all familiar with friends and family who find any violence as morally problematic and who hold the position that those who consume it as entertainment are in need of re-education. I'm sure many of you reading this book right now feel that way! My sister-in-law, for instance, despises violence in film and television, and she leaves the room if football is on, greatly complicating family visits during the fall season. I certainly don't feel the same way about violence as a form of entertainment, but I too have my limits. I love stories of political intrigue and I love fantasy role-playing games, but I hate *Game of Thrones*. Violence is part of the human condition, but I like to think that it is not a human aspiration.

Gwynne Dyer, a Canadian historian and public intellectual of international politics, once offered the following reflection on the deep-rootedness of political violence in the human condition:

> It can never be proven, but it is a safe assumption that the first time five thousand male human beings were ever gathered together in one place, they belonged to an

## 1. The Aspirations of MMA

army. That event probably occurred around 7000 BC—give or take a thousand years—and it is an equally safe bet that the first truly large-scale slaughter of people in human history happened very soon afterward.[8]

Any student who has taken an international relations course in Political Science has been encouraged to think about human nature in the context of war.

The late Kenneth N. Waltz, one of the most influential international relations theorists of the twentieth century, if not the most influential, suggested that there have been three "images" used to explain the presence of war and organized violence over the last 5,000 years of human history.[9] The first image of war is based on the nature of man. It perceives us as inherently disposed to avarice, division, and genetically privileging aggression. It is a theory of man that is, in part, inspired by a Judeo-Christian tradition of the sinfulness of human nature and the fall of man. The first image proposes that the prospect of war will forever exist due to this fundamental and immutable condition.

Waltz's second image interprets war as a product of our governmental institutions, especially the proliferation of authoritarian regimes that are not only lacking in accountability to their public, but actually base their legitimacy on a perpetual enmity with other states.

The third image, and the one that Waltz believed to be the correct "ordering principle" for inter-state behavior, one that he dedicated his career to understanding, was the contest of the surrounding structure. For states in international systems, this has been a condition of anarchy. Not chaos, but the absence of a global state to enforce a political order on the international relations of states. Anarchy does not force states to adopt any specific policy, but it is rather the context of policy. Waltz did not believe that human nature is a useful tool for understanding the continuity of war in history. It is murky and vague to disassociate what is socially learned and what is a product of our genes, and probably facetious even to think about them as distinct realms at all.

Just as an appreciation for the context of structure allows one to understand the continuity of war, so too does it matter when thinking about violence in sport. The Unified Rules of MMA, when passed in 2000, represented the structure that indelibly changed the sport. It is hard to imagine the sport even being entertained by mainstream society without them. However, these rules are not the sole influence on MMA and the expression of violence in the sport. Context and structure is more than a

## Mixed Martial Arts and the Quest for Legitimacy

defined set of rules. It includes the surrounding norms of the sport and society in general. It includes the shared meanings and interpretations held by fans of the sport, and the understood limits placed on both violence and personal conduct. It pertains to our ethics—a realm of contested ideas on what is acceptable and unacceptable in social relations.

Perhaps violence is in our genes, perhaps not, but it is clear that violence is not something everyone intuitively likes or "gets." It is quite the opposite. Violence can make many very uncomfortable, or, as the anthropologist Clifford Geertz might say, "disquietful." It is impossible even to think of a sport like MMA conforming to a set of ethical norms that can make it palatable to all in society. A sizable proportion will recoil at a fight, no matter the aesthetics and the packaging that high-priced marketing experts use to fetishize the violence. But asking questions about the normative and ethical context surrounding MMA is part of an important discussion to have for those who are fans of the sport, those who are interested in it, and especially for those who utterly detest it.

This book is not a history of MMA or the UFC. The agenda of this book is not to extol the business genius of Dana White, who as legend has it, convinced the wealthy and powerful owners of Stations Casinos in Las Vegas, the Fertitta Brothers, to invest in an all but dead brand and lead it into an immensely profitable future where they were able to sell it for $4 billion to WME-IMG. Nor is the book intended to vilify the sport or the UFC. It is, instead, a collection of essays meant to reflect on a young sport, perhaps the fastest growing sport in the world, one that is alternately defined as "mixed-martial arts" and "ultimate fighting."

There is a politics to these names, as they inspire different reactions from society and stand for starkly different things. The exact same phrase will elicit very different reactions from different people and groups. "No holds barred fighting" had been used by enemies of the sport, such as U.S. Senator John McCain. So too have promoters historically used this phrase to sell their product, winking at unmentionable levels of violence in the pre–Zuffa era when the UFC was owned by Semaphore Entertainment Group (SEG). MMA invokes an ethics of what we associate with martial arts, such as frugality, discipline, humility, and defense of oneself and others. Ultimate fighting invokes a very different set of impressions, of lessons learned on the street, or in the back alleys behind countless bars and clubs around the world. Ultimate fighting represents an ethics that is often in opposition to martial arts, reflecting values of decadence, excess, vanity,

## 1. The Aspirations of MMA

and aggression. What we have today is neither entirely MMA nor ultimate fighting, it is instead both of these things. It is the dialectic, or the tensions, between frugality and decadence, discipline and excess, humility and vanity, defense and aggression. It is a sport in its infancy, evolving and being shaped by this dialectic of sport and spectacle.

The dialectic between MMA and ultimate fighting is clearly on display with the twin opening segments of UFC pay-per-view broadcasts. Since 2002, every UFC pay-per-view event has opened with a selection of statements from fighters on the main card promising violence to their opponents, reaching a crescendo with the metal band STEMM's song "Face the Pain." The lyrics are surprisingly reflective, commenting on how one can lose a sense of control in life, and of facing fears and personal torment. The music, though, cut with brutal highlights of the fighters on the card, knocking out previous opponents while screaming and flexing to the crowd, is pure aggression and incitement. It is the foreplay of violence, provoking anxiety, increasing heart rate and blood-flow in expectation of an orgy of violence.

In 2012, the UFC introduced a new opening to precede the confident assertions of violence promised by fighters. It, too, features rock music, but is subtle, less abrasive than STEMM. The accompanying visuals depict not just highlights from the history of the UFC, but perhaps *the* history of the UFC itself. Cut by James Cameron's production company, Digital Domain, the opening captures pivotal moments of the UFC, from Royce Gracie submitting Ken Shamrock in UFC I, to the powerful double-leg takedowns that wrestlers like Matt Hughes and Tito Ortiz brought to the sport during their era of dominance. It also includes changing of the guard clips, such as GSP (Georges St-Pierre) defeating Hughes, Brock Lesnar's polarizing rise and fall as heavyweight champion, the Griffin-Bonnar fight, Penn, Edgar, Aldo, Jones and others, at one time concluding with Anderson Silva's iconic front kick KO of Vitor Belfort.

The opening unveiled in 2012, known as "Evolution," was a presentation of violence. Crushing knockdowns, wild exchanges, and one-shot knockouts. The history of the UFC, and MMA more broadly, is itself a history of violence. Some clips in the opening ostensibly remove fighters from the octagon and the arena and instead give the illusion that UFC bouts are contested in the street and in alleys. And yet, this montage does not evoke the bloodlust of "Face the Pain." Rather, it evokes tradition, legitimacy, and most importantly, sport, perhaps comparable to ESPN's opening for

## Mixed Martial Arts and the Quest for Legitimacy

Monday Night Football during the 2015 season. While "Evolution" now opens the pay-per-view broadcasts, it is still followed by the assurances of violence given by fighters, and STEMM's "Face the Pain," though STEMM has never been used as the introduction to a UFC on Fox broadcast. The UFC, and the sport itself, is caught between "Evolution" and "Face the Pain." It is both the ethos of MMA and the anger, bloodlust, and negativity of ultimate fighting.

I never took karate lessons as a kid, but my understanding of martial arts was that it was *not* okay to pummel a clearly unconscious opponent. I also have a hard time imagining that martial arts is something to be practiced in front of screaming fans, drunk with excitement or just plain drunk. Or held in a casino where viewers are informed of the upcoming round by women who look a lot like my comic book heroines. No, it is a sport of fighting, ultimate fighting, in the Ultimate Fighting Championship.

And yet it isn't. The champions of today, and in recent history, are not the tough guys at your local bar in Hamilton, Ontario, or Nanaimo, British Columbia, or any other city or town around the world. No, they are disciplined in every sense of the word. Men like Cain Velasquez, an NJCAA champion and two-time NCAA Division I All-American. Or GSP, a man who exudes the spirit of the classic martial artist—reserved, intelligent and classy—while clearly a high-level athlete, and a man who was not above incorporating gymnastics into his strength training.

The goal of this book is to take advantage of the relative youth of MMA and reflect on this sport before a rigid sense of tradition sets in, a reactionary conservatism that is unthinkingly hostile to any criticism. The thoughts presented here are personal and hopefully act as a vehicle for reflections made by the reader as well, whether they are fans of the sport, implacable opponents, or something in between. It is hoped that these reflections are not exclusively personal, though, but instead manifest as collective actions by those who follow the sport and as consumers, to shape the market forces that provide the structural context for the business strategy of the UFC and its new era under the management of WME-IMG. This is a sport that is evolving, as evidenced by the expansion of the UFC to include lighter weight divisions (125 lb, 135 lb, and 145 lb), and even to include three women's divisions at bantamweight (135 lb), straw-weight (115 lb), and finally the controversial featherweight division (145 lb). One of the most profound developments that illustrate this period of dramatic

## 1. The Aspirations of MMA

change is the banning of testosterone replacement therapy (TRT) by the Nevada Athletic Commission (NAC) in 2014.

This book can be understood as a political inquiry. I don't mean the narrow interpretation of politics as the actions of government, but the broad interpretation of politics as the communities and identities that are manifest within societies and between them. In the *Politics,* Aristotle famously remarked that "a human being is by nature a political animal" and "by nature, then, the drive for such a community exists in everyone." For Aristotle, "as human beings are the best of all animals when perfected, so they are the worst when divorced from law and right.... Justice is something political, for right is the arrangement of a political community, and right is discrimination of what is just."[10] We need to reflect on justice in government, absolutely, but also on justice in other social realms, such as in market relations, our consumptive patterns in marketplaces, and even in sport. According to Aristotle, it is our ability to think about justice at all that separates human beings from the other social animals, even animals that can be described as gregarious, such as bees, and it is our ability to communicate our reflections on morality to the community that defines us as a species. A modern work of political science by Harold Lasswell describes politics as the discernment of "Who Gets What, When, How."[11] Lasswell's study is mostly on the control of public goods and influence over public policy, but really we are thinking politically whenever we ask these questions in any context, whether they pertain to the decisions of government, the dynamics of an industry or major corporation in the marketplace, or the promotional decisions of a sports organization. These particular questions are especially important when we are thinking about a sport where the means of accessing wealth largely revolve around athletes trying to bludgeon an opponent with fists in four-ounce gloves (you know, to protect delicate hand bones), feet, shins, knees, elbows, and at one time, even your head!

I can assure you, dear reader, that this is not one of those books that uses entertainment or popular culture to insidiously lecture on obscure debates within academia. I think that the UFC in particular would work very well as a metaphor for neoliberal economic theory, but that is not what I am attempting here. Instead, my interest lies in offering a personal tale or two and in engaging with the tensions of MMA, the dialectic of ethics, experienced through expressions on themes such as nationalism and class. To comment on a sport where promoters and athletes alike often utilize highly gendered language to dominate and ridicule. This is a book of reflections on justice and cage-fighting, promising not philosophy, but an experiment to create a bit of space to talk about the good, the bad, and the ugly, of the octagons, hexagons, decagons, circles, pentagrams (okay, that one is a joke) and rings of the most inherently violent sport to be found on network TV.

The second chapter of this book considers the nationalism inspired by the sport. In some ways, nationalism can be a positive experience, uniting people under a common identity, forging the bonds of citizenship, making brothers and sisters out of strangers. However, as any student of politics will tell you, nationalism is Janus-faced. It also inspires enmity, delineating the boundaries of friendship and citizenship to separate "us" from "them." The connections between nationalism and tribalism in sport have been widely commented on in the contexts of soccer, baseball, hockey and the Olympic games, but very little has been collected so far on cage-fighting, not for lack of source material.

The third chapter reviews the TRT era of cage-fighting, the controversies it provoked, its heroes and villains, and why banning it was the right decision to make. The fourth chapter reflects on violence, mostly on the nature of head injuries and the growing recognition of chronic traumatic encephalopathy (CTE) as a major problem in professional sports. This chapter will also critically reflect on the narrative that cage-fighting is "safer" than boxing.

The fifth chapter focuses on the gender roles that are part of the industry—not just the inclusion of women fighters in the UFC, but also the gendered language used by fighters, the projection of hyper-masculinity and the insults of feminization hurled around. A book of reflections on cage-fighting would not be complete without a consideration of class, and the impossibility of the UFC being held in an even remotely similar regard as the NFL when minimum wages in the UFC are so obscenely depressed. The seventh chapter evaluates the tensions emanating from the global expansion of the sport, specifically on the debate over whether the UFC is a "monopoly" or a "monopsony," and what that means for fighters past, present, and future. There is one fighter who receives a whole chapter all to himself. He represents the epitome of MMA and this dialectic between martial arts and outrageous spectacle. You should be able to guess that I'm talking about Conor McGregor if you have been following the UFC at all during the 2015–2016 campaign.

## 1. The Aspirations of MMA

It is not my intent to convince you of any particular perspective on MMA, but instead to have a conversation. The UFC, coming very close to holding powers of monopolization of the industry, is not going to create the forum to hold such a conversation. It operates under market-based logics, perhaps now more than ever after the sale to WME-IMG and the powerful need to achieve a very high rate of return on their investment to service the debt payments. WME-IMG might only concern itself regarding the tension between MMA and ultimate fighting when it threatens the marketability of the brand. The UFC needs the MMA ethos for legitimacy to enter into mainstream sports, especially since its ambition is to outcompete well-established leagues like the NHL and the NFL. However, the UFC is not willing to jettison ultimate fighting from its brand. It wants the extreme violence of ultimate fighting, the flexing of muscles, the triumphant screams to the gods of violence, the vanity, the shameful Russian prison tattoos, the fake tans, the waxed bodies, the enmity, the surgically enhanced busts, the hate, and the insecurities and anxieties of young men.

This dialectic between MMA and ultimate fighting is ongoing and will defy reconciliation. The UFC is not the only organization promoting a contact sport that is experiencing this tension between ethics and entertainment. The NFL and the NHL are similarly attempting to re-negotiate the boundaries of what is acceptable as entertainment in their respective sports as medical research continues to unveil the frighteningly high rates of CTE amongst their athletes. The position of the UFC is different due to its relative youth as a sport, and because its violence doesn't aid a victory secured through goals and touchdowns, but is the only means available to win.

As mentioned, my greatest fear for MMA is that the violence is too unforgivable for polite society, and the new ownership of WME-IMG might recognize this and go entirely toward spectacle. I think that we have already seen a transition to spectacle over legitimacy in recent years with respect to who gets title shots, who headlines events or is a co-headliner for an event, and who gets offered a UFC contract. Fun brawlers who are fan favorites, and even worse, polarizing trash-talkers, are often receiving title shots over more deserving contenders with a more proven recent record. The GSP-Nick Diaz title fight comes to mind, though the origins of that fight are more connected to the desire of GSP than Dana White and the Fertittas. I love watching Carlos Condit, one of my favorites, and he had a fight-of-year against the champion of the time, Robbie Lawler.

## Mixed Martial Arts and the Quest for Legitimacy

I feel bad about using this example, but at 2–3 in his last five fights, and 1–1 in his last two fights, he was not deserving of a title shot over Tyron Woodley, who had beaten Condit by an injury-TKO. It was booked because everyone who followed the sport knew that it was going to be an awesome fight to watch.

Conor McGregor, who will receive a lot of attention in the book toward the end, received a lightweight title shot against Eddie Alvarez, despite never defending his featherweight belt, going 1–1 against a lightweight gatekeeper, and leap-frogging contenders like Khabib Nurmagomedov and Tony Ferguson, who held winning streaks of notable significance in the UFC. Another decision where spectacle overruled talent was to feature Paige VanZant as the headliner of UFC on Fox 22, and Sage Northcutt in the co-headliner bout. Both of these fighters may prove themselves to be contenders at some point, and I enjoy seeing them compete, for what it's worth, but they were still very young prospects, elevated to such a high status on the card because of their Barbie and Ken-doll blond hair and perfect bodies, and VanZant's celebrity status that came with competing on *Dancing with the Stars*. Bryan Barberena, who had recently defeated Northcutt, languished in the undercard, and more significantly, top-five men's bantamweight and all-time great, Uriah Faber, was placed lower on the card than VanZant and Northcutt, despite it being his high-profile retirement fight. Both VanZant and Northcutt lost by submission early in the fight, but the event peaked at over three million viewers.

It is my conviction that the sport will benefit most if MMA emerges as the more dominant influence in the sport and that the values of ultimate fighting, the values of spectacle, are less pronounced. However, I respect dissenting opinions on this. I do not believe for a moment that the aggression of ultimate fighting is going to disappear from the UFC under its new management of WME-IMG, or in cage-fighting of any other organization. Pure MMA, one entirely grounded in an ethics of martial arts, might be too bland and boring for mainstream entertainment, but pure ultimate fighting is unethical and repulsive for mainstream audiences. Either extreme has the potential of stopping the growth of the sport, which is not at all what I want to happen. My concern is that if the pendulum is to swing too far toward the spectacle of ultimate fighting, then culture becomes assaulted by the demons of nationalistic hatred, dehumanization and empathetic failure, misogyny, patriarchy, and exploitation, with both the sport and society the worse for it.

# 2

# National Pride and Prejudice

On a chilly night in December of 2010, my brother Paul and I, along with two of his friends, Sohaib and Craig, found ourselves driving around to various sports bars and getting turned away. Our regular haunt was not accepting any more customers, as maximum occupancy had been reached hours earlier, and neither were the various other bars of somewhat diminishing respectability accepting more patrons. Finally, a sympathetic waitress made a call for us to a "dive" she thought was airing the bouts and might still be able to accommodate our modest party. We arrived at the bar, one that none of us would otherwise have ever set foot in, found a table, and cheered along with our fellow Hamiltonians for the multi-year recipient of the Rogers Sportsnet "Canadian Athlete of the Year" award. The match, fought in Montreal's Bell Centre for the UFC welterweight championship, was a showdown between Georges St-Pierre (GSP), widely regarded as the greatest welterweight of all time, and Josh Koscheck. The title fight was the culmination of a *TUF* season in which GSP coached against the brash American, Koscheck, one of the most despised housemates from *TUF I* who had become a "heel" of the sport.

The expression heel is derived from the realm of "professional wrestling." The term is a misnomer of entertainment if there ever was one, as the so-called professional wrestling of the past few decades has been rehearsed and scripted, and features a great number of bodybuilder/actors/stuntmen and women who never even wrestled at the high school or the collegiate level. It is certainly an inherently dangerous spectacle for the participants involved, as injuries are very common, and the toll taken on these athletes is as punishing as it is in real sports, as director Darren Aronofsky vividly portrayed in the critically acclaimed film, *The Wrestler*.

# Mixed Martial Arts and the Quest for Legitimacy

One of the central devices for advancing narratives in professional wrestling, and to foster intense, visceral responses from the audience, is to cast some wrestlers as the heels. Often, the villain is selected based on ethnicity and geopolitical tensions, most notably Middle Eastern and Soviet characters when I was a boy, but also exaggerated caricatures of the ultra-rich who are made into decadent villains and oppressors of the working classes.[1]

The heel elicits enmity from the viewer, a sense of contempt that can only be satiated with the humiliation of losing in combat. The UFC, and many of its fans, are uncomfortable with the perceived overlap between MMA and professional wrestling business models and history. However, the overlap exists. The Japanese organization Pride debuted in 1997 to feature pro wrestler Nobuhiko Takada as its main star. Ken Shamrock, semi-finalist of UFC I, finalist of UFC III, and a "Superfight Champion," left the UFC in his MMA prime in 1997 to join pro wrestling for more money. In 2014, CM Punk, aka Phil Brooks, a WWE stalwart and former champion, signed with the UFC despite having no professional or amateur experience in MMA, or even any collegiate wrestling experience, only to be submitted within seconds of the bout beginning. And of course, Brock Lesnar, pay-per-view kingpin of the UFC between 2008–2011, largely owed his immense popularity to his WWE fan-base. The WWE connection drove people to the UFC, just as it caused many older MMA fans to root against Lesnar, who represents the kind of guy you learn martial arts to defend yourself against.

The heel dynamic Koschek presented on *TUF*, and in the lead-up to his 2010 showdown with GSP, was fundamental to the interest the match drummed up, especially for Canadian audiences. To a Canadian, losing was one thing, but the prospect of losing to Koscheck, a cocky American, was something else entirely! While GSP exuded class, dignity, and the grace that many associate with martial arts, Koschek played the part of the ultimate fighting heel. In Koschek's previous fight, which earned him the coaching gig on *TUF*, and most importantly, the shot at GSP's title, he had put on a wrestling clinic in a smothering decision victory over heavy-handed British kick-boxer Paul Daley. The trash-talking between the fighters during the bout, though banned by the unified rules of MMA, had been so intense that Daley ignored the buzzer to signify the expiration of the contest and gave a cheap shot to the head of Koschek as he was walking away, which resulted in Daley getting booted from the UFC.

## 2. National Pride and Prejudice

Koschek's ability to instigate his opponent could only have been seen as "marketable" to the UFC, providing the perfect foil to act as ultimate fighter to the martial artist personified by GSP.

GSP won in dominant fashion over Koscheck that night, breaking an orbital bone in Koschek's face with a stiff jab in the first round, which caused gruesome swelling and allowed GSP to land that same jab repeatedly over five rounds. GSP took his revenge at being insulted over the weeks leading up to the match, with Canadians, and the vast majority of American fans, celebrating the beat-down of the abrasive challenger in bars and homes around North America.

The impact of GSP in Canadian culture has been entirely positive. Watching GSP compete generated an enormous amount of national pride amongst Canadians, even from those who barely followed the sport. Canadians who could not fathom watching a UFC event all the way through looked up the result after a GSP title-fight, or even made it out to their own local dive to watch him in person. Nowhere was this pride felt as strongly as GSP's home province of Quebec. With his *fleur-de-lis* tattoo on his calf, GSP transformed Montreal into one of the most important cities of MMA, vaulting it to the same tier as Atlantic City, Newark, Anaheim, Rio, and London. Tom Wright, the director of UFC operations in Canada, Australia, and New Zealand, claimed to the Canadian Press that "on a per-capita basis, no nation in the world consumes MMA like we [Canadians] do." This is flatly unimaginable without GSP and has not been true during GSP's quasi-retirement, as the most important MMA market outside of the U.S. has now become Brazil.

One of the key reasons why GSP has had this positive impact on Canadian culture is the way that he has bridged at least three of the "solitudes" of Canadian society. Hugh MacLennan, in his 1945 novel, *Two Solitudes*, popularized the conception of a cultural, political, and linguistic "solitude" between Francophone Quebec and the rest of Canada, with the exception of a bilingual yet Anglophone New Brunswick. GSP grew up Francophone but developed English language skills during his UFC career, becoming a Canadian who bridged the traditionally most divisive solitude in Canadian politics, and was cheered for by both French and English Canadians. From Saint-Isidore, an Eastern township of Quebec with a population of just over 2,000, to training at Tristar Gym in Montreal, Canada's second largest city, GSP also transcended the rural-urban solitude of Canadian political life, and has inspired people from both walks of life in a way that few non-hockey athletes have done in Canada. What is likely to be the defining solitude for Canada in the twenty-first century, and for many other Western societies, is the widening disparity of income and opportunity in Canadian economic life. As someone who went from working as a bouncer and a garbage collector to being the top pay-per-view draw in the UFC for a time, a darling of sponsors, and one of the sport's richest athletes, GSP has been that increasingly rare example of a working class young person who became a phenomenal success. Not from privilege, not from speculation on Bay Street/Wall Street, or from impoverishing the lives of others, but from honest, hard work, discipline and complete dedication. GSP is a Canadian national treasure.

Other UFC fighters have similarly inspired the best in their fellow citizens. Antônio Rodrigo Nogueira, a heavyweight champion of Pride and an interim UFC heavyweight champion, is revered as an elder statesman of the sport in Brazil. Kazushi Sakuraba is similarly held in very high regard in Japan, once christened as "The Gracie Hunter" for his notable victories over the first family of jiu-jitsu. These competitors have evoked enormous national pride in their home countries for those who have followed their professional careers, and these men have been highly respected, even outside of the insular world of MMA. They are notable not just for the spirit of nationalism they have fostered, but for the style of nationalism, not based on ethnocentrism, or enmity with "outsiders," but representing a martial arts ethics that recognizes universal human dignity. One does not need to be Brazilian to be a fan of Nogueira, or "Big Nog," as he is affectionately known as, or be Canadian to have been a fan of GSP.

These are some of the athletes who have transcended national borders and citizenship by acting as ambassadors for all of us who have been fans of competition. They represent the ambassadors of MMA in the sport, but they are not alone. The other half of the dialectic of the sport, the spectacle of "ultimate fighting," has thrived on prejudice, insecurities, and national enmities.

Chael Sonnen is the other side of the coin. Calling himself "The American Gangster" and claiming to have "once out-boxed Hemingway" on his twitter account, Sonnen became *the* polarizing athlete of the sport up until his disgraceful long-term suspension for failing a drug test. He was the UFC's ultimate heel. Sonnen became one of the top-earning athletes in UFC history by creating a character. Sonnen, a one-time journeyman,

## 2. National Pride and Prejudice

made himself into a PPV superstar by transforming himself, in the most calculated possible manner, into the bad guy. It was his feuds with Brazilian fighters that gained him the most notoriety, often crossing the line from promoting a fight to playing upon national tensions and prejudice.

Following a five-year layoff after his first professional fight in 1997, Sonnen bounced between organizations as a middling fighter, going 1–2 in the UFC between 2005–2006, more known for his spectacular submission losses than for any of his victories. That all changed leading up to his first title fight with Brazilian middleweight champion Anderson "The Spider" Silva.

Bursting into the UFC with a 49-second destruction of Chris Leben, Silva was vaulted to a title shot against champion Rich Franklin, a former math teacher who had the appearance of a champion who had dug himself in for a lengthy reign on top of a mediocre UFC middleweight landscape. Silva laid waste to Franklin in the clinch, gruesomely breaking Franklin's nose, and then smashing a game Franklin again for a second time a year later. On his way to setting the record for most consecutive UFC title defenses and most consecutive UFC wins, Silva defeated Dan Henderson, unifying the Pride Welterweight belt with the UFC middleweight belt, defeated three light-heavyweights in their own division, including one deposed champion, and defended the belt six times leading up to the first meeting with Sonnen.[2] Silva had established himself as the best "pound-for-pound" fighter in the world by 2010, and in that year was increasingly being seen by commentators of the sport as the "Greatest Of All Time" (GOAT), and was unquestionably the GOAT to Dana White and UFC commentator Joe Rogan.

This remarkable winning streak did not directly translate into pay-per-view buys for Silva. While his wins over Henderson, Griffin, and both of his wins over Franklin, had been acknowledged as brilliant feats, other victories appeared less inspired to MMA fans. Silva's back-to-back wins over Canadian Patrick Côté and fellow Brazilian Thales Leites were lackluster, but it was his title defense over Damian Maia at UFC 112 that drew the ire of fans and UFC President Dana White.

UFC 112, held in the stifling heat of Abu Dhabi, was intended to be something of a showcase event for Zuffa's new investors from the Gulf. It featured two title fights involving challengers who were not seen as particularly compelling match-ups going into the event. Maia, for instance, had suffered a KO loss to Nate Marquardt seven months earlier, and

## Mixed Martial Arts and the Quest for Legitimacy

Frankie Edgar, the lightweight challenger, was not too far removed from a loss to Gray Maynard. However, Frankie Edgar shocked the MMA world when he edged out the dominant champion of the lightweight division, B.J. Penn, in a very close co-main event. Anderson Silva however showcased his talents in the desert by ... clowning.

Early in the fight, a KO or TKO win for Silva seemed inexorable, with Silva showing cat-like reflexes, landing jabs with ease and breaking Maia's nose. As a counter-striker with an iron chin, Silva was known for sometimes dropping his hands and drawing opponents into striking range where a barrage of elbows, knees and punches awaited them. In Abu Dhabi though, something was off. Silva incessantly taunted Maia, at one point yelling, "*Bate na minha cara playboy*," which roughly translates into "Come on, hit me in the face, playboy." It was an insult to Maia's abilities as a martial artist, as well as a totally unfair accusation that Maia is a spoiled brat who has enjoyed a life of hedonistic pleasure. But it was his actions in the octagon that were more apparent to viewers at home, and in the desert that night, what generated the most resentment.

At first, it almost appeared comical. Silva lifting his knees high as he turned his back to Maia, running away from him in the most exaggerated manner. Silva even hid behind the referee on more than one occasion during the fight. It became a lot less funny as his antics escalated, and Silva seemed to have lost interest in mounting any offense against his opponent, who had unwisely attempted to clear his sinuses by blowing out of his broken nose, causing an eye to practically swell shut. While Maia earned fans that night for persevering in a fight he was desperately over-matched in, Silva was derided. Paying fans felt cheated, and there was something unsportsmanlike about Silva's conduct and unbecoming of his greatness. White left before the fight was even finished, forgoing his tradition of wrapping the belt around the waist of the victor, and instead handed it off to Silva's manger, Ed Soares, to do the (dis)honors. Immediately after the fight, White stated that he had never "been more embarrassed in the ten years of being in this business," adding an overblown observation that it "was the most horrible thing I have ever seen."

It is within this context that the Silva-Sonnen title fight was booked. So low was confidence in Anderson Silva that Dana White even commented to ESPN's Jim Rome on the possibility of stripping Anderson Silva of his belt and cutting him from the organization. Chael Sonnen, however, made sure that the ethics of stripping a UFC champion of a title,

## 2. National Pride and Prejudice

after successful defenses, was not going to be debated in the summer of 2010.

Looking back on the years of hateful vitriol Sonnen spewed about Silva, his training partners, and even Silva's wife and country, Chael Sonnen has reflected somewhat honestly when asked by the media about what he was doing at the time. "I was jealous when I watched Anderson fighting on TV. I didn't think he was the best in the world, and I wanted to fight and beat him." Sonnen made sure that everyone interested in the sport was going to want to tune in to see if he really could beat the champ.

A couple of months after the fight in Abu Dhabi, Sonnen went on an unusually personal attack of Silva's skills during a Q&A session. Not content to dismiss Silva's jiu-jitsu abilities, which have clearly been Sonnen's serious weakness, Silva proceeded to mock Antônio Rodrigo Nogueira and his twin brother, light-heavyweight competitor Antônio Rogério Nogueira, but in press conferences and via social media. "He's [Silva] got a black belt under the Nogueira brothers. I think a black belt under the Nogueira brothers is like saying, 'I got a free toy in my Happy Meal.' I don't really understand what the big deal is. One of em's a punching bag, and the other one I just ignore; he's really irrelevant."

The comments were, of course, ludicrous. Both men had remarkable careers during their prime, fighting in Pride, and fought, and won, against elite opponents in the UFC. What made the comments incendiary was the respect the Nogueiras earned, amongst Brazilians, and fans of the sport around the world, for the class they have conducted themselves with. Sonnen, reducing them to being a "punching bag" and "irrelevant," was being insufferable, intolerable, irrational, and spiteful. He was trying to play off of a nationalistic enmity and paint Silva, his training partners and coaches, and Brazil itself, as hated outsiders to an American fan-base.

Another example of Sonnen verbally attacking the Nogueira brothers leading up to his match with Anderson Silva was in the following message he sent to MMA journalist Ariel Helwani.

> I was in Las Vegas when the Nogueira brothers first touched down in America. There was a bus, this is a true story. There was a bus that pulled up to a red light, and Little Nog tried to feed it a carrot, while Big Nog was petting it. He thought it was a horse. This really happened. He tried to feed a bus a carrot, and now you're telling me this country has computers? I didn't know that.

Sonnen is a promoter, and a shameless one at that. Sonnen was playing a character, and everything he said was done in a calculating fashion. However, he did not stop to question whether or not an entire people should be insulted and robbed of their dignity. As a "BRIC" country, with the seventh-largest GDP in the world and an important member of the G20, the Brazilian economy will likely have a bright future in the coming decades. But it is still a country that is dealing with extreme poverty, where more than one in five live below the poverty line. It is also a country of demoralizing inequality, with a Gini coefficient of almost 50, representing one of the largest divisions in the world between those with wealth and income and those with very little. Brazil is classified by both the World Bank Group and the IMF (International Monetary Fund) as a less developed country (LDC). None of this mattered to Sonnen. Poverty in Brazil is a joke to sell a fight. The heel does not respect peoples and societies. The heel is just trying to promote a fight. The heel represents spectacle.

The problem of crime in Brazil? Another opportunity for Sonnen's jokes. "Brazil isn't a bowing country. You bow in Brazil they'll hit you over the head and take your wallet out of your pocket." In 2011, the United Nations Office on Drugs and Crime (UNODC) ranked Brazil amongst the worst sixth of countries for homicides, when adjusting for population. Dismissing the enormous contributions of Brazil to martial arts, and MMA in particular, a culture is instead defined by the behavior of the worst of its people, in a narrative where victims are the punch-line.

Leading up to that first Sonnen-Silva fight, Sonnen tweeted to Ed Soares, Silva's long-time manager, to "pray to whatever Demon effigy you prance and dance in front of with your piglet tribe of savages that I decide not to CRUCIFY you." Wanderlei Silva received similar insults from Sonnen in 2011, brashly declaring that; "If it wasn't for me, you would be thrashing around the jungle w/a blowgun trying' to catch breakfast," or "sellin' barbecued monkey on the street in Manaus." I'm sure that Sonnen hasn't spent much time reading linguistics journals, but that never stopped him from dismissing Portuguese as a "half-step up from pig-Latin," and saying that Silva was going to thank Sonnen for "re-baptizing" him with a beating, in perfect English, of course. During a visit to Brazil in the summer of 2011 to support his training partner, Yushin Okami, in his bid to claim the middleweight title from Silva, Sonnen unleashed such a torrent of vindictive tweets about the country and its athletes that his Twitter feed even went noticed by the Brazilian media outlet *Globo*. Below is a selection of just some of his tweets:

## 2. National Pride and Prejudice

Greetings from Sao Paulo! I'm learning the language: breakdancing in the Special Olympics is called capoiera and cocaine is called brunch.

I'd beat up Machida [a former Brazilian UFC champion] on the way to the ring to beat up Anderson, and I'll kick Nogeria's ass in the parking lot on the way to my after party.

Machida is not a bad guy; he's a victim of the Brazilian education system. There are better ways to get electrolytes than drinking piss.[3]

Brazil likes to boast that it's the power seat of MMA, yet it's so-called champions bow to the man behind "Under Siege 2." [Steven Seagal]........ Classy.[4]

Yushin and I are in Brazil to follow in Andy's ways. Got ballet shoes, a team of has-beens, even brought a fat talentless celeb for trainer.

In April of 2012, just a few months before the re-match with Silva, Sonnen, when asked by the Brazilian media what he thought of Rio, Sonnen offered the following:

I don't have anything against the Brazilian people.... I've got something against a Brazilian sitting a few feet from me [Anderson]...Your women are all OK with me, so feel free to give me a call or pay me a visit. But, as far as my impression, it's a lot like America ... when I was a little kid, I'd go outside with my friends and we'd talk about the latest technology, in medicine, gaming and American ingenuity—and Anderson and the Brazilian kids are sitting outside playing in the mud.

I think this might be the most offensive comment made by Sonnen. It plays upon every trope found in ethnocentric nationalism and does so in a particularly reprehensible way. By prefacing his comments with what appears to be a conciliatory concession, he then proceeds to sexualize Brazilian women, trumpeting lascivious intentions for the purposes of inflaming male pride. Sonnen even insulted Anderson Silva's wife once. Even though this is a person who has clearly wanted to keep her privacy over the years Silva was champ, Sonnen warned to "tell Anderson Silva I'm coming over. I'm kicking in his back door and I'm pattin' his old lady on the ass and I'm telling her to make me a steak, medium rare just how I like it."

The second part of his comments on Rio followed the same pattern as the gendered comment. First, Sonnen offered a reflection of the common lived experiences, hopes, and aspirations of the American and Brazilian people. Instead of following through on that point, he contemptuously mocked Brazilian children. Is it funny to imagine children living in conditions of absolute poverty? Does a mixed-martial-artist laugh at the unfortunate to sell a fight?

The thing is, Sonnen does not even claim to be a martial artist. Leading up to the rematch with Anderson, Sonnen predicted the following: "He's a martial artist [and] I'm a cage fighter and there's a tremendous difference. And on Saturday night, there's going to be one more in the win column, one more for the highlight reel and one more for the bad guy."

Sonnen constructed a public identity of himself as the antithesis of the mixed martial artist. He is the "American Gangster," the "cage-fighter," the "bad guy." He mocks the Brazilian all-time greats of his sport, jokes about making a woman into his servant, and expresses contempt for children from LDCs. For Sonnen, the promotion of the event is not even real. There is going to be no physical violence between the U.S. and Brazil, just him and Silva. It's all just a fight.

Another tactic of Sonnen had been to deny the Brazilian identity of his opponents by painting them as Americans. "Anderson Silva, their big national hero, just put two million dollars down on a mansion in LOS ANGELES. Los Angeles is in America, for those of you that aren't good at geography, it's not in Brazil." "People ask me if I wanted to go to Brazil for the fight. Sure. It'd be neutral territory! Anderson lives in a mansion in Beverly Hills. Las Vegas, Nevada is closer to him than it is to West Linn, Oregon. He's got home-court advantage."

Wanderlei Silva, another Brazilian who is renowned for his legendary run as middleweight (205-lb) champion in Pride, who even competed against heavyweights, also became the subject of Sonnen's insults.

> I am attempting to pick a FIGHT with some Brazilian fighters. Not fighters that care about you, Brazil. Fighters that have abandoned you. Fighters that claim they're from Brazil, like Wanderlei Silva, but he lives in a gated community in Las Vegas. He drives an Aston Martin. Do you guys even know what that is? That's what James Bond drove! It costs 200 grand. Wanderlei could have bought a fully-loaded Lexus, drove around in style for forty-one thousand, sent a hundred and fifty-nine grand back to your country, built two schools ... but he didn't.

This is not only meant to be an insult to his Brazilian opponents, but also to rob Brazilians of the athletes they identify with, attempting to cast doubt into the minds of fans and portray them as plutocratic Americans. Simply put, divide and conquer.

Sonnen used controversy and sensationalism to turn himself into a major star of the UFC, someone who could "move the needle." The first Silva-Sonnen bout earned around 600,000 pay-per-view buys, a high number, but the rematch hit almost one million buys. It is uncontestable that Sonnen deserved that first fight with Silva. He went 3–0 in the UFC

## 2. National Pride and Prejudice

leading up to that bout, all unanimous decision victories that were uncontroversial. His opponents included top-ten fighter Yushin Okami and a top-five fighter, Nate Marquardt, who was coming off three straight KO/TKO victories, the last of which was against Maia, who had tapped Sonnen out in his last fight before his three-fight win streak. Sonnen had earned that fight against Silva and he made the most of it. Dominating the champ throughout the fight, Sonnen threw reckless punches, transitioned his striking into take-downs, where intelligent positioning and persistent, if light, ground-and-pound made a Sonnen decision win all but certain. Improbably, Silva took advantage of a momentary lapse in Sonnen's judgment. Falling too low in Silva's guard towards the end of the fifth and final round, Silva caught Sonnen in a triangle-armbar, eliciting a reluctant tap from Sonnen in his first submission attempt of the fight.

At first, it seemed as if a re-match was mandatory. Silva had lost rounds before, in the infamous fight against Maia, as well as in the first round against Dan Henderson. Furthermore, Silva had lost bouts before, though never in the UFC. It was thought that perhaps Sonnen had the right tools to dethrone the champion. A tenacious wrestler who wasn't intimidated by the mystique that seemed to surround Silva in the cage looked like a toxic match-up for the Spider. But then the California State Athletic Commission (CSAC) revealed that Sonnen had failed his drug test. Sonnen had been taking testosterone replacement therapy (TRT), which was not illegal at the time, but he never disclosed this information to CSAC. Even more damning was his testosterone-to-epitestosterone ratio, 17 times higher than the average man and three times the limit allowable under CSAC.

Instead of being given an immediate rematch with Silva, Sonnen was thrown back to face two more top-ten fighters. With his TRT usage now officially disclosed, he first easily dispatched the highly respected Brian Stann with a second-round arm-triangle submission, and then fought to a controversial unanimous decision victory over *TUF III* winner, Manchester, England's Michael Bisping. Though Silva-Sonnen I still felt tainted by Sonnen's cheating, which we will discuss again in a later chapter, there was an enormous amount of enthusiasm for the rematch. Fans wondered how much of Sonnen's success against Silva in the first fight was the product of Sonnen's absurd testosterone levels, and some sort of rib injury that Silva allegedly sustained before the fight that compromised his takedown

## Mixed Martial Arts and the Quest for Legitimacy

defense. And of course, there was always Sonnen's vitriol, venomously attacking Silva, his training partners, and his country. The rematch was deserved, in the eyes of most, and the tension was electrifying. Sonnen appeared to start the first round of the rematch where the previous bout was fought, with Silva on his back and Sonnen working moderate ground-and-pound. The second round ended abruptly; with Sonnen having difficulty scoring a takedown, he chanced an ill-delivered spinning elbow, missing Silva and stumbling to the canvas. With Sonnen on his knees, Silva ripped a perfectly placed knee to the solar-plexus, and then slammed punches to a turtled-up Sonnen until the referee intervened.

Sonnen's follow-up bout was a sham of match-making, a pure case of spectacle over sport. UFC 151 was scheduled for September 1, 2012, in Las Vegas. It was headlined by light-heavyweight champion Jon Jones defending his title against Dan Henderson, a man who once held Pride's 183-lb and 205-lb titles at the same time. Henderson was Strikeforce's last light-heavyweight champion and not long removed from a KO victory against Fedor Emelianenko, the greatest heavyweight of all time, and a front-runner, along with Silva and GSP, for GOAT in the sport. An event featuring Jones, a young champion who looked to be on a path toward legendary status before he even hit the age of 30, was not one to be missed. However, for a UFC pay-per-view event, it resembled more of a boxing main card. The problem was that it was centered around one marquee matchup without much else in the way of compelling bouts. Approximately three weeks before the event, Dan Henderson experienced a partial tear of his right MCL in his final sparring session. Rather than immediately notify the UFC, Henderson briefly kept the situation quiet, hopeful the injury would not prevent him from competition. Once the extent of the injury was revealed, just over a week before the scheduled event, the UFC was desperate to find a replacement to fight against Jones.

After an announced rematch between former light-heavyweight champion Lyoto Machida and Jon Jones fell through, Sonnen positioned himself in the role of challenger. Jones, highly conscientious of the legacy he was in the process of establishing in his young career and once known for methodically preparing for his opponents with Greg Jackson and Mike Winklejohn, as a true student of his sport would (this is likely before Jones' downward spiral), prudently declined to face Sonnen on eight days' notice. Although Jon Jones would accept a short-notice fight against former light-heavyweight champion Vitor Belfort later in the month, UFC 151 was a

## 2. National Pride and Prejudice

lost event, causing some public relations issues with fans who typically center a trip to Vegas around a UFC event.

As a reward for agreeing to fight Jones at the doomed event, Sonnen was offered a gig coaching against Jones for a season of *TUF*, and got his shot at the light-heavyweight title, despite not having a win at 205 lbs in years, and coming off that second-round TKO loss to Silva. The *TUF* assignment felt like a punishment of sorts for Jones. White derided Greg Jackson, Jones' trainer, as a "sport-killer" for valuing the career of his young champion over the organization, and a tense period ensued between White and Jones. Having Chael Sonnen around Jon Jones for the weeks that a taping of *TUF* requires, was, for the UFC, the perfect opportunity to have Sonnen in Jones' face, hopefully getting under the champ's skin, and to beat the drums of fan interest. The UFC brass must have been gleeful in anticipation of a heated rivalry developing between the abrasive Sonnen and the proud, increasingly volatile champion.

The rivalry never blossomed into what UFC execs, and fans probably expected. Jones remained aloof, not allowing his feelings toward Sonnen to manifest into anything more than some fierce staring into the distance, and Sonnen, for his part, seemed entirely focused on his team of young fighters, giving himself over to them and sincerely concerned with improving their skills. The fight between the two confirmed everyone's suspicions. The result was a first-round blowout victory for the champion, though one that left him with a badly mangled toe.

All professional sports are haunted by the specter of racism in one form or another. Racial and ethnic exclusion defined sports such as baseball, golf, football, soccer, tennis, boxing, and hockey. Some of the greatest athletes from the pantheon of their respective sports held racist attitudes of pure hatefulness, such as baseball great Ty Cobb. This shameful and despicable legacy makes the more empathetic and thoughtful observers sensitive to racist language and behavior in sports and concerned about the process by which racist behavior and commentary can be normalized.

The enmity expressed in Sonnen's comments between 2010–2013 about Anderson Silva, Brazilian competitors, and Brazil more generally, were such that media observers who don't normally show much interest in MMA started to take notice. Tim Marchman wrote a particularly insightful piece in *Deadspin*, making the argument that Sonnen had been race-baiting the public into supporting him in his fights against Anderson Silva and Jon Jones. Marchman opened his comments by asserting that

## Mixed Martial Arts and the Quest for Legitimacy

Chael is "a well-known asshole," and made a comparison between him and Skip Bayless, an ESPN commentator who has built a career out of disputing the undeniable greatness of Lebron James. The author noted Sonnen's use of "boy" in reference to Jones, and calling him "an entitled brat." Another article published about the Sonnen-Jones fight, this one by Tomas Rios for *Pacific Standard,* made a similar claim that Sonnen used "racially coded language."

Both Marchman and Rios discussed how Sonnen derided Silva's counter-striking style as a man who "prances and dances, and does his little jigs." More fodder came from Sonnen in the lead-up to the rematch, with him saying that Silva was "a grown man with saggy pants, pink T-shirts, and crooked hats," and that the champion should "join a gang." A particularly racist shot that Sonnen threw at Silva was the notion that parents bought their kids Anderson Silva toys for Christmas, mistakenly thinking the action figures depicted fan-favorite Quinton "Rampage" Jackson. Rios believed that Sonnen had taken a page out of the playbook of Lee Atwater, a political consultant who advised Republican candidates in the Southern U.S. during the 1980s to substitute slurs that have been denounced nationally as racist, the traditional slurs of Southern white populism, in favor of innuendo and racially coded language—the dog whistles for those with racial enmity in their hearts and in their cultures.

It does appear as if Sonnen was tapping into what is sometimes referred to as "white anxiety" in promoting his fights, but I seriously doubt that Sonnen is a racist. I think Sonnen's tirades are less examples of racism than of ethno-centric nationalism. Calling light-heavyweight champion Jon Jones "boy" and a "brat" were probably less about Jones as a black athlete and more about his very young age at the time and his remarkable financial success. Another quote, used by Marchman, was of Sonnen ruminating on why Jones didn't want to fight him at the canceled event, wondering if he needed to be "wine tasting at a racetrack or something." At 25, Jones became the youngest champion in the modern UFC, which he translated into being the first UFC fighter to have inked a sponsorship deal with Nike, and before horrendous decisions in his personal life interrupted his career, he was on the precipice of becoming the UFC's marquee pay-per-view draw.

Sonnen's ludicrous accusation that Jones would rather attend a wine tasting event represents an intention to label the champ as an immensely wealthy elitist, a well-known troupe in professional wrestling. I can't say

## 2. National Pride and Prejudice

for certain, but I don't think that there exists in American culture a stereotype of black men going to wine tasting events. What must be understood, though, is that Sonnen's verbal assaults against Jones were tame compared to the mean-spirited barbs hurled at Anderson Silva. Much to the disappointment of the UFC brass, Sonnen was never in Jones' face during the filming of *TUF*. Instead he remained focused on training his team of young athletes. When Sonnen fought against Rashad Evans, a black former UFC champion and a fellow commentator of Sonnen's on Fox's UFC broadcasts, the mutual respect was clearly evident, bereft of any racially-coded insults or dog whistles. Maybe the biggest insult to Jones that Sonnen delivered was the poem to the champ that he recited on *UFC Tonight*. It begins,

> "I got a call one day from Dana, he said 'Chael, I'm putting you to work.
> 'You see, I overpaid for this light heavy, who I now realize is a jerk.
> 'He's been winning fights, but not with brains or with brawn.
> 'And his matches and his one-armed cartwheels are making
>    the whole crowd yawn'."

And, after a lengthy string of insults, closes with:

> "Jon, I'm coming to New Jersey, because I've got a job to do.
> I'm a fully-loaded cannon, boy, and I'm pointed right at you.
> A little advice, go get in your car and hit another tree.
> Do whatever you gotta do to stay away Jon, you don't want to fight me."

The poem is notable for not really playing on racial tropes, aside from calling Jones "boy," which is offensive, but I think it was more a reference to his age. He brings up Jones' DUI from 2012, and calls his fights boring, but phrases like "snoozefest," "Dancing with the Stars," "*Cirque de Soleil*," and the *lack* of "brawn" really don't fit with conventional dog-whistles that racists use. He also uses the poem to tease two Brazilians (Machida and Vitor [Belfort]) and three Americans (Bonnar, Bader, and Ortiz), none of them black competitors.

I don't dispute that there had been a racial subtext to Sonnen's outlandish comments to the media, but I think it was more about him constructing an American-Brazilian rivalry in the sport. The targets of some of Sonnen's most inflammatory remarks have been the Nogueira brothers, Lyoto Machida, and Vitor Belfort. I wouldn't described any of these men as black. The main target of Sonnen's mockery, possibly even more than Anderson Silva, had been Wanderlei Silva, another Brazilian who you also wouldn't think was black by looking at him. The Sonnen-Wanderlei rivalry in particular consumed both athletes, as the fires of their hatred burned out of control in front of *TUF* cameras, and looks to have basically ended both of their careers.

UFC 134 in 2011 was the first UFC event in Brazil since UFC 17.5, which took place back in 1998. One Brazilian was featured in every bout, almost all of them competing against non–Brazilians. This general pattern of matchmaking has been followed for most Brazilian cards, the only exception being the *TUF: Brazil* finale episodes where the entire cast is Brazilian. One of the striking characteristics of these Brazilian cards, one that could be heard to a certain extent at Las Vegas cards that featured Brazilian fighters, has been the chant from the crowd of "*Uh, Vai Morrer!*" The direct translation, "You're going to die," is certainly a classless chant that speaks to the spectacle of MMA, but it is probably a little misleading, as the chant is also heard at Brazilian football matches, especially those featuring the national team, and might be better understood in a cultural context as a tasteless way of saying "You're going down." Nationalistic American fans have been known to offer their own nauseating chant of "U-S-A," and Canadian fans, especially in Montreal, enjoy a round or two or ten of "*Ole Ole*" in support of their own. Even Japanese fans, known for their much more subdued presence in arenas, will unabashedly wear headbands and a gi to show an unbreakable patriotic support for their countrymen. However, I certainly wouldn't equate the wearing of headbands with a chant of "You're going to die!"

Fighting has the ability to bring out the tribalism in people, but it is partly the content expressed in the Brazilian chant, and partly the aggression in which the chant is delivered, that makes Brazilian fans appear as the most passionate and partisan. Wanderlei Silva became a major star in Japan by utterly laying waste to some of the greatest fighters Japan ever produced. Anderson Silva rose to popularity in the U.S. MMA market by beating Americans like Rich Franklin, Dan Henderson, and Forrest Griffin in states like Ohio and Pennsylvania, all despite his reluctance to demonstrate his improving English language skills to the American public. It is hard to imagine an American fighter rising in popularity in the Brazilian market, being placed against Brazilian fighters, and thoroughly smashing them. And yet, almost impossibly, this happened with Chael Sonnen of all people during 2014.

Chael Sonnen vs. Wanderlei Silva finally looked like a match that would be booked. First, the two had to coach against each other for a Brazilian installment of *TUF*, no doubt anticipating that the intense rivalry

## 2. National Pride and Prejudice

between the two could reinvigorate the floundering reality show and set up major interest in the eventual coaches' fight. The UFC had always found itself in a difficult position with *TUF*. They wanted to show how UFC hopefuls were relatable people, with dreams of elevating themselves and their families out of poverty through a tireless dedication to their craft. *TUF* was intended to bring MMA into the mainstream, proving to American audiences that these athletes were like athletes of any other major sport. On the other hand, *TUF* was also intended to create drama, appeal to fans who wanted to see honest expressions of violence between men who detested each other. This meant that narrative also include a lot of guys who didn't seem that ordinary. They were men unable to fit into civilization, angry at everyone around them, on the edge, just an inch away from "losing their shit," as one could put it colloquially. It is a stark example of this tension between MMA and ultimate fighting that has defined the sport.

Santino DeFranco was an aspiring mixed-martial artist trying to find a path into the UFC who wrote an article for *Vice* describing his ill-fated attempt to be cast for *TUF II*.[5] After watching the first season of *TUF*, DeFranco sent the UFC his audition tape where he attempted to portray himself as a "100% obnoxious asshole." His tape got him a plane ticket to Las Vegas to be interviewed for the show. DeFranco stuck to his character of obnoxious asshole, boasting of his skills, indignantly dismissing questions posed by his interviewers, and scoffing at the inclusion of Canadian Jason Thacker on *TUF I*, an unseasoned amateur with zero professional fights before coming on the show. After demanding to know which "asshole" let Thacker on the show, Dana White made his appearance, identifying himself as "the asshole responsible for putting Jason Thacker on the show." DeFranco asked the president, his potential future boss, "what the hell were you thinking?" White responded by saying that, "Well, we need different types of personalities on the show. We need your good, nice kids like Thacker, and we need your foul-mouthed, mother-slapping nut jobs like yourself." At a second interview, this one including a number of TV executives, Craig Piligian, whose producer credentials included the first few seasons of *Survivor*, asked White, "what the fuck are we going to do with this kid?" White wryly replied that he didn't know, "but I like him."

The success of *TUF*, for UFC management and the television producers hinged on creating drama between contestants, some of whom were meant to be slightly unhinged, but to avoid actual fighting outside of the bouts. The idea was to promote hateful grudges, anger, and indignation, but to maintain the illusion that these men were trained athletes, professionals who were above fighting each other out of competition. This delicate balance was impossible to keep, with fights between contestants occasionally bringing the righteous wrath of Dana White to bear on the belligerents, even resulting in their dismissal from the show for violent confrontations, sometimes not. The season of *TUF Brazil* with Sonnen and Wanderlei was intended to promote this state of enmity between coaches, and to become what was probably hoped for but didn't materialize during the Sonnen-Jones season.

Wanderlei could not play by the rules, and the script that Sonnen was trying to build, of himself as the bad guy and Wanderlei as the white knight, was doomed. The disrespect Silva felt from Sonnen, a man who insulted his country and laughed at the impoverished children of Brazil, demanded justice. Sonnen, much to the surprise of audiences in North America and Brazil, was respectful to his Brazilian team, and they in turn largely respected him. Gone was the showboating, nationalistic blowhard whose incendiary comments over the past few years enraged Brazilians so much that Dana White feared for Sonnen's safety when visiting Brazil. In his place was Sonnen the coach, the dedicated leader of a group of young men, who had nothing but their best interests at heart. Rather than Sonnen acting as a foil for the beloved Wanderlei, it was Wanderlei who was acting as the foil to Sonnen. Wanderlei appeared disinterested in his team, far more committed to mean-mugging Sonnen at every available opportunity than running a training camp that could meaningfully help his students. Attuned to the role reversal that was happening, Sonnen, as he revealed to Dave Meltzer, got in touch with Paul Heyman, an instrumental piece of the Extreme Championship Wrestling during the 1990s who became a fixture of World Wrestling Entertainment during the first decade of the century.[6] He told Heyman how Wanderlei

> gave me the silent treatment for ten days. I never knew what I'd get. It could be passive aggressive, aggressive, just passive, angry, or confrontational. Every day I had to take his temperature. I didn't know what mood I was going to see him in. Some days he'd walk right past me, and that was a good day, with no shoulder bump, and no scowl. Some days I'm coming in and he would put in his mouthpiece, like we're about to fight.

He confided to Heyman, "I'm losing my grip on my character as a heel. I can feel it slipping away. He's being aggressive. He's skipping practices.

## 2. National Pride and Prejudice

He's partying. I don't know what to do. I don't know how to handle this." Heyman, according to Sonnen, advised him to "drop everything and come clean," and be "completely real" if Wanderlei wasn't going to follow the tacit script.

It certainly got real at a weigh-in for two of the season's competitors. Wanderlei, staring at Sonnen, menacingly pounded his fist into his palm, telling Sonnen, "soon, soon." Sonnen returned fire, remarking that he had challenged Wanderlei for years. Wanderlei responded by spitting in the direction of Sonnen and stalking toward him, closing the distance, with Sonnen insisting that it was "weird" that now he seemed so eager for the fight. Bickering about the date of the fight, Sonnen asking when the fight was supposed to happen, with Wanderlei affirming that he knew when it would go down, getting amped up with his swearing and pointing a finger into Sonnen's face. After a moment of quiet, Sonnen, asked softly and smoothly, "can we talk then?" Wanderlei threw up his arms, announcing, "I don't want to talk. I'm done talking." Sonnen, still trying to defuse the situation, let Wanderlei know that "sometimes, I'd like to say 'hello.'"

Wanderlei continued his descent into losing control, angrily deriding the idea of saying hello or shaking hands, dismissing Sonnen's overture, spouting the f-word into Sonnen's face, saying "I don't want to like you and I don't want to be one of your friends." Eventually, Wanderlei walked away, clapping his hands. Perhaps mistakenly, Sonnen broke the silence, pleading, "I don't know the date. Can you tell me the date?" The date in Wanderlei's eyes was right then. Slapping Sonnen's face, demanding that the date was "now." With Wanderlei blustering "you want it now," Sonnen calmly told Wanderlei, "you have to stop. Please stop it." As Wanderlei moved closer, Sonnen shoved him, stating, "I can't let you get close." The two immediately squared off, Sonnen in a southpaw stance, and Wanderlei stalking in, ready to let his fists fly from his waist. Sonnen continued to ask Wanderlei to "stop." Wanderlei swung at Sonnen's head with an open hand, but Sonnen ducked under the blow, landing a double-leg takedown and putting Wanderlei on his back. With Sonnen punching from top position and Wanderlei crashing elbows from below, the two teams rushed in, most trying to separate the coaches and stop the fighting, with one, Wanderlei's assistant coach, Andre Dida, cowardly punching Sonnen in the back of the head. With the fighters separated, Wanderlei called out to Sonnen to go finish it. Sonnen, quite hilariously, apologized to his student

## Mixed Martial Arts and the Quest for Legitimacy

who was supposed to weigh-in for his fight, telling him that "I hope this isn't a distraction," whereas Dida and Wanderlei said "to hell with this" and took pride in the shots they landed back in their dressing room.

Only 30 percent out of 60,000 fans said they would be cheering for Silva in a poll done by Brazilian media outlet UOL, conducted in Portuguese! Wanderlei Silva, exasperated with the support Brazilian fans started to show for Sonnen, appealed to them, saying that "this guy is a racist and he doesn't deserve our respect." The heel had become vulnerable and then became the hero. However, the bout is now unlikely ever to occur, at least in the UFC. Wanderlei and Sonnen were temporarily forced into retirement, their careers tainted by performance-enhancing drugs (PEDs), the subject of another chapter. The fight still has a chance of happening in Bellator, but now lacks any meaning and would be pure spectacle if it ever gets booked.

It is hard to imagine that comments such as those made by Chael Sonnen around his two fights with Anderson Silva would not result in fines or suspensions in just about any other professional sport. When NHL forward Sean Avery remarked that he did not understand why fellow hockey players were dating his ex-girlfriends, or as he detestably put it, "his sloppy seconds," the league suspended him for "conduct detrimental to the league and the game of hockey," and his team, the Dallas Stars, wanted him gone. Sonnen was never punished for his comments. He was never asked about the ethics of hurling insults at the children of a less developed country.

It does seem evident that Sonnen's behavior violates the UFC's own Code of Conduct:

> Derogatory or offensive conduct, including without limitation insulting language, symbols, or actions about a person's ethnic background, heritage, color, race, national origin, age, religion, disability, gender or sexual orientation.
> 
> Inappropriate physical, verbal, and online behavior (such as inappropriate statements made via e-mail, text messaging or social networks).

Even if we assume, as I do, that Sonnen's vitriol was leveled at Brazilians, regardless of race, the Code of Conduct clearly specifies both "heritage" and "national origin" as an offense. It is also hard to imagine jokes at the expense of children living in poverty to be anything but an "inappropriate statement."

Chuck Liddell, a former light-heavyweight champion who endeared himself to fans with his reserved personality out of the octagon but wild-

## 2. National Pride and Prejudice

man, gladiatorial style of "go out on your shield" within the cage, offered his assessment of Sonnen.

> Chael's a nice guy. I've met him and hung out with him. I like him, and he's a nice guy. I can't stand the way he promotes fights. I understand what he's doing; he wasn't the most exciting fighter, so he made himself exciting by promoting the fight really well, and he got himself a couple of title shots for it. It works, but that whole crazy WWE-type stuff, that over-the-top stuff when you're fighting a guy, doesn't make sense to me, and I don't like it.

For the UFC, it is the drama and the spectacle. Sonnen turned the greatest cage-fighter in the world into a pay-per-view draw, and that is what counted. MMA as a sport has thrived on nationalistic and, perhaps, even racial tensions, fostering a type of tribalism and reaping enormous profits off it. After all, those tensions are not real, are they? Those kids living in absolute poverty in Brazil *are* real, though. Can a sport that builds a profile off of laughing at poverty and crime, even if it is disingenuous, ever become mainstream? And if it does build a profile off the heels of the sport, men who scoff at the very prospect of respecting others and treating people with dignity, then what exactly is this sport trying to foster in society? What becomes of a people who are told a narrative that degrades others for cheap laughs? It is just a fight, right?

Josh Koscheck, with his competitive professional career seemingly coming to a close, offered a perspective on his career as a heel to MMA journalist E. Spencer Kyte:

> I've done very well with my personality and being the so-called bad boy. It's part of the entertainment factor; you have to have some value. If you don't have any value, you can't sell tickets, and you can't put butts in seats. If you can't do that, you're useless.... You either have to have a character or just be a plain bad-ass fighter, but sometimes being a bad-ass fighter isn't enough. If you look at the WWE, they've done it for years—building characters and storylines—and I think that's a big part of our sport.... People always seem to want to watch a Josh Koscheck fight. They want to see me either get my ass kicked or they want to see me win. Either way, I don't really care what people's opinions are of me. I'm not here to make friends; I'm here to make money and win championships, and that is the opportunity I have Saturday night.

Though he may call himself the "godfather of integrity" on Twitter, Sonnen's public antics were never honest. When not promoting a fight, Sonnen can be articulate, even thoughtful. Sonnen is a calculating fighter/promoter who created a character to loathe. He was a professional in his duties as a broadcaster for UFC events on Fox, and now with ESPN and color commentating for Bellator. Following his loss to Jones, Sonnen said that he was finished speaking ill of Anderson Silva, and after Silva's gruesome TKO loss to Chris Weidman in 2013, he said that he hopes Silva "can look back and feel proud of his career and understands that we all see him as a great champion." Though Sonnen would not really be Sonnen if he did not let the competitor out: "I wish him an amazing life, but I still want to beat him."

# 3

# The Rise and Fall of TRT

Leading up to Sonnen-Silva I, there were more than a few who thought that Sonnen's wrestling could have some success against the Spider, whose takedown defense against BJJ fighters was very good, but a little suspect against wrestlers. Sonnen, it was thought, might have success for a round or two, maybe even two and a half, but eventually, Silva was expected to either submit Sonnen, as Anderson confided to the older Nogueira brother leading up to the fight, or blast Sonnen away with some combination of knees and laser-like punches.

Silva got the submission, but not when most were expecting it to happen. Sonnen charged Silva with a flurry of punches at the beginning of round one and then dumped Silva on his back, smothering him with top control. The ground and pound was nothing too damaging, but it was dominant. Silva's triangle-armbar attempt with time dwindling away was desperate. The champion, in his prime, stubbornly refused to wilt under the challenger's pressure. With less than two minutes left in the match, Sonnen hesitantly tapped his submission to Silva's choke, and the audience witnessed the most incredible defense of Silva's championship career in the UFC.

As it turned out, it wasn't a conventional defense. If Sonnen had won that unanimous decision, the bout would certainly have been declared a "no contest," and Silva would remain champion. After the fight, it was revealed that Chael Sonnen had been taking testosterone replacement therapy (TRT). At the time, TRT was not banned by the California State Athletic Commission (CSAC), under whose jurisdiction the bout was contested, but Sonnen never disclosed his use of the drugs to CSAC. What was perhaps even more damaging to the legacy of the first fight between Silva and Sonnen was that Sonnen's testosterone to epitestosterone ratio was three times above the limit CSAC allows for athletes who had a license to use TRT, and a shocking 17 times the male average.

## Mixed Martial Arts and the Quest for Legitimacy

Sonnen's defense was as exaggerated as all things Sonnen. In an interview with the *LA Times*, Sonnen was asked to explain his hypogonadism, which was the supposed reason why he was taking TRT. Sonnen flatly responded that taking TRT was not an option. "I either take this medicine or die. I'm not asking if I can take it. It's up to them to let me take it. It's a substance that's often abused, and I deal with taking it in shame. But a blood test can clear you, and show I take the appropriate amount. I'm paying for the tests. I've taken four so far. And they'll do a day-before and morning-after test as well." In just a few short years, a second PED scandal would force Sonnen into retirement, deny him the grudge match against another Brazilian, Wanderlei Silva, further erode whatever legacy he had managed to build for himself, and, largely due to another multiple offender, TRT itself would finally be banned.

TRT, the addition of exogenous testosterone to one's body, is traditionally authorized through a medical prescription for two injections of testosterone per week, or sometimes through the application of gels and one pill to block the production of female sex hormones. Dr. Johnny Benjamin, a medical doctor who is also a MMA commentator, has iterated five reasons why a man in his 20s or 30s might require TRT to attain average levels of testosterone. Reasons include testes that did not develop during adolescence, damage or the removal of one's testes, damage to the pituitary gland, a temporary drop in testosterone levels due to excessive weight-cutting and overtraining, and previous steroid usage.

What made Dr. Benjamin a controversial figure, back in the days when TRT was sanctioned, was his disbelief in the legitimacy of TRT prescriptions for MMA. Less than one percent of males in the general population under the age of 45 are clinically diagnosed with low enough testosterone levels to warrant TRT. If a preponderance of mixed-martial artists are legitimately in need of TRT, then the sport really needs to take further measures to ensure that accidental groin kicks do not happen, prevent excessive weight-cutting, or refuse to license fighters with damaged pituitary glands, as this would actually indicate brain damage. Dr. Benjamin had insisted that the diagnosis of low testosterone levels was linked to prior steroid use.

Dr. Karen L. Herbst, an endocrinologist with the University of Arizona, reviewed Sonnen's medical files leading up to his fight against Rashad Evans, when he had applied for a TRT usage exemption. In a letter sent to Sonnen's management and to the Nevada Athletic Commission

## 3. The Rise and Fall of TRT

(NAC), the body that was reviewing Sonnen's TRT exemption, Dr. Herbst concluded that Sonnen had medical grounds to be given the exemption. However, the letter sent by Dr. Herbst expressed two alarming qualifiers. Firstly, she expressed that Sonnen was "likely permanently hypogonadal" from his usage of testosterone that went back at least five years. She posited that "the suppression of his gonadal axis for that long may never allow a return to normalcy," and that going off of TRT "would be very disruptive to his career." Secondly, and even more damning, was Dr. Herbst's review of the original medical decision to prescribe Sonnen TRT, claiming that it is "not clear that there was a definitive [without a doubt] diagnosis of hypogonadism."

Taking synthetic testosterone has the potential of making one dependent on this external source, effectively shutting down the internal production of testosterone. The athlete becomes trapped in a negative feedback loop where the ability to compete is severely compromised by the body's inability to produce testosterone. There do not appear to be any cases of fighters who were publicly taking TRT, stopped their injections, and then continued to enjoy successful careers at the same level of competition as during their days of taking TRT.

Dr. Herbst's questioning of the initial TRT prescription is profoundly troubling, and potentially a view into a medical establishment that was all too eager to recommend professional fighters for injections. One of the most entertaining fights in UFC heavyweight history occurred in Brisbane, Australia. Antonio "Bigfoot" Silva, a massive heavyweight known to cut water-weight to reach the 265-lb limit of the UFC's heaviest division, squared off against Mark Hunt, another fighter who often cut weight to make the 265-lb limit. A K-1 kickboxing champion who entered the UFC with an overall losing record in MMA, he had endeared himself to fans by winning four straight fights before getting stopped by former champion Junior Dos Santos. Their five-round fight was a compelling, back-and-forth affair, fraught with electrifying swings in momentum. The judges tasked with deciding the winner turned in a majority draw decision, a just call for the big men who gave so much of themselves in the octagon.

The decision was not to last for Bigfoot, as his drug test revealed elevated levels of testosterone and his record was altered for the bout to stand as a no-contest instead. On the one hand, Silva's medical prescription for TRT appeared to be more on the level than most. Silva has acromegaly, a condition where tumors on the pituitary gland cause excessive growth hormone. Fearing the onset of diabetes and heart disease, Silva, at 33, elected to undergo surgery for acromegaly, putting his pituitary gland under the knife and therefore compromising his body's ability to produce testosterone. Silva seems to have more of a case for TRT than anyone else fighting in the UFC. On the other hand, Silva is no stranger to PED controversy, having tested positive for the steroid boldenone in 2008. He dismissed the 2008 CSAC ban of one year, electing to fight in Japan, where athletic commissions are basically non-existent. Silva's $50,000 bonus went to Hunt, the failed test tainted what could have been a fight to define his legacy, and he surely lost a number of fans, including Dana White.

White was enthused during the contest, tweeting that the bout was the "Sickest HW fight ever!!!" and that he "might buy them both their own private ISLANDS!!!!" The failed drug test changed his tune measurably, and he said that the revelation "bummed" him out and caused him to issue a stern warning to fighters on the UFC roster. "So all you guys out there that are on TRT, and it's legal, you won't go fuck around and take that shot after you've been tested, there's the consequences. The consequences could not be worse. Now you're on suspension for a year, you lost your win and your bonus money, and I'm sure your sponsors aren't thrilled either."

The problem is that the supposed decision for Bigfoot to take additional testosterone, above his prescribed amount, came from a medical doctor who is also employed by the UFC. The call to take an extra dosage of testosterone came from Marcio Tannure, who was hired by the UFC to liaise between Silva's own medical doctor, the UFC medical staff, and UFC executives, such as Marc Ratner and Mike Mersch. Tannure was supposedly chosen because of his fluency in English and Portuguese. However, in addition to Tannure's paid consultant position with the UFC, he was also the medical director of the Brazilian Mixed Martial Arts Commission (CABMMA). Tannure insisted that he was simply passing along advice that came from Silva's medical doctor, and not the advice of anyone else. Silva, at least initially, disagreed, taking to social media to blame Tannure as the "UFC doctor" who advised him to jack up his testosterone treatment.

White expressed what was obviously frustration over the prescription to take the additional shot, and at fighters who are using TRT. "I told you we test the shit out of these guys that are on TRT. We gave him his last

## 3. The Rise and Fall of TRT

test the week of the fight, and he was perfect. He took another shot. It put him over. And what does that extra shot really do for you? What did it really do for you the week of the fight? It destroyed everything."

As White admitted early in 2013, it is not hard to abuse TRT and still get your testosterone limits under control at the time of the bout, the only time when UFC fighters were traditionally tested during this era. "What I believe guys are doing, is jacking up this stuff through the roof through their entire training camp, then getting back down to normal levels right before the fight, which is cheating."

That is exactly what Chael Sonnen was doing leading up to his fight with Wanderlei Silva. Sonnen tested positive for Anastrozole and Clomiphene in late spring of 2014, weeks before the bout was scheduled. His initial excuse was that there are distinctions between "gameday" testing and out-of-competition testing. For example, cocaine is a prohibited substance on fight night, but it is not against the rules to test positive for cocaine metabolites leading up to the fight. Jon Jones tested positive for cocaine in an out-of-competition test leading up to his fight against Daniel Cormier and was never fined or suspended for that violation. Whether the fight between Jones and Cormier should have taken place at all, when one of the athletes was at the very least dabbling in a highly addictive and dangerous drug, is a whole other issue. Jones did check into a rehab facility after the fight against Cormier, but was only there for a few hours.

The flaw in Sonnen's logic is that PEDs are banned outside of competition. The idea that you are receiving a performance enhancing benefit in your training camp that will not lead to an enhanced performance on game day is totally absurd. It was not until NAC disclosed the full extent of Sonnen's violations, enough chemicals to make a Soviet strength and conditioning coach blush, that he even came remotely close to coming clean. Faced with the revelations that he was also taking human growth hormone (HGH) and recombinant human erythropoietin (EPO), Sonnen finally admitted to getting caught. What he wasn't willing to do was issue any kind of apology. An apology might have been fairly meaningless considering that when the lab came to collect Wanderlei's out-of-competition sample, the Brazilian simply ran away. Sonnen was slapped with a two-year ban on his fight career that prompted him into a temporary retirement, whereas Wanderlei was issued a lifetime ban that was overturned just over a year and a half later, though both men exited the UFC in disgrace.

## Mixed Martial Arts and the Quest for Legitimacy

In 2016, Chael Sonnen went on the Joe Rogan Experience, the UFC color commentator's excellent podcast, to explain not only his side of the story, but also the context of Wanderlei's alleged run from the NAC sample collector. Sonnen explained that the individual tasked with collecting the sample ambushed him at the MGM, insisting on taking both a urine sample, which requires the regulator to see the athlete undress and to watch him pee, and to collect a blood sample in a dirty custodian's closet. The collector, according to Sonnen, did not even present any ID, nor did he allow Sonnen to take his picture. Sonnen went along with the urine sample and the blood test, but Wanderlei, when met with the same suspicious testing procedure, being communicated to him in his second language, did not feel comfortable with either getting naked in front of the regulator or letting him draw blood, and eventually got in his car to make it to an event promoting the fight against Sonnen. Surely, experiences like the one Sonnen described are not an acceptable methodology of sample collection. Sample collectors must carry documentation to corroborate their identity, and sample collection must be done in sanitary conditions. At least Sonnen and Wanderlei will always have that tussle on the set of *TUF*.

Mark Bocek, a Canadian veteran of the sport and former training partner of GSP at Tristar in Montreal, announced his retirement in August of 2014. Bocek held a very respectable lifetime UFC record of 8–5, and was 3–1 in his final four fights with the organization. During an interview with *MMA Fighting*'s Ariel Helwani, Bocek listed a number of reasons behind his retirement, with PEDs informing a major part of his decision. "I know everyone's saying it comes off weak, don't mention [a PED problem] unless you're going to mention names, blah blah blah, but, I don't think it's classless to mention there's a PED war going on. It's classless to mention names. That's not fair. That's not right."

> We all lift weights, and we know what weight-lifting does. Weight-lifting doesn't turn one into a superhuman freak that doesn't get tired. It doesn't really work like that. [PEDs are] not a magic bullet, or anything. You still have to do the hard work. It's not like you can give this to anyone and they'll become the world champion. But when you have someone who is highly evolved, and highly trained, and highly motivated, and highly focused with training and work ethic and diet and big money on the line … of course it's going to be an issue, unfortunately.

When asked by Helwani to comment on a figure recently quoted by another fighter, who speculated that as much as 90 percent of the UFC roster is on PEDs, Bocek thought that it is likely close to the reality. "We

## 3. The Rise and Fall of TRT

can only speculate, we can't put a number on it, but maybe someone like me can go further into this area than your average Joe. Maybe 90% sounds about right. You could say that, yeah."

The highest profile fighter to call for changes to drug testing is Bocek's former teammate, the greatest welterweight of all time, Georges St-Pierre. In early 2014, GSP explained that his concerns regarding PEDs were central to his decision to "take a break" from competition.

> I wanted to do something to help people who are honest in their sport. And whether or not you believe me, I have never taken drugs in my life. I am willing to take a lie detector, I do not care. I'm all for drug testing. I'm not accusing anyone of taking steroids and I'm not judging anyone. I have internal information. I am an athlete and I know what's going on.
>
> Everyone knows who, when, where and how. There are people, some doctors, and everyone will see the same. It's like all sports. Where there is money, there are ways to cheat, and it will always be so. But I think we should take steps to minimize those things, because it is not fair. I tried to change things remaining diplomatic. Unfortunately, people were not ready to change. This is OK, but I was disappointed.

Leading up to what might have been GSP's last fight as a professional mixed-martial artist at UFC 167 in November of 2013, a debate erupted on testing for PEDs. The challenger for UFC welterweight gold, Johny Hendricks, had established himself amongst the elite of the division at the time, knocking out then-top-ten fighters Martin Kampmann and Jon Fitch, and earning close decisions against two other top-ten fighters, Josh Koscheck and Carlos Condit. In the months leading up to the bout, GSP publicly raised the possibility of having the PED testing performed by the Voluntary Anti-Doping Agency (VADA), an independent lab that tests for prohibited substances and methods listed by the World Anti-Doping Agency (WADA), the governing body responsible for identifying the International Olympic Committee's (IOC) prohibited substances since 1999, and for establishing the template intended to harmonize all sports.

Weeks before UFC 167, GSP stated his intentions to have his testing performed by VADA, calling upon Hendricks to do the same and even offering to pay for those tests. Hendricks instead suggested that WADA conduct the testing, seemingly unaware that WADA is not responsible for actual lab-work, and that VADA's list of prohibited substances is based on the WADA list. Not unreasonably, Hendricks expressed a feeling of insecurity as he was uncomfortable with the notion of his opponent paying for his testing that was being conducted by an agency that featured this same opponent quite prominently on its website. The debate went nowhere, eventually ending with GSP submitting himself to VADA testing and Hendricks complying with the NAC testing.

Two months before UFC 167, MMA journalists Matt Roth and Brent Brookhouse reported on the email correspondence between GSP's camp and the NAC that Keith Kizer, executive director of the NAC, provided to the journalists. It began in the summer, with GSP suggesting VADA for drug testing and offering to pay for Hendricks' lab work. Hendricks initially responded to the offer with, "Heck, ya!" UFC president Dana White was less enthused about the idea, calling it "a little weird" and insinuating that enhanced testing beyond the NAC was superfluous. Hendricks' manager, Ted Ehrhardt, became uneasy with VADA, recommending instead that GSP and Hendricks be tested by the NAC, but based on the WADA list of prohibited substances, recommending a lab based out of Salt Lake City, Utah, that was equipped for the enhanced testing required. The email correspondence between Rodolphe Beaulieu (a representative from GSP's camp) and Kizer illuminated the reluctance of the GSP camp to agree to that particular method of enhanced testing.

During the month of August, with the NAC waiting on GSP's camp to confirm the enhanced testing through the NAC, Beaulieu asked Kizer a litany of questions, many of which aroused the suspicions of Kizer, such as the exact list of substances that the competitors would be tested for, asking about specific steroids, such as 19-norandrosterone, as well as asking about human growth hormone (HGH) and erythropoietin (EPO). Beaulieu inquired about detection limits for prohibited substances, the name of the medical review officer, and details on the collection procedures. With still no confirmation from GSP's camp, despite the email correspondence, Kizer sent an email to Beaulieu outlining his assumption that GSP was refusing the NAC-WADA enhanced testing. Exasperated at the level of questioning coming from the GSP camp and concerned that the GSP camp had overstepped boundaries, Kizer also wrote, slightly peevishly, that "the Commission does not allow any licensee to dictate or craft the testing. Not only is this inappropriate, it is not something the Commission would even consider." Beaulieu responded to this email on August 17, one day after Kizer's email, to confirm GSP's participation with the NAC enhanced testing. However, Beaulieu also requested that all the documentation pertaining to the enhanced testing be sent to his office, but he would not be unable to respond to email or voice messaging until

## 3. The Rise and Fall of TRT

August 27. Based on Beaulieu's email, Kizer decided that the enhanced testing was off. GSP went ahead with his original plan to submit to VADA testing, and Hendricks complied with the standard testing performed by the NAC.

GSP-Hendricks was an evenly contested bout. Many observers, none more than Hendricks himself, believed the challenger to have triumphantly dethroned the long-dominant champ. Hendricks clearly won rounds 2 and 4, hurting GSP badly in both rounds. GSP, however, narrowly defeated Hendricks in rounds 3 and 5. Round 1 was a toss-up, but all three judges scored it for the champ. GSP's interview with Joe Rogan became an awkward encounter, with the champ seemingly wanting to say something to the crowd, but unsure if he should. Rogan's insistence that GSP reveal what he was thinking eventually won out, and GSP announced that he was going to go away from MMA for an indeterminate period of time.

Both GSP and Hendricks passed their tests. In an interview conducted in August 2014, GSP flatly stated that a condition he has to fighting again in the UFC is that both he and his opponent must submit to drug testing based upon the WADA list of prohibited substances and methods and performed by either VADA or the U.S. Anti-Doping Agency (USADA). That condition now appears to be met through USADA.

The perceptions surrounding Dan Henderson's TRT usage and that of Vitor Belfort represent a study of contrast. Both are old-school veterans of the sport, Belfort turning pro in 1996 and Henderson in 1997. Both men are UFC tournament winners, Belfort winning the UFC 12 heavyweight tournament and Henderson the UFC 17 middleweight tournament. Belfort was also a UFC light-heavyweight champion, and Henderson captured both the Pride middleweight (205 lbs) and welterweight (183 lbs) championship titles. Both of these men have defined their careers with crushing knockout victories.

Henderson captured the Pride welterweight title in 2007 with a spinning back-fist knockout of the Brazilian, Wanderlei Silva. Silva's reign in Pride's middleweight division was one of the most legendary championship runs in the history of MMA. With a penchant for vicious onslaughts of knees in the clinch and winging punches, Silva decimated his competition, earning 22 victories in Pride, 15 of them by KO or TKO. Henderson's flattening of Silva enshrined him a special honor in the sport as the first athlete to hold championship belts across two weight classes simultaneously in an organization that featured elite talent of multiple top-15 fighters by weight class. Though Henderson would fall short in his bids to unify his Pride belts with their equivalents in the UFC, his KO of Michael Bisping has stood out as the archetypal one-punch knockout for a lot of fans of the sport. Henderson captured light-heavyweight gold in Strikeforce with a massive KO of Rafael Cavalcante, and in his last fight in Strikeforce, knocked out the greatest heavyweight in the history of the sport, Fedor Emelianenko, in a heavyweight matchup where Henderson just barely made the lower limit of the weight class, drinking a bottle of water to tip the scales at 207 lbs.

Henderson's return to the UFC was a thrilling five-round contest with former UFC light-heavyweight champion, and 2005 Pride Grand Prix tournament winner, Mauricio "Shogun" Rua. Henderson's right hand found Shogun early and often during the first three rounds until Henderson began to fade, allowing Shogun to take over, connecting on Henderson and taking him down relentlessly during the fifth round. The title fight Henderson earned with the decision win over Shogun was not to be, as Henderson had to pull out of the fight due to an injury suffered in a final sparring session, therefore losing his shot at the title, and even causing the whole event to be pulled when champion Jon Jones refused to fight Sonnen on short notice.

Henderson's usage of TRT is not without controversy. The Manitoba Provincial Athletic commission was skeptical of his application for a TRT exemption leading up to his match against Rashad Evans, requesting a direct medical reason for the exemption. Henderson never provided a reason for the exemption, but neither did he pull out of the fight. Instead, Henderson fought the former UFC light-heavyweight champion without TRT, losing a close decision.

Henderson never quite returned to the same level of success in the twilight of his career after getting off of TRT. He lost badly to Daniel Cormier, who tossed Henderson around the octagon at will, and suffered first-round stoppage losses to Vitor Belfort for a second time over a span of two years and to Gegard Mousasi. Henderson earned two final victories to close his legendary career, knocking out the durable Tim Boetsch and coming back from the brink against Bellator middleweight kingpin Hector Lombard with a brilliantly timed elbow. Henderson even came within a hair of capturing the elusive UFC gold, nearly knocking out Michael Bisping a second time, only to have the Brit recover his wits and secure the decision victory.

## 3. The Rise and Fall of TRT

However, whatever controversy surrounded Henderson's TRT usage pales in comparison to controversies surrounding Vitor Belfort.

Vitor Belfort's professional career has been marked by incredible highs and soul-searching lows. His knockout wins have dominated highlight reel specials on late-night TV. The notable difference between Belfort and Henderson is that although Henderson always looked the part of a high-level athlete, Belfort, at certain times in his career, looked like something else entirely. He had the appearance of a jacked-up monster when he debuted in the UFC at the young age of 19, five years before the NAC had *publicly revealed* that it caught its first UFC competitor on PEDs.[1] However, Belfort's losses defined him as someone who would break if the match got out of the first round.

Following his split-decision loss in 2006 to Henderson, it was revealed that Belfort had tested positive for 4-hydroxytestosterone, failing his drug test. Belfort had a list of excuses, suggesting that the steroid was in some over-the-counter product he was using and suggesting that it was present in injections he was given by an endocrinologist in Brazil while rehabbing a torn meniscus. Though the NAC suspended Belfort for nine months, he disregarded the ruling by fighting on a card in England, honoring less than half of the NAC suspension for steroids.

What has really made Belfort into a lightning rod was the destruction he wrought during a run throughout 2013. Previously, the only connection between kicks and Belfort was the front-kick to his face in a loss he suffered at the foot of Anderson Silva. However, in 2013, Belfort smashed Michael Bisping, Luke Rockhold, and Dan Henderson with brutal head-kicks. The victory over Rockhold was especially incredible as it was a spinning heel-kick, a technique that rarely works in MMA, and what would be an ill-advised tactic against a fighter with an absolutely devastating top-position ground game like Rockhold. The idea of a veteran like Vitor Belfort effectively adding kicking weapons to his repertoire at a relatively advanced age (for a professional athlete, of course) became pretty hard to imagine outside of the advantages TRT provides. It was not just Belfort's wins that raised the suspicions of thoughtful fans, it was the man's appearance. In 2013, Vitor Belfort looked like a bodybuilder. He was this transhuman specimen whose very face looked like it had developed musculature.

Part of the appeal of Henderson, and why many had not made as big an issue with his TRT usage, is undoubtedly connected to his personality.

## Mixed Martial Arts and the Quest for Legitimacy

Henderson, without any discernable concern for his public image whatsoever, has been perceived as an elder-statesman of the sport. Vitor Belfort, though as much of a veteran of the sport as any man currently competing can claim to be, has not been granted that same amount of respect. His expression of faith, completely honest and unquestionably fundamental to his tremendous professional success in the wake of the personal tragedy he's endured with the apparent kidnapping and murder of his sister, has irked many MMA fans as hypocritical and contradictory.

The stated position of UFC President Dana White on TRT has migrated over time. Ben Folkes, a MMA commentator who is a regular contributor to *USA Today*, has defined White as "against TRT—after being for it, against it, and for it again." He had alternatively promised to test the "shit" out of fighters who were taking TRT, and trumpeted the wonders of modern sport science to revive a man's testosterone levels to their peak. In fact, White's flip-flopping on TRT is especially evident with Vitor Belfort, expressing contempt at journalists who found it suspicious that Belfort appeared to be fighting exclusively in Brazil, where testing and oversight is marginal, while known to be taking TRT.

To White, Vitor Belfort was "fucking awesome" when he became the first man to KO Dan Henderson. He was a destroyer of men, with a physique straight out of a Mr. Olympia contest, likely tapping into the kind of fans who followed Brock Lesnar primarily because of the aesthetics of his size. The less said about Belfort's hair during this time, the better. He seemed to have earned another shot at UFC middleweight gold as a clear contender for Chris Weidman's title. Then, a drug test in February of 2014 almost derailed a title shot for Belfort, and did much more.

No title fight between Belfort and Weidman was actually booked yet, and Belfort had not applied for a TUE for the much-discussed fight. However, as a TRT user, and the most controversial one there was, Belfort was asked to undertake a random test by the NAC while he was in Las Vegas for the World MMA awards. He later claimed the test was "irrelevant" and refused to release the results. The NAC could not legally release the results without consent from Belfort, but they could deny him a license to fight in the state of Nevada until he voluntarily agreed to release the results to the public.

Belfort eventually relented, showing to the MMA community that he had been flagged for inhumanly high serum testosterone and free testosterone. The results of his test showed that his score for serum testosterone,

## 3. The Rise and Fall of TRT

at 1472 ng/dL, soared above the accepted range of 348–1197 ng/dL, and his free testosterone, ambiguously listed at >50.0 pg/mL, was well above the 8.7–25.1 pg/mL range.

A scandal involving Vitor Belfort that is perhaps even more shocking was made public in 2015. Three years prior, the UFC accidentally emailed the results of a test administered to Belfort to approximately 30 UFC fighters and managers. The test, administered before Belfort's hastily assembled fight against Jon Jones for the light-heavyweight title, showed that Belfort had testosterone levels well above the maximum range allowed by the NAC. Realizing who the recipients were of the test results, a paralegal with the UFC sent an email to retract the original email, and then another email demanding that recipients delete the lab results. A few hours later, Lawrence Epstein, the UFC's executive vice president, sent out a threatening email to the original recipients. Warning the recipients to destroy the email and keep its contents confidential, Epstein promised to "seek all available judicial remedies against you in both your professional and personal capacities." Instead of publicly releasing Belfort's failed test, the UFC covered it up. Instead of pulling Belfort from the bout, the fight against Jon Jones went on. What personal repercussions Epstein had in mind can only be left to the imagination.

February 17, 2014, marked a turning point in MMA and a victory against the forces of spectacle that damage the legitimacy of the sport. The Nevada Athletic Commission unanimously voted to ban TRT in the state of Nevada and encouraged other athletic commissions to follow suit. Most other athletic commissions that oversee MMA competitions surely did, and most importantly, the UFC issued a statement affirming their belief that "our athletes should compete based on their natural abilities and on an even playing field. We also intend to honor this ruling in international markets where, due to a lack of governing bodies, the UFC oversees regulatory efforts for our live events. We encourage all athletic commissions to adopt this ruling."

It is likely not coincidental that the NAC's decision came during a period of heightened scrutiny. About a month before the decision to ban TRT, the Association of Ringside Physicians issued a call to remove TRT from MMA, and Dana White had started to question the presence of TRT in the UFC, threatening to start "testing the shit" out of those with a TUE for the duration of their training camp.

Two days before the NAC's landmark vote, ESPN published an expose

## Mixed Martial Arts and the Quest for Legitimacy

in *Outside the Lines* chronicling the prevalence of TRT and blurring the distinction between TRT prescriptions and PED abuse. Mike Fish, with assistance from Josh Gross, revealed that while the NAC had issued only 15 TUEs, that number is actually very high compared to other sports. For instance, the International Olympic Committee (IOC) did not issue a single TUE for the 2012 Olympic Games in London, England, an enormous event with almost 6,000 male athletes. A particularly damning interview that Fish conducted was with Dr. Don Caitlin, identified as the leading anti-doping expert in the U.S., who described the athletic commissions who were granting TUEs as following "Mickey Mouse rules." The doctors were depicted as signing off on TRT prescriptions in just about any case of a fighter describing tiredness and lethargy, a very common predicament for people who are training two or three times a day. Furthermore, the allegations surrounding these medical professionals as having ambiguous relationships with the UFC helped to sway public opinion against TRT. According to Caitlin, "It's just a farce that is perpetuated in MMA. It is doping. It is cheating. It is both."

The investigation leaves the reader flummoxed over how TRT could have been prescribed to mixed-martial artists by medical professionals. Hypogonadism afflicts fewer than 0.1 percent of healthy 30-year-olds. Men who are diagnosed as having "low-normal" testosterone are not immediately prescribed TRT. Professional sporting leagues only grant TUEs for serious medical conditions, such as in cases of cancer or physical trauma. Defenders of TRT in MMA have argued that low testosterone is significantly more common for fighters because the blows to the head that they receive in training and competition damage the pituitary gland, causing hormone irregularities. However, no boxers have applied for a TUE, and it is exceptionally rare in the NFL. It is actually quite dubious to be granting someone a license to fight *at all* if they are believed to have suffered the kind of serious brain trauma that would cause a reduction in the production of testosterone to levels that are so dangerous that the quality of life enjoyed by athletes is impaired. If fighters do have low testosterone, and this is a really big "if" because we are assuming that TRT was not simply being used as a PED, then it is most likely caused by some combination of overtraining, weight-cutting, and prior steroid use.

The tragic irony of TRT in MMA is best captured by Michael "The Count" Bisping. During a UFC middleweight run between 2008–2013, Bisping lost only to fighters who had been linked to TRT and Wanderlei

## 3. The Rise and Fall of TRT

Silva, a fighter who refused a random test. Two of those losses were concussive blasts, by the right hand of Dan Henderson and the shin of Vitor Belfort, crushing KOs destined to live on in highlight reels of the sport for decades. Bisping told Fish that the combination of TRT and the experience of those fighters in their 30s and 40s who use it to foment a new biological prime is "ridiculous." The irony of TRT in MMA is that fighters "are not trying to hit a ball with a bat or throw it in a hoop. We're trying to knock our opponents out. So somebody is going to get hurt one day." As we will consider in the next chapter, many, if not all, competitors in MMA have likely been seriously hurt in this sport. It is also a kind of poetic justice that Bisping, a man whose career has been hurt by PED probably more than anyone, improbably captured UFC gold in 2016 as a huge underdog while nearing the age of 40.

There is a certain symmetry to the TRT era in cage-fighting. As Dan Henderson was the original UFC fighter to make transparent requests for exemptions, so too was he the last UFC fighter to use TRT legally for his re-match with Shogun Rua. Henderson held on in the first round, coming very close to a TKO loss as the buzzer sounded. In fact, to viewers at home, it almost looked like the referee had in fact stopped the fight before the round ended, as the production cut to a commercial break without a moment's pause. Despite looking more and more like a man his age, Henderson eventually landed his patented "h-bomb" on Rua, following it up with more headshots until the referee called off the fight, revealing a violently broken nose on Rua's face. Henderson characteristically referred to getting "dinged" in his post-fight interview, having left fans with another thrilling fight. But he also left us with the sense that such fights will be fewer and farther between for aging veterans. Not just for Henderson, but for all UFC fighters as they advance in their 30s, inexorably fading and dealing with slower reflexes and longer post-workout recovery times. In his next bout, only two months after the Shogun Rua fight, Henderson took on former Olympic wrestler Daniel Cormier. Cormier, a training partner of UFC heavyweight champion Cain Velasquez, was a former heavyweight, a Strikeforce tournament champion, and undefeated in 14 fights. Cormier effortlessly tossed Henderson around the Octagon, completely overwhelming the former Pride champion, until mercifully ending the match with a rear-naked-choke.

TRT likely prolonged Henderson's legendary career and gave fans some memorable bouts. Competing in a sport as grueling and as violent

## Mixed Martial Arts and the Quest for Legitimacy

as MMA is not feasible for fighters closing in on 40 years old, especially for those who have been competing in the fight business since they were young men, nor is it sensible. Fighters will no longer have the TRT option to prolong their careers artificially going forward, and that is surely a good thing.

In 2015, the UFC made one of its most important decisions in bringing MMA into the mainstream and transforming it into a legitimate sport. It was a decision that has surely had a notable impact on Zuffa's bottom line, but it was a decision that has gone far in cleaning up the sport. Since the summer of 2015, UFC fighters undergo testing conducted by the U.S. Anti-Doping Agency (USADA). This allows for an independent and reputable institution to not only test fighters on fight night, but to also randomly test fighters out of competition. The move to incorporate USADA is commendable and far-sighted on the part of Zuffa and is a relationship that WME-IMG must continue. It has had costs on the sport, though. Numerous bouts, including headliners, have been scratched, and lingering question marks hover over the records of legends.

Anderson Silva, a man who twice defeated Chael Sonnen on TRT, and no less than Dana White's own choice of GOAT, failed a USADA-administered test a couple of weeks before a fight against Nick Diaz. The Spider tested positive for anabolic steroids Drostanolone and Androstane, in addition to drugs for anti-anxiety and sleep deprivation. Rather than accept responsibility, Silva inexplicably blamed the positive test on a tainted Thai sexual enhancing blue liquid that was given to him by a guy he couldn't remember. Silva's decision victory over Diaz was overturned to a no-contest, and he was fined almost $400,000, but the consequences for his legacy are far worse.

Another GOAT front-runner, and possibly future legend of the sport, tested positive in a pre-fight test, almost ruining the much-anticipated UFC 200. Light-heavyweight champion Jon Jones was stripped of his title in 2015 when he ran a red light with his rental car, colliding with a pregnant woman, fleeing the scene on foot, and briefly returning to grab a wad of cash from his car before taking off again. After winning an interim title in 2016, Jones was booked to rematch against current champ Daniel Cormier, whom Jones had already defeated, in the headlining bout of UFC 200. The fight was called off close to the event after Jones tested positive for Clomiphene, an estrogen blocker, and Letrozole. Jones blamed the failed test on what he described as a "dick pill" that a buddy of his

## 3. The Rise and Fall of TRT

purchased online, an arbitration panel of NAC met to reach a disciplinary decision. Maintaining that Jones' decision to take the erectile dysfunction pills was behavior that "verged on reckless" and that the story "lacked the clear ring of truth," the panel cleared Jones of intentional wrong-doing, limiting his suspension to a year. However, when this friend who allegedly supplied the "dick pill" to Jones submitted the invoice of the purchase for the erectile dysfunction medication to NAC, the invoice also listed clomiphene as having been ordered![2]

The new marquee fight of UFC 200 instead featured Mark Hunt against a rejuvenated Brock Lesnar, the former heavyweight champion who had catapulted UFC 100 to PPV success, making a return to the octagon from the WWE. Lesnar took Hunt down and won a decision, utilizing ferocious ground-and-pound that pummeled a shell-shocked Hunt. Unlike other fighters competing in UFC 200, the announcement of Lesnar's return occurred only a few weeks before the event, meaning that he was not subjected to the same possibility of random drug testing that other fighters, like Hunt, would have had to pass. Lesnar received an exemption from earlier testing, but did undergo a densely concentrated regime of pre-fight tests. After the revelations of Jones' failed drug test surfaced, Lesnar even questioned Jones' professionalism. Only a few days removed from the UFC's biggest event since UFC 100, Lesnar failed one of the pre-fight tests, also for an estrogen blocker, which was blamed on foot cream.

Lesnar's failed drug test was an especially infuriating predicament for Hunt, who once again fought an opponent who was chemically enhanced. Hunt had goaded Lesnar during the build-up to UFC 200, doubting that Lesnar was clean. Lesnar responded by telling Hunt that he was a "jacked White-boy" and to "deal with it." The failed drug test clearly radicalized Hunt, as he publicly considered retirement, demanded all of Brock Lesnar's money from UFC 200, and even threatened legal action against Zuffa for helping Lesnar attain the pre-fight drug testing timetable exemption.

These are but the highest profile fighters to test positive during this new USADA era, but there are many, many, MANY others. It will be hard for WME-IMG to stomach the loss of champions and contenders from cards, especially after paying $4 billion to Zuffa for the UFC, but it is a relationship that must be maintained. The legitimacy of the sport depends on it.

MMA is a sport that can be decided by the slimmest of advantages,

## Mixed Martial Arts and the Quest for Legitimacy

and matches can end very quickly. I earlier suggested that *fortuna*, or luck, might be experienced more acutely in MMA than most sports. It is not surprising to see that mixed-martial artists are also desperate for whatever advantage they can find. The stakes of eradicating PEDs from MMA are so high, higher than in most other sports, because of the inherent violence of the sport, the subject of our next chapter.

# 4

# The Spectacle of Violence

In 2012, Nick Denis entered the UFC as a promising young talent for the organization's newly established bantamweight division. For the UFC, signing fighters who are born outside of the U.S. and Brazil represents an imperative for international expansion. Hailing from beautiful North Bay, Ontario, a fighter like Denis was perfect for a Canadian market that had been catching fire thanks to the enormous popularity of Georges St-Pierre. Even with an impressive 11–2 record, Denis exceeded everyone's expectations in his UFC debut with a series of brutal, standing elbows to the temple of his opponent, Joseph Sandoval, knocking him out in less than 30 seconds. Denis earned a "Knockout of the Night" pay bonus for his devastating victory. Denis was then submitted in his next bout to fellow Canadian Roland Delorme. How shocking was it, less than a year later, when Denis announced his retirement from the sport.

As Denis is a PhD student in Biochemistry, it is an understatement to say that he is not your average cage-fighter. Following Denis' first loss, a knockout to Marlon Sandro where, as Denis describes it, Sandro "dribbled my head on the canvas like a basketball," he used his library privileges at the University of Ottawa to review the research on head trauma in sports. What deeply concerned Denis was the growing literature on the relationship between "sub-concussive trauma," all those blows to the head that do not cause a loss of consciousness, and the probability of neurological decay. In November of 2012, Denis announced his retirement on his blog. It was his fear, not just the certainty of the trauma that his brain would be subjected to in the event of another knockout loss, but also the certainty of knowing that if he pursued a career in MMA he would be punched, elbowed, and kicked in the head at sub-concussive levels. Furthermore, this exposure to trauma would not be isolated to professional competition, maybe three times a year, but far more often than that.

## Mixed Martial Arts and the Quest for Legitimacy

Instead, he was forced to reflect on whether it was worth it to continue sparring at Montreal's Tristar gym and endure an endless barrage of blows to the head while working through a camp to prepare for a bout. Every. Single. Week.

In his retirement notice, Denis said that he was forced to ask himself if he could willingly sacrifice his brain for this sport. "Could I fight in the UFC, against the best fighters in our solar system, literally trained killers, without sparring in training? Not really, so what was a I to do?" Denis expressed his dilemma in the next paragraph:

> Maybe I have already suffered brain injury, maybe I never would have. That is the problem with the brain. You can't really see the injury, it will take years and decades to manifest itself. When you get rocked in sparring, you shake your head and regain your composure, and within 10 seconds say, "ok, I'm good let's keep going." But are you actually ok? You are no longer dizzy, true, but do you have any idea what physical trauma your brain has just experienced? I have told this to a few people before. I make the analogy of my love for MMA as being a drug addict—I know that it isn't healthy for me, but holy fuck do I love it. I love MMA, and I have loved my experience with the UFC, Sengoku, and every other promotion along the way, but I am a human being first. I don't define myself by my work, and nor should you. I am a human being, and I was born with only one brain, and I want to take care of it so that I will recognize the ones I love when I get older.

Denis' "drug addict" comment is particularly revealing. It speaks of the months and years of hard work and self-sacrifice that is unleashed in competition against another, one just as prepared as you are. I can't be too confident, as I have never come remotely close to being a professional athlete myself, but there is an important dimension to the drug addict comment of Denis. It is the rush, the exhilaration of feeling 10,000 people celebrate your triumph, a celebration no more intensely experienced than when you club your opponent unconscious with an elbow, a knee, a shin, or a fist.

The promise of any UFC event is the KO. A one-strike thud to the head of an opponent. The freezing of a body as it stiffens and falls straight back like a tree that has been cut across close to the stump. This is the focus of UFC trailers used to promote pay-per-views. Strikes thrown by men out of time, savage reminders of a pre-modern existence when life was "solitary, poor, nasty, brutish, and short." This is what the people have paid for, and this is what has them screaming. When you are the victor, the explosion from the crowd is your drug. And you are financially compensated for your success. A fat "Knockout of the Night" bonus doubles

## 4. The Spectacle of Violence

your combined "show" money and "win" bonus, in some instances quadrupling it, or even quintupling it.

It is an addiction that causes you to take risks. Push things that much harder in the gym. Escalate the sparring session. Turn it into a "war" like you might experience on fight night. Forgo caution during the bout. Put it all on the line and "swing for the fences." Don't admit defeat, even when losing badly. Suffer a couple of knockdowns. One punch is all it takes. Round number is lost. Hard to focus. A fog sets in. Musashi's void of automatic movement. Unsure of what has happened. This is what sparring is for. Been through it. Instinct. Fight on instinct. Fighting is instinct. It is in our genes.

Denis has not been alone in citing brain trauma as a key reason to walk away from the sport before his time is more obviously up. Mark Bocek, as we discussed in the previous chapter, had reflected on PEDs as a principle reason behind his early retirement, but he also expressed his fear of how brain trauma might impact the quality of his life as the years pass. Incredibly, despite a long career in the UFC, Bocek had only been TKO'd once, at the hands of former lightweight UFC champion Frankie Edgar back in 2007. Still, Bocek worried what a career of fighting has done to his brain. For Bocek, a palpable pressure was coming from the UFC to put on slugfests, insinuating that career advancement and money go to those who risk personal brain injury for themselves, while dishing out some brain injuries to their opponents.

> Let's take the PEDs out for a second, let's even forget about that as rampant as they are. With certain fights and certain fighters and certain people, you don't even see who the best fighter is. Because you know if you take someone down, you're probably going to end up on the undercard in your next fight, because they hate grappling. The UFC doesn't even like grappling, because the uneducated fans don't like grappling. So you start doing things like that, you end up on the undercard. If you stand in the middle and abandon strategy and just put on a slugfest and see who stays standing until the end, that's what people want. That's what they want to see, but now the chances of you winning the fight are much lower.

The main attraction for the UFC is the big knockout and it is no secret that the big knockout is what gets fans off their butts and excited, and even more importantly, it is the *anticipation* of the knockout that causes fans to order the PPV.

Unfortunately, while our bodies can be conditioned to pour out violence on each other (with hand wraps and gloves), and we can condition our bodies to not recoil into a fetal position when under attack, we cannot condition our brains to better absorb traumatic blows. Once known as "no-holds-barred" fighting, the introduction of the unified rules and the banning of head-butts, groin shots, hair pulling, 12-to-6 elbows on a grounded opponent, etc., was imperative in the movement to transform cage-fighting into a sport that we might be able to call MMA without deceiving ourselves entirely. These rules are, justly, invoked in the defense of the sport, proof that Senator McCain was ignorant in his identification of it as "human cockfighting." It may not be the arts to Meryl Streep, but associating MMA with the NFL in 2017 is a win that MMA fans will take.

UFC President Dana White has been the most prominent defender of the safety of the sport.

> Concussion is a huge dilemma right now for the NFL. Here's the difference between the UFC and the NFL as far as concussions are concerned. First of all, if you get a concussion, if you get knocked out or you get hurt whatsoever in the UFC, three months suspension. You are on suspension for three months and you cannot come back until you are cleared by a doctor. You can't have any contact whatsoever. In the NFL, you're not going to lose Tom Brady for three months, man. You lose Tom Brady for three months and your whole season is wiped out. So, the UFC, listen, we don't hide from it, it's a contact sport and that's what these guys do, [is] much safer. In the 20-year history of the UFC, it will be 20-years in November, there has never been a death or a serious injury. Never been a death or serious injury in 20 years because we go above and beyond when it comes to the safety of these guys. When you know you have two healthy athletes getting ready to compete, they get the proper medical attention before and after, it's the safest sport in the world, fact.

White raises some very good points about mandatory suspensions for fighters after KO and TKO losses, especially for those of us who have seen players on the New England Patriots come right back on the field after some fairly serious-looking hits. However, I don't know of too many people who consider cage-fighting, where the goal is to defeat your opponent in unarmed combat, as the "safest sport in the world."

There is a deeper and more troubling problem that this insistence on "cage-fighting as safer than boxing" narrative obfuscates. Josh Tucker, a journalist of the sport and, like myself, one of its conflicted fans, problematized the issue in the following way:

> While other combat sports face similar issues, and deal with them poorly, they tend to display some vague awareness that violence has consequences. (Boxing people, especially, know that their sport has been and continues to be a goddamned tragedy.) From top to bottom, though, many people involved in MMA don't.[1]

## 4. The Spectacle of Violence

The *Deadspin* article in which this quote is featured in is poignantly titled, "If MMA Doesn't Change, Someone is Going to Die." It is written in the aftermath of a particularly violent bantamweight beat-down in the WSOF (World Series of Fighting) between a sizable underdog, Josh Rettinghouse, and the well-known Marlon Moraes. Moraes punished Rettinghouse with crippling leg kicks, teeing off on the prospect at will, with Rettinghouse beaten, but refusing simply to crumble in a way that would typically cause a referee to call a TKO.

It is one of the tragic ironies of this sport that MMA has a taboo against throwing in the towel. Keith Kizer, the Director of the Nevada Athletic Commission (NAC) between 2006–2014, describes the reluctance of instituting an official policy of towel throwing as stemming from fears surrounding a "knucklehead fan" from throwing a towel in the octagon and causing an alteration in the behavior of fighters not directed by the referee. When Nick Diaz threw in the towel after his brother Nate suffered a massive head-kick thrown by his opponent, Josh Thomson, and appeared unable to defend himself or fight back, MMA fans like myself were left wondering when they last saw a towel thrown into the octagon. In MMA, the procedure is for a corner-man and the inspector to walk up to the cage and then for another inspector to signal to the referee to end the bout.

It is disturbing that corner-men in the UFC almost never stop a beatdown in progress. Rather than protecting their fighter from serious trauma, corners are reluctant to use even this mechanism for stopping a fight, and they seem disinterested in even entertaining the idea of intervention. While it is understandable that a corner wants to support the fighter, no matter what, it is ludicrous to imagine that a corner can defer to the judgment of their fighter. Yes, fighters are going to be angry with a corner that stops a fight. Joe Frazier was livid with corner-man Eddie Futch for stopping the fight before the start of the 15th round against his hated rival, Muhammad Ali, in the "Thrilla in Manila." Frazier was terribly swollen, practically blind, and Ali had famously said to his corner after the ninth round, "Man, this is the closest I've ever been to dying." Futch had cornered boxers who had actually died in competition, and he was not going to let Frazier risk his life. What is a legacy without life?

A fighter who has suffered multiple head-shots cannot make rational decisions regarding long-term health. In fact, they are not going to be thinking about the long-term whatsoever. They are in survival mode, going on instincts honed in the gym. They have moved into what Miyamoto Musashi described as the "void" in his 17th-century treatise on dueling. Musashi theorized that the void is the place where you react on instinct on an unconscious level. How often have fighters revealed that they have no memories of rounds? Corners are hoping for something to happen to dramatically change the momentum of a fight. To be fair, this does sometimes happen, and when it does, it is incredible. But it rarely happens. Ever since gloves have become mandated for MMA events, promoters have commented on how small and light they are. "Anything can happen in 4-oz. gloves," is the often-heard line. Corners are hoping for that "anything" to happen, which occasionally does.

Scott Smith immortalized himself in the sport for appearing to be a finished man when he knocked out his tormentor, Pete Sell, and then allowed himself to crumple over in pain. Even more incredible was that he replicated a similar comeback three years later in Strikeforce against Cung Le, an even more dangerous striker.

Another type of comeback a corner is praying to see happen is for the opponent to "punch himself out," "gas," or as UFC commentator Joe Rogan has elegantly put it on the air, "blow their wad." They are hoping that their opponent will smell blood and turn up the volume on power punches that will come too fast for their shoulders to recover. Gray Maynard clobbered Frankie Edgar, then UFC lightweight champion, in the first round of both of their title fights, only to appear flat and tired in later rounds and have Edgar come back to life, forcing a draw in their first title fight, and then actually knocking Maynard out in their second fight for the championship. Brock Lesnar took an incredible beating at the monstrous hands of Shane Carwin during the first round of their heavyweight title fight. But it was Carwin who was the fighter who could barely move at the beginning of round 2. Carwin was promptly put on his back and submitted by the battered, but comparatively fresh-looking Lesnar. The two fights between Mauricio "Shogun" Rua and Dan Henderson each followed one of these narratives. In their first fight, in 2011, Henderson brutalized Shogun with overhand rights, leaving viewers in awe of Shogun's chin. Momentum shifted at the end of the third round, when Henderson started to fade, and Shogun, impossibly, poured it on, threatening Henderson with dominant top-control positioning and ground-and-pound in the fifth and final round. The rematch, in 2014, saw Shogun drop Henderson early in the fight, nearly finishing him at the end of round 1.

## 4. The Spectacle of Violence

Henderson, always one punch away from victory, found that punch in the third round, breaking Shogun's nose and winning the fight.

These fights have become some of the sport's most memorable contests, winning fight-of-the-night bonuses for their participants, they are typically the fights that are shortlisted for various fight-of-the-year awards, and they earn accolades and respect from men like Dana White and fight-fans around the world. I couldn't even sleep that night after watching Henderson-Shogun I. Perhaps the comeback win is so memorable and enduring we overstate how often it occurs and how probable it really is for a concussed fighter to get the win. Smith's comeback wins are something special and deserving of recognition and celebration. They are anomalies, though, and it is a misperception in the sport to understand comebacks from the brink as a common occurrence. A recent study has shed light on the statistics behind KOs and TKOs, showing how KOs rarely end with the shot that causes unconsciousness, and TKOs rarely come out of nowhere.

A study out of the University of Toronto, whose findings were published in 2014, conducted video analysis of UFC events numbered 66 to 146, spanning the time period between December 2006 and May 2012.[2] The researchers found that KOs (knockouts) occurred in 12.7 percent of the 844 matches surveyed, and TKOs (technical knockouts) occurred 19.1 percent of the time, for a combined rate of 31.9 percent of the total matches surveyed. These KO/TKO rates demonstrate that the chance of an athlete suffering traumatic brain injury (TBI) in the UFC is twice the rate of an athlete in the NFL, a sport that already has an alarmingly high frequency of TBIs, and that TBIs in those UFC events surveyed occur approximately seven times more often than the observed rate in the NHL.

A disturbing revelation of the study pertains to the barrage of strikes, overwhelmingly to the head, of the defeated opponent leading up to the stoppage. The report reveals that the average time between the KO strike, which knocked out the fighter, and the match being stopped was 3.5 seconds.[3] During this period of time between the KO and the actually stoppage, the defeated opponent sustains an additional 2.6 strikes to the head on average. The losing fighter, in the 30 seconds leading up to the KO blow, sustained an average of 6.2 strikes, with 88.2 percent of them landing to the head.

The findings regarding TKOs are even more disturbing. During the 30 seconds leading up to the stoppage, losers were struck an average of

18.5 times, with 92.3 percent of these strikes landing to the head. If the jab is the most under-utilized weapon in contemporary MMA, then the body shot must be next. Body shots have surely been a decisive factor in some fights, such as Nick Diaz's pummeling of B.J. Penn, and JDS-Stipe Miocic in a 2014 Fox headliner, not to mention the body kicks of lightweight champion Anthony Pettis and Lyoto Machida, but they are not employed nearly as often as head-shots.

Another dimension that the study brought to light was the higher KO/TKO risk for fighters 35 years old and older. It is a reminder that professional sports is unforgiving to its elder statesmen, especially so for MMA, a sport which seems to include more athletes on the north side of 35 than any other major North American sports organization, and a disproportionate number of guys on the wrong side of 30 in the heavyweight division, where the shots are harder. A lot of it has to do with the comparative youth of MMA, meaning a lot of guys who were always going to go into it one way or another did not know about the sport until they were already well into their athletic primes. A further contributing factor is that most who get into MMA do so after spending their formative years in a sub-discipline, such as wrestling, which is very different from guys in the NHL who have been playing hockey since they were four years old. It does seem like this trend is going to be less pronounced in the coming years. Already there are fighters establishing themselves as elite mixed-martial artists, such as Rory MacDonald, who have been training in MMA since they were kids, not just a single martial discipline, such as wrestling or kickboxing.

The researchers also demonstrate that the risk factor of receiving a KO/TKO in future matches after being knocked out or stopped due to strikes is significantly elevated. Perhaps the most disturbing note is that the study only considers KOs and TKOs, ignoring those fights that go to a judge's decision, but still involve one fighter, or both, sustaining serious head trauma. The ongoing research into CTE is in its infancy, but it is proving that head-shots in general cause traumatic brain injuries, not just the experience of getting knocked out. The study also omits the head-shots suffered by the eventual winners, and, what research is likely to prove to be the greatest contributing factor of CTE, the constant low-impact blows, and sometimes very high-impact blows, from sparring in training camps.

There was a time when concussions remained a dirty secret in contact

## 4. The Spectacle of Violence

sports. More than dirty, it was shameful to acknowledge them, as if a concussion showed one to be weak and ill-suited to manly pursuits. I think that it is important to tell these stories, though. Do not deny experiences with traumatic brain injury. Only by discussing them in an open way can we learn anything from these experiences, if there are such lessons that can be learned. I mentioned my distaste for fighting in hockey, but what was more influential in my life was to experience a serious concussion playing on the high school varsity team and to not have anyone at the school or on the team care about what had happened. Below is my own concussion story.

I was always a fairly serviceable defenseman playing hockey as a kid. I never scored many goals in the season, but I had more than my share of assists, pretty good +/- ratings, and I took home more than a couple of MVP awards for tournaments. In grade 11, I decided to try out for the high school team. Why did I do this? Why does a teenage guy do anything? Girls. I remember sitting in homeroom in grades 9 and 10 and listening to the points sheet being read of the high school team's games. I thought these guys were giants at the school. I was only in grade 11, at a time when high school in Ontario went up to grade 13, but I wanted in then. I had a small group of friends but I was always treated as an outsider (perhaps that's why I heard the calling of an academic career), and, let's face it, I thought being on the hockey team would help me to meet girls.

I made the team, despite being on the young side, and the season was off to a fine start. We were the best team in the district by far, easily winning almost every game. My production wasn't anything to notice over the PA system in the morning, as I doubt I was the envy of any kid in grade 9 at the time, but I was playing well defensively as a fifth defenseman to back up the first two defensive pairings, getting plenty of ice-time.

It was during a mid-season, weekend-long tournament when my season went off the rails, or maybe off my skates. We had advanced to the championship game, but were down one or two goals late in the third period. I don't remember anymore. The captain of the other team, a brick shit-house of a guy, was fearlessly skating through the neutral zone with the puck. Not one to pass up what looked like a beauty of an opportunity for a hit, I grew up on those *Rock'Em, Sock'Em* videos same as Steve Downie, and had laid out some guys during the season so far, and so I went right at the guy. Of course, slamming yourself into someone who is at least 50 pounds heavier than you while on skates is usually a pretty dumb thing to do. It certainly was for me this time. My recollection is spotty, but I'm pretty sure that I bounced off the guy, lost my footing on the ice, and hit the back of my head on the ice, the worst place to suffer a blow to the head. I came around in a moment or two, looking up at the ceiling of the arena. The play went on, and I got to my feet to get off the ice, so that my team could get someone on the ice who wasn't in dreamland.

I sat out the final couple of minutes of the game on the bench. I felt nausea, like I was going to vomit, but I was still lucid enough to hear the guy from the other team taunt me as he skated by while I sat on my butt knowing that I couldn't do a damn thing about it. I skated off the ice and walked to the dressing room after the game ended. My coaches, Mr. Hunter, who was our physics teacher, and Mr. McLellan, the head coach who was not a teacher but a father of one of our part-time players, never checked up on me, and honestly, didn't seem to give a shit. My teammates didn't seem to care much either. So much for making friends. Mike, a senior and a real good guy on the team, came over to sit beside me just to make small talk and hold my gaze. He said that he thought my eyes seemed a little off and that I should see a doctor. Nearby teammates, already peeved about losing the tournament championship, erupted at Mike, telling him off and telling me that I was fine and to get over it. After all, in high school hockey in Canada, what is a concussion that a kid suffers compared to losing a game?

My coaches never checked up on me, never called me, and never suggested that I see a doctor. They never said a damn thing about it. We had another game a week later and I showed up to play, with not a single person questioning whether that was a good idea. I had felt ill all week since the hit, but I was also hungry, mad at myself, and eager to prove myself. I can't for the life of me understand why I wanted to prove myself to a bunch of coaches who didn't care what happened to any of their kids on the ice, or to my teammates I was invisible to, but I did. I played this game, where we won in a huge blowout. I played very aggressively, jumping up into the offense as often as possible and intent on getting on the score sheet. As I was carrying the puck around the other team's net, I got checked solidly off the puck. I fell down but I wasn't out. However, I felt really close to vomiting. I played the rest of the game, but on the long drive home, I knew that I had not recovered from that hit in the previous game, and that I was maybe even seriously hurt.

What bothers me about people like Dana White who insist that

## 4. The Spectacle of Violence

fighting and violence is in our genes is that they must never have had violence done to them, because if they did, they would be a lot more critical about violence existing as a pillar of the human condition. Concussions, and sub-concussive blows, take a real, human toll on your health and wellbeing. The naivety, or maybe it is just a dehumanizing cruelty, that exists in contact sports prevents an honest conversation about how to maintain the integrity of sport while showing a modicum of empathy toward those physically harmed by its violence and at least try to protect someone who has suffered a TBI, least of all from themselves.

Over the next couple of days, after what might have been my second concussion within a week, I made a difficult decision. I contacted my physics teacher, Mr. Hunter, to let him know that I needed to take some time away from hockey, on account of the head trauma that I recently received. Incapable of expressing compassion, Mr. Hunter looked at me blankly, eventually nodding and telling me to do what I had to do. I focused more on my courses and began a membership at a local gym, taking out my frustrations and self-loathing by vigorously training (which is probably not a good idea after suffering a TBI) to an extent that makes my 35-year-old self envious. After withdrawing myself from the team for only about three weeks, I returned to my first practice. Mr. Hunter was obviously avoiding me, but that wasn't entirely unusual. The head coach, Mr. McLellan, seemed to be shooting me the stink eye at every possible opportunity, adding an extra sneer to his permanently scowled visage whenever he looked in my direction.

The coaches wanted us to participate in a new drill that we hadn't done before, digging the puck out of our own end while under forechecking pressure. The defense had to get to the puck and intelligently pass it out of the defensive zone while being forechecked by the offense. At first, I thought that the suspicions that the drill aroused in me were entirely in my head, but it became very clear that I was the only defenseman who was actually getting hit during this drill, all while Mr. McLellan screamed that this is "what high school hockey was all about," and bellowing that this "wasn't house-league."

The funny thing was that I played on a house-league team with Paul, the *captain* of our high school team and another classy leader on the team, to get extra practice in a still semi-competitive environment. Paul wanted to chat with me alone before our next house-league game. He told me that the coaches told the offense to hit me, and only me, as hard as they could

## Mixed Martial Arts and the Quest for Legitimacy

during that drill. Paul also confided that he was truly sorry for not standing up to the coaching staff, but he assured me that no one wanted to do it and they tried to make it look like they were hitting me harder than they were. This is contact sport for you, though. You take a bit of time off out of concern for possible brain injuries, and you get some additional brain injuries in practice for it.

I grudgingly played the rest of the season, despite a toxic relationship with a coach whom I loathed and now seethed around, and for a team where I struggled to make friends. My weight training at the gym was paying huge dividends over the weeks, though. By the end of the season, I was as strong as the strongest seniors on the team. Of course, this just further alienated me from the rest of the team, as a number of the senior egoists on the team adamantly accused me of doing steroids. I found those accusations too crazy to offend me because I have always been way too scared of potential side-effects, and I'm actually pretty spiteful against people who take that stuff.

I continued to train regularly throughout the summer while working in a grueling manual laborer position. After a long and careful consideration, I decided once again to try out for the varsity hockey team when grade 12 started. A year older and much more physically capable, I felt like I cruised through the challenging tryouts, easily a starting defenseman. At the end of the last tryout, Mr. McLellan made a bizarre announcement. He told everyone to hit the showers, and when we were ready to leave, a list would be posted for everyone to see. The list would include three categories: those who made the team, those who didn't, and another category. It was a list of people who made the team but only if they really want it bad. As I stopped to look at the list on my way out, with more than a few butterflies bouncing around in my stomach, I felt crushed not to find my name amongst those who made the team.

I was not a vain teenager. I was a pretty withdrawn introvert, in case you haven't already put that together, but I knew that I was objectively the second-best, or the very best, defenseman during those tryouts. I failed to see my name on the cut list, and so I thought that I must be on this other list. I was. In fact, my name was the ONLY one on that list. I could play for the team, but only if I really wanted it. I could not believe it. I was being singled out, again, for telling my coach last season, who was also my physics teacher, that I needed a break on account of the head injuries that I suffered in back-to-back games.

## 4. The Spectacle of Violence

The next day I was using my lunch period to study in the library when the new team captain, Greg, blustered into the library, head held pompously high, attended to by a little entourage of sycophants, to announce to everyone around us that he was told that I could be found here. He then ostentatiously told me, on orders from the coaching staff, that my name was put on that list because of last season when "you quit on us."

I had felt really good about the start of a new season. I thought that I had a chance of contributing effectively to the team, and that I could help our school dominate our conference again. I even, quite foolishly, thought of myself perhaps even standing out to a girl! I went to see Mr. Hunter to explain to him that I wasn't going play this season because of this indignity I was being subjected to, reminding him that I only needed time off to recover last season because I was knocked out in a game. This time, Mr. Hunter never said a word. He just grimaced and walked away, while I stood there hoping we could have engaged in something like a conversation.

The UFC is caught in a very difficult position, much more difficult than the NFL or the NHL, because violence is *the* attraction. Bone-jarring hits are a major component of North American football and hockey, but it is peripheral to the sport. The real attraction is scoring goals, touchdowns, runs, and passes. In fact, hockey and football typically get more exciting with stricter rules around contact, opening up the passing game in football or allowing fast skaters open ice in hockey. Reduce the KOs/TKOs of MMA, and you are left with submission grappling contests, events that television networks are not going to be interested in showing during primetime. Head trauma is a part of the sport, and it is not going anywhere, nor should it.

What the sport does not need is the discursive culture that proudly boasts of the violence. It is the narrative found in the ultimate fighting culture, a culture that is far more spectacle than it is sport, that revels in the physical violence, spitting on the values and norms of martial arts itself. Sonnen, a man who has claimed that there is no such thing as "MMA," only cage-fighting, perfected the tough-guy routine. Toward a former UFC champion from Brazil, Lyoto Machida, Sonnen barked the following: "News flash, Lyoto: the spotlight is part and parcel for the gig. Go join a monastery if you want to pretend that fighting is about honor or integrity. And who are you to talk about being a big man? I don't see you changing diapers on flipper babies in Chernobyl."

## Mixed Martial Arts and the Quest for Legitimacy

One of the most wonderful dimensions of MMA is the respect that athletes will show to each other before and after the fight, and sometimes even during it. The vast majority of fights in the UFC, and in the small organizations, end with the competitors embracing each other, showing respect, and acting with a lot more class than you see in sports such as boxing and hockey. There are exceptions. Jon Jones' "suck-it" gesture to Daniel Cormier. A Paul Daley sucker-punch. Erick Silva faking to touch gloves only to wing a punch at a fighter with his guard down. Occasionally one or both fighters will simply ignore each other after the buzzer. But these are anomalies. Shamefully, there is some push-back against this. Sonnen once vented, "You know, these guys are out there making man-love all the time, giving high-fives and huggin' one another. You deserve to be knocked out if you're trying to hug a man in the middle of a fist-fight."

Excessive hugging in the middle of a bout is not a good idea, but apologizing for accidental groin shots and eye pokes is one of the finer characteristics of MMA today. How often do guys in the NHL apologize to each other for a dirty hit? After illegal contact has hurt an opponent, the response of the offender is usually to look for the ref and to make excuses or act like he didn't do anything. This mentality is expected from fans who want their team to show no quarter to opponents, and coaches who demand to see their guys as "hungry," no matter how low the stakes might be in the game. Hockey is impoverished by the unwillingness of NHL players to take accountability for times when they hurt opponents by intentionally or accidentally breaking the rules. The fact that mixed-martial artists express concern for the safety of their opponent is one of the more noble aspects in an otherwise unforgiving and cruel sport.

The victor, screaming and spitting to the crowd after winning by KO, is one of the less noble dimensions of MMA. There is something immensely "disquietful" about that sight, especially, as the stats reveal, and many of us know from watching the sport on TV, that TKOs typically occur after a lot of violent head-shots to an all but vanquished opponent, and KOs rarely end after the knockout blow. The theatre that follows the vicious damage dealt to a beaten man feels gladiatorial, even unsportsmanlike. It is the realm of ultimate fighting and spectacle, far removed from MMA. Nick Diaz, a UFC veteran and former champion of Strikeforce who has been one of the more polarizing figures in the sport, known for flipping the bird at fans and television cameras, has long expressed his

## 4. The Spectacle of Violence

disapproval of when guys "go crazy" after a knockout. "Have you ever seen me knock somebody out and make a big scene? Hell no. I threw my hands up and walk around pissed off because, fuck, that could have been me. That wasn't fun."

There persist a few ongoing controversies since the introduction of the unified rules of MMA that relate to the discussion of brain trauma. One rule that is occasionally derided by members of the MMA community, particularly irksome to UFC commentator Joe Rogan, is the ban on elbows against a downed opponent that follow a 12 o'clock to 6 o'clock arc. First of all, there is the ambiguity of whether the clock "moves." That is, if the ban on 12-to-6 elbows is limited to the conception of a clock mounted on a wall, does the clock go flat? Does the ban apply to any elbow that cuts high to low? That is the movement your arm makes during a chin-up, for instance. "Big" John McCarthy, a highly respected MMA referee and one of the authors most responsible for drafting the unified rules, has stated that the clock doesn't move, but this interpretation is not always recognized. The real controversy however, is whether this move should stay illegal.

Joe Rogan likes to tell the story during UFC broadcasts that the authors of the unified rules watched a karate expert break blocks of ice with 12-to-6 elbows and became worried about the amount of damage that could be done to a human skull. The concern is that they overlooked how sweeping elbows from top position can be even more powerful. Those who think that 12-to-6 elbows should be allowed want to see a more dangerous ground game in MMA. They think that wrestlers will not be as likely to "lay-and-pray" on opponents because they can cause significant damage to opponents with little effort or danger to them, and that fighters will be more desperate to scramble to their feet if they are threatened by 12-to-6 elbows.

Changing this rule would be a terrible mistake. It is an attack that requires little skill but one that can be delivered with a punishing effect. Not only would such a move make MMA even more traumatic to the brains of athletes, it would also present a major danger to the eyeballs of fighters, likely leading to instances where fighters lose their eyesight. It would likely also diminish the effectiveness of a fighter working from the bottom, attempting sweeps, armbars, or triangles, because they would be busy trying desperately to avoid punishing elbows.

Another controversy about the unified rules is the ban on knees to a grounded opponent. Under the old unified rules, you could not throw a knee to the head or face of a grounded opponent. The problem here is what constitutes a "grounded" opponent. An opponent was grounded if they were in a three-point stance, meaning either a knee or even a fingertip was touching the canvas. Fighters who are bent over in a clinch will drop one hand to the canvas to protect them against knees to the head, in a classic sporting move of "cheating within the rules." At the opening of the Jon Jones-Vitor Belfort title fight, Jones crawled toward Belfort with his hands touching the canvas. Belfort swung a big kick aimed at Jones's head. Jones looked at referee Big John McCarthy with an expression of "what the fuck?" McCarthy dismissed Jones' protest by warning him not to play games with the rules.

In one way, granting knees or kicks to the head of a grounded opponent would give wrestlers a dramatic advantage. They could employ a front-headlock to force an opponent to his knees, something they've done 10,000 times in practice, and then unload with a knee or two to the head. This would inevitably lead to TKOs and significant strikes that an opponent would not readily recover from. This rule change could also place wrestlers at a distinct disadvantage, as tired takedown attempts could be brutally punished by a sprawling opponent. The unified rules did recently change the definition of a grounded opponent so that one hand on the canvas no longer constitutes being grounded. I think that this change seems fair, but kneeing an opponent with one or two knees on the mat would be a step too far, and I'm glad that this change has not been implemented. This is a seriously violent sport, and we are just getting a glimpse into the quality of life those who have participated in it can expect to live after retirement. My advice to the new owners of the UFC, WME-IMG, is to leave the rules as they are. Adding to the violence, especially the brain trauma, is unconscionable and unethical at this stage of the sport.

I'm not even going to entertain the idea of a soccer kick to a grounded opponent or the head stomp, two of the more gratuitous allowances of Pride, and even allowed today in OneFC, an MMA organization based out of Singapore. I know a lot of diehard fans of the sport who continued to follow it during the late 1990s and the first part of the first decade of the twenty-first century are going to disagree with me on this, but I respectfully have to say my piece. Yes, Shogun's Pride victories are something to behold, but kicking your opponents in the head when they are down represents a serious betrayal of some basic values that cement the

## 4. The Spectacle of Violence

foundations of martial arts. Soccer kicks and head stomps have no place in a legitimate sport. They are a relic of the no-holds-barred days when promoters played to the lowest levels of bloodlust, lasciviously promising the viewer that "anything can happen." Any jackass can knock someone out by kicking a man who is down in the head, but only an athlete, or martial artist, can do it to a man standing in front of him.

These controversies pale in comparison to the stipulation of the unified rules that bouts are scored under a 10-point-must system by a panel of three judges. It seems almost incredible that the early UFC events never had judging, thanks to the Gracie family's derision of the practice. Sakuraba even joked, many years later to Sherdog.com, that if Royce Gracie got to write the rules for the Pride 2000 Grand Prix, the fighters would have been forced to wear diapers for fights that went on for hours. Judges are instructed to "evaluate mixed martial arts techniques, such as effective striking, effective grappling, control of the ring/fighting area, effective aggressiveness and defense."

Specifically, effective striking is evaluated on "the total number of legal strikes landed by a contestant," and effective grappling is judged by "the amount of successful executions of a legal takedown and reversals." Fighting area control, aggressiveness and defense all seem somewhat vague at first glance, but they too are defined in at least some measure of detail by the unified rules. They are weighted secondarily to effective striking and grappling and should be invoked when it is hard to evaluate who had the more effective striking and grappling. Area control is determined by "dictating the pace, location and position of the bout," aggressiveness means "means moving forward and landing a legal strike," and effective defense "means avoiding being struck, taken down or reversed while countering with offensive attacks." The unified rules also detail that if the majority of a round is fought on the canvas, then grappling is weighted first, followed by striking, and the weighting is reversed if the majority of a round is fought on the feet. What counts as "effective" is how momentum can be gained by one fighter over another. A knockdown is more meaningful if the fighter who suffered it is visibly wobbled by the blow, compared to an occasion when the fighter instantly recovers and keeps up his own offense.

A point at which the sport of MMA is lost to the spectacle of ultimate fighting occurs when, at the end of the fight, commentators, fans and people in the media want to award the decision to the athlete who finishes the fight the strongest, or who causes the most facial damage to his opponent. There is an expressed sentiment that disregards the ideas of rounds, disregards the idea of sport itself, and merely wants to crown the victory to who "fucked up" the other guy best, or if there were no time limits, you know, so the narrative goes, like in "a real fight" that doesn't stop when a horn blows, who would win. It is a mindset that is fundamentally opposed to fighters who are able to exploit a weakness in an opponent and ride it to decision victories, most notably wrestlers like Jon Fitch, who in his prime was known for grinding away the will of opponents with a steely determination, but was also unwilling to take unnecessary risks to secure a stoppage.

Dana White has been especially irked by the "lay-and-pray" style of wrestlers who execute strong takedowns, but use minimal striking and rarely attempt meaningful submissions. Also derided is the practice of "wall-and-stall" clinching, when a fighter, unsuccessful at taking an opponent down, instead holds opponents against the cage through underhooks or by controlling their hips. MMA loosens its claims to being a sport and descends into the spectacle of ultimate fighting when fans, and even the president of the UFC itself, whine about boring "point-fighters." The problem that MMA has is that fighters who approach the fight with the intent of winning, strictly within the rules of the sport, are denounced as harming the sport.

One of the defining characteristics of contemporary MMA is this profound sense of insecurity that the sport has. It has a paranoid fear that anything less than a card of slobber-knockers is going to kill interest in the sport. Fighters are expected to engage in reckless "wars," headhunting their opponents without any regard to their personal safety or long-term mental health. It is a sport defined by an organization that elects to keep Diego Sanchez, a *TUF I* veteran who stalks forward, headhunting while absorbing tremendous damage, but cuts Jon Fitch, Jake Shields, and Yushin Okami after a single loss, about which more will be said in a later chapter.

It is interesting to note that the unified rules are perhaps less ambiguous than they are commonly understood to be, both by fans and judges. Rounds that are mostly contested on the canvas weigh effective grappling more than effective striking. A takedown is certainly effective grappling, but so too are submission attempts. A wrestler who succeeds at a takedown is going to have to advance position once the fight is on the ground,

## 4. The Spectacle of Violence

move to half-guard and make a bid for side control or full mount. Otherwise he could be subjected to submission attempts or reversals if he is too content to sit in an opponent's guard. Too often a wrestler cruises to victory sitting in guard, even though the grounded opponent could actually be scoring the advantage, if the judge was adhering to the unified rules.

Another issue has to do with the wall-and-stall technique for winning rounds. If the majority of a round is contested on the feet, then effective striking should prove decisive for that round. If a fighter is simply holding the other fighter against the cage and is not actively attacking in the clinch, then the round should be determined by what happens on the breaks and who gets the better of those exchanges. If a fighter is going to implement a wall-and-stall technique, then he needs to be active with short body and head punches, as well as short knees, the likes of which Cain Velasquez was able to use to chip away at the formidable defenses of JDS in the third fight of their storied trilogy, and what Randy Couture was able to do to opponents against the cage in his prime.

There is nothing inherently wrong with debating the rules of MMA, or sports in general, and the UFC has at times touted the unified rules as proof of the legitimacy of the sport. However, at other times, White and others have seemed to question the unified rules, perceiving them as a nonsensical straightjacket that has harmed the entertainment value of the product. Plenty of professional sports leagues over time have tweaked the rules to increase the entertainment value of the game.

When MLB stipulated that baseballs must be kept clean and visibly white, it was informed as much by the tragic death of Ray Chapman as it was by the prospect of a swing in the balance of power from defense, particularly pitchers, who could put all kinds of things on the ball, to the offense, thereby helping to usher in a golden age of home run hitters like Babe Ruth. The NBA cut out the physical contact that defined the play of the hard-nosed Detroit Pistons of the 1980s to open up the game for the offensive dominance of Michael Jordan and similar players at the end of that decade and into the 1990s. More recently, the NHL forced defensively minded teams to abandon "the trap" by simultaneously getting referees to enforce hooking and holding penalties, eliminating the two-line pass as illegal, and by reducing the size of the neutral zone by tightening the distance between the blue lines.

Perhaps the most cynical move of all to restrict defense and allow for a dramatic unshackling of offensive output can be found in the NFL. After

## Mixed Martial Arts and the Quest for Legitimacy

shamelessly dismissing the work done by doctors, such as the work of NFL fan Dr. Ann McKee, a medical doctor who statistically showed a correlation between playing football, even at high school and collegiate levels, and the prevalence of CTE, the NFL finally recognized the scientific consensus. By changing the rules to protect quarterbacks and defenseless receivers, the NFL gave the illusion of being proactive to reduce the occurrences of head trauma. The fact that doing this, combined with a much stricter interpretation of holding (which is totally unrelated to head trauma), opened up the game to new levels of offensive excitement was far from being unintentional on the part of the NFL brass.

The UFC does not have the same flexibility that the NFL and the NHL have to make their sport moderately safer for its athletes. MMA is simply not viable without KOs and TKOs. But the spectacle of violence cannot completely disregard fighter safety. Surely there is room to cut down on the head-shots to knocked-out fighters, one of the more serious examples of where the values and norms of ultimate fighting have overtaken mixed martial arts. The other area where something should be done is with respect to TKOs and the overwhelming barrages that typically precede the end of the fight. An admirable change the UFC made was to replace "knockout of the night" bonuses (as well as the submission bonus) with "performance of the night" bonuses. Most of these bonuses are still awarded for knockouts, so it might just be a discursive change. However, discourse matters, and changing the name of a bonus has an impact on the culture of the sport.

Commissions also need to re-evaluate exactly what they are regulating and allow themselves to take a more critical look at the levels of brain trauma that are dished out on a card on any given Saturday night. There is going to come a time when we will start seeing retired fighters in their 50s and 60s talking about neurological problems that they are having. And what do you think medical professionals, such as Dr. Ann McKee, are going to find when these athletes pass away and their brains are examined? Can athletic commissions, MMA organizations, and trainers legitimately say that they did the best they could to protect the brains of the athletes? And will fans, at least on some level, not have some measure of responsibility for cheering on the slobber-knocker wars of obviously concussed men, and taking to the internet to denounce early stoppages?

# 5

# Feminization, Fighting for Recognition and Octagon "Girls"
## *Spectacle and Patriarchy*

Ever since Art Davies first read about the "Gracie Challenge" in the pages of *Playboy*, gender dynamics has been central to the world of MMA, and if we are to be honest, painfully apparent in all professional sports. MMA is a place where the men are overdosed with testosterone and women dress in booty shorts and bikini tops to inform the masses of the impending round. After all, a typical match can have as many as *three* rounds. A championship match, or a UFC main event, can have as many as *five* rounds! Surely one requires a beautiful woman with a card to attract the attention of the audience in order to keep all of that straight.

Mixed-martial arts is a sport where masculinity is the supreme virtue and femininity is a trait that is disgraceful and maligned amongst the men, but nearly demanded of any women associated with the sport. MMA represents a world that is too often defined by the numerous troupes of patriarchy, such as silencing critically minded women, using feminine characteristics as a vehicle for hurling insults, and sexually objectifying those women who are publically associated with the sport, card girls and fighters alike. This is a sport that the UFC's president reminds us is "in our genes," a primal ritual to determine alpha male status and property claims to females. It is marketed as a throwback to a Hobbesian state of nature that may have never existed. The spectacle of MMA echoes a prehistoric world where might meant right, with one of the most important rights being the right to dominate women, and where being a woman, or representing feminine traits, is the greatest disadvantage. The values of ultimate fighting are inherently patriarchal and as often expressed are deeply misogynistic.

It is not easy to be a fan of professional sports for those who care about gender and are sensitive to the power relations formulated by patriarchal hierarchy. This is not even remotely isolated to MMA either. Stories of professional athletes being responsible for sexual and physical abuse grab headlines on a regular basis. When Ray Rice, the running back for the Baltimore Ravens, cold-cocked his fiancé (the two got married soon after the incident) in a casino elevator, the story smacked of a cover-up, with NFL commissioner Roger Goodell unconvincingly (to many in the media) denying allegations of having seen the video of the disturbing attack.

Such behavior is not limited to professionals. The University of Ottawa hockey team was met with a long-term suspension from competition in March of 2014 after two of their players were charged with sexually harassing a woman in a hotel in Thunder Bay, Ontario. The investigation into the players and coaching staff of Baylor University football team raised many eyebrows. The damning revelations of the behavior of the coaching staff of the football team at the prestigious Penn State University point to the most deplorable and heinous acts of sexual violence as having occurred for years.

Acts of patriarchy showcase the culture of patriarchy and the assumptions of a patriarchal worldview. Sport, especially team sports that hold lucrative earning potential and prestige, is a patriarchal world. It is a realm of perpetual contests between men and one that is dominated by men.

It is important to acknowledge that a great number of men in amateur and professional sports have values that hold women to an equal status, or pretty close to it. They are sympathetic to the women who are abused by teammates, and many express their horror when cases are brought to light. In fact, NFL players are less likely to be arrested for criminal behavior than the average American male between the ages of 25 to 29. However, the world of sports, and the world of MMA in particular, is a patriarchal domain that almost seems to revel in misogyny.

One of the more difficult examples of hateful, misogynistic vitriol to listen to in the world of MMA happened in the spring of 2009. Loretta Hunt, a news editor for *Sherdog*, wrote that two anonymous sources informed her that the UFC had been preventing backstage access during events to agents and managers that were currently unpopular with the organization. Dana White, hardly known for his patience or discretion, erupted in a

## 5. Feminization, Fighting for Recognition and Octagon "Girls"

YouTube video that was uncharacteristic, even for him. White called the piece "fucking retarded" and barked that Loretta was a "fucking moron" and "fucking dumb." The anonymous sources also became the subject of the tirade, venomously denounced as "a fucking pussy and a fucking faggot and a fucking liar." Then, suggesting that Hunt might have fabricated the whole thing, White concluded with a final, "Fuck you, Loretta Hunt!"

In an interview with ESPN's Mary Buckhelt, White emphatically apologized for the abhorrent language he used, though he insisted that he "absolutely, positively meant to attack the reporter." White recounted a story about when he protected a lesbian couple from harassment in his old neighborhood in South Boston, and White even spoke with GLAAD (the Gay and Lesbian Alliance Against Defamation) to atone for his hateful tirade. In one of his more poignant remarks, White offered the following:

> The thing that sucks is that video rant, the feedback I got was not negative. It was overwhelmingly positive from our fans. It was, "Yeah, you go, Dana. You're the man."
> At the end of the day, the worst thing for me is that I don't want anybody thinking that it's cool to say that word, especially now that I know the word fuck is as powerful as the n-word. I don't want these kids out there watching me and thinking it's cool. I don't want that.
> I want them to know that I agree with the issues of people in the gay community and shouldn't have said that word. The reality is—I swear a lot, you know that. I swear all the time. It's not just a thing I do on blogs or on TV or at work—I swear all the time. I swear everywhere. I swear. Am I going to turn over a new leaf and stop swearing? Who knows? Maybe I will. But right now, that's what I do.

That is about as close as Dana White gets to public contrition.

Accusations of homosexuality are incessantly employed by cagefighters to mock and emasculate other fighters. Fighters accuse each other, through the media as well as in social media, of being "fags," "pussies," and most often, a "bitch." The UFC does not have nearly the same kind of profile as the NFL in the U.S., but if it did, the language used by some fighters would surely be unconscionable for a more aware public. You would expect to see a great deal of pressure from sponsors, mindful of the product they are putting up their money to endorse, to clean up the sport and confront the misogyny that delegitimizes it. It is even hard to imagine that such a thing as MMA even exists as a sport with the current state of public discourse used by a number of its athletes. These are not the virtues of martial arts. This is ultimate fighting.

Nate Diaz, no stranger to controversy in the UFC, launched a public tirade at Josh Thomson during an interview with BJPenn.com in 2013, a few weeks after Thomson beat him in the cage.

> The last guy I fought, Josh Thomson, he was scared shitless when I was fighting him. It's unbelievable how scared he was in there.... He was making bitch ass lady sounds and that's not bullshit. I'm not here talking shit on him, this is reality. He was making woman sounds. He was running out of the clinch. I hit him in the face and he was going "Oh, oh, ehh" making woman sounds I've never even heard out of a man before during a fight. I'm hearing his corner telling him to smile and I'm like, "Yeah, smile motherfucker" and not a single smile came out of his mouth.

In case you didn't know, Thomson won that fight via TKO from a head-kick.

Only a month after his incendiary comments about Thomson, Diaz attacked bantamweight fighter Bryan Caraway. Caraway was given bonus money that had originally been promised to lightweight Pat Healy, after Healy tested positive for marijuana. Diaz, very open about his enjoyment of marijuana, stated that he felt "bad for Pat Healy that they took a innocent man's money and I think the guy who took the money is the biggest Fag in the world." Diaz was briefly suspended by the UFC, and it was even suggested by White, who was concerned for the credibility of the UFC, that Diaz could actually get cut from the organization, even though he had recently fought for the lightweight title.

The only thing that more painfully demonstrates the degree to which elements of cage-fighting is misogynistic than Nate Diaz calling Caraway a "fag" is the public defense that his manager gave. Mike Kogan, who had just taken on the role of Diaz's manager a few months before this went down, gave one of the sorriest and frustrating apologies for the use of "Fag" imaginable.

> Guess what? The word faggot, at least in Northern California, and where Nate is from, means bitch. It means you're a little punk. It has nothing to do with homosexuals at all. So when Nate made the comment that he made, he didn't make it in reference to homosexuals or calling Caraway a homosexual. He just said it was a bitch move.

Well, it is nice that Diaz has a manager to clear that up and prevent him from looking like an immature playground bully. He wasn't intending to disparage homosexuals by calling Caraway a "fag," he was only trying to call him a "bitch."

And in case you thought that Diaz now understands that he did anything wrong, Kogan is there to dispel any illusions.

## 5. *Feminization, Fighting for Recognition and Octagon "Girls"*

Nate doesn't feel remorse for what he said. I don't feel remorse for what he said. I don't feel remorse for defending what [Diaz] said or elaborating on what he said. Because it was not a homophobic statement. It was not intended to offend homosexuals. We weren't even talking about homosexuals. One can debate the multiple uses of this term. We can sit here and debate in the English language, there's a lot of words that mean a lot of different things, but whatever. As it is, it wasn't intended to be used the way people tried to twist the way it was being used. So therefore, what does he have to feel bad about?

What people don't seem to understand, according to Kogan, is that to some Northern Californians, when you call someone a "fag" you are actually calling him a "bitch." Diaz isn't trying to express his hatred by insulting LGBT communities, instead he just intends to denigrate women.

Light-heavyweight champion Jon Jones and his challenger, former Olympian Daniel Cormier, got into a much-publicized altercation at a press conference in the summer of 2014 to promote their upcoming fight. The photo-op for these asinine events typically requires the two fighters to stand in front of each other for the "stare-down." Jones came toward Cormier, bringing his forehead down to the challenger's own forehead. Cormier interpreted the gesture as a head-butt, or close enough to one, and pushed the champion away, the traditionally respectful challenger seemingly aiming the shove at Jones' neck. A head-to-head sometimes occurs during these staged confrontations, usually at the weigh-in, but occasionally at the photo-op weeks or months before the fight, and there is often a shove involved with at least a couple of contestants on a card. This was not even remotely like a traditional photo-op, though. Shane Holler, Senior Director of Public Relations for the UFC, who was standing in for Dana White, the man who typically moderates these events, was thrown off the stage by Jones with a powerful backhanded push as the champion stalked toward Cormier. Jones winged punches, and as the fighters fell to the ground in the commotion, Jones continued to throw vicious punches at Cormier.

The two fighters were quickly ordered to make the rounds of sports channels to offer the least sincere apologies for the scrum that you could expect from a couple of proud light-heavyweights. While off the air during one of these pretend apologies, an ESPN hot-mic caught the continued barbs and threats the two fighters were spewing at each other. Cormier threatened to spit in Jones' face, Jones threatened to kill Cormier if he ever did that, and everyone had a good time.

Of course, what set it all off was a gender-related comment from the champ. While waiting for the interview to resume, Jones asked Cormier, "Hey pussy, are you still there?" Cormier laughed at Jones, expressed his incredulity over how quickly Jones' personality changed when the cameras are off, and called Jones "fake," a word that has attached itself to Jones ever since the build-up to the Jones-Evans fight a few years ago, and intensified as Jones' public expression of Christianity has not convincingly meshed with the revelations of a reckless and hedonistic personal life. Jones thoughtfully reflected that "the fact that you're a pussy hasn't changed." Not to be out-done, Cormier remarked that Jones too was "such a fucking pussy."

In the lead-up to their much-anticipated title fight, Jones responded to the increasing number of fans who called him "fake," by saying that these people "sound like a girl." Cormier's wrestling-heavy performance against Anderson Silva at UFC 200 was also denounced by lightweight/welterweight contender Donald Cerrone as fighting like a "fag."

At the end of a hard-fought lightweight bout between Danny Castillo and Tony Ferguson, Ferguson got his hands raised with a split decision by the judges. It was a close fight, with Ferguson getting better of the majority of the striking exchanges, but Castillo putting Ferguson on his back. Castillo, frustrated by the decision rendered by two out of the three judges, whined into the microphone that "If we were in jail, he would have been in trouble." Fortunately for everyone, effective grappling is not defined by the unified rules of MMA as the ability to simulate a sexual assault in missionary position. Effective grappling is actually defined as takedowns mixed with advancing position and attempting submissions, two things that Castillo struggled with. Missionary position in MMA actually means that you are in the guard of your opponent where the fighter on the bottom can control your movement, limit the damage from ground-and-pound, neutralize basic submissions, threaten with a sweep, and even threaten with submissions of their own.

Allistair Overeem, a K-1 kickboxing champion and Strikeforce heavyweight champion whose tenure in the UFC quickly came under fire after a slew of disastrous performances and a failed drug test, took exception to his former teammate, Anthony "Rumble" Johnson. Rumble, a one-time welterweight who reignited his career as a top-three light-heavyweight, didn't like how Overeem seemed to injure fighters intentionally during sparring and even challenged Overeem to a heavyweight contest. Overeem

## 5. Feminization, Fighting for Recognition and Octagon "Girls"

shared his thoughts on the matter by stating that "Where I come from, if I have a problem, I'm coming directly to you and I'm asking you what's up. For me, that's like pussy behavior."

Potential opponents, and past ones, aren't just rivals or opponents. They are pussies, bitches, and fags. I don't think that anyone has used misogynistic attacks as often as Chael Sonnen did, though. One of Sonnen's favorite methods of insulting Brazilian fighters was to question their sexuality. "Machida is a gentleman. MMA is very cutthroat, and it's sweet that Lyoto promised to never fight his girlfriend Anderson. That's devotion."

Sonnen, whose 15 losses included nine by submission, had often disparaged jiu-jitsu as lacking manly toughness.

> Listen Wanderlei, I will do a home invasion on you. I will cut the power to your house and the next thing you'll hear is me climbing up your stairs in a pair of night vision goggles I bought in the back of Soldier of Fortune magazine. I'll pick the lock to the master room door, take a picture of you in bed with the Nogueira brothers working on your "jiu-jitsu." I'll take said quote unquote photograph, post it at dorksfrombrazil.com, password—not required, username—not required. That, Wanderlei, is how you threaten someone. Dummy.
>
> Even if I thought I could get a submission I'm not laying underneath a grown man with my legs spread on worldwide TV. Some guys subscribe to that theory but I am a Republican and we don't do that.

This hyper-masculinity is a reflection of the ultimate fighting side of the dialectic that is shaping this sport into something that is closer to spectacle. The UFC and Bellator have little control over how fans act, but they do have some powers of oversight with respect to their fighters under contract. According to the UFC's Code of Conduct, fighters are "ambassadors of the sport of mixed martial arts," and their "responsible conduct advances the interests of the sport and the fighters."

> Fighters shall conduct themselves in accordance with commonly accepted standards of decency, social conventions and morals, and fighters will not commit any act or become involved in any situation or occurrence or make any statement which will reflect negatively upon or bring disrepute, contempt, scandal, ridicule, or disdain to the fighter or the UFC.

There are a lot of troubling examples of fighters who ridicule other fighters through the gendered language of "bitch" and "pussy." Does this not count as a violation of "accepted standards of decency"? Are these not the social conventions and morals that are deserving of rebuke? What comes to mind is the American adage that freedom of expression does not give one freedom from consequences, and the UFC should at least try to discourage the shameful language invoked during the promotion of a fight.

The significance of language is in the shared meanings that it represents. When MMA is discursively overwhelmed by insults of "fag," "pussy," and "bitch," it is giving us a disturbing window into the highly patriarchal and misogynistic norms of a subculture. The reification of these words as insults has consequences for a society that thinks it is okay to use them with increasing frequency and not even feel shame about their usage.

As demoralizing as the gendered use of language is, the physical violence against women represents a whole other level of cruelty.

A *Salon* article published in the summer of 2014 by Tracy Clark-Flory suggested that there exists in the subculture of MMA a "horrific misogyny."[1] The article chronicled a litany of horrifying cases where (mostly) former UFC fighters were responsible for violent domestic abuse and for threatening the lives of women. One of the examples Clark-Flory cited was Josh Grispi.

Grispi, who went 4–0 in the featherweight division of the WEC before it was folded into the UFC, was first in line to fight against the champion, Jose Aldo, in what would have been the first title fight at 145 lbs in the UFC. Aldo had to withdraw due to injury, so Grispi risked his number-one contender status against a fellow prospect in his early 20s, Dustin Poirier. Poirier beat the doors off of the legitimacy of Grispi as a future contender during the three-round fight, effortlessly winning a judges' decision. Grispi's career continued to falter, as he went 0–3 in his next three matches and was inevitably cut from the UFC. Largely forgotten by the MMA community, Grispi made headlines in early August of 2014 when he assaulted his wife, concussing her, while also threatening to murder her and to use his pit-bull to do it.

Clark-Flory also mentioned the case of Thiago Silva, once a staple of the UFC's light-heavyweight division. He fought against some of the best in the division, such as Lyoto Machida, Rashad Evans, and Alexander Gustaffson, going 7–3 during his time in the promotion. Despite the respectable record, Silva's tenure in the UFC was plagued by unprofessional and even unethical behavior. His record might have been a 9–3 if two wins were not converted into no-contests after he submitted a non-human urine sample for drug testing and then failed another test for marijuana. He did not make weight for one of his wins and demonstrated an

## 5. Feminization, Fighting for Recognition and Octagon "Girls"

unsportsmanlike attitude on multiple occasions, such as when he played the bongos on the back of an opponent who was clearly going to lose a judges' decision, and when he glared over the body of an unconscious opponent, menacingly pointing his finger down at him. In early 2014, Silva allegedly held a gun in his wife's mouth, threatening to kill her. A week later, Silva allegedly showed up at a jiu-jitsu gym run by his estranged wife's boyfriend, threatening to shoot everyone. The drama did not end until an armed stand-off with police at his home in Florida played out and with Silva finally getting arrested.

What makes the article even more disturbing is that there are even more high-profile examples that Clark-Flory does not even bother to mention, such as an incident involving two students of Lloyd Irvin who assaulted and raped a fellow student in a garage in early 2013. Irvin, a Brazilian jiu-jitsu black-belt who had helped train a number of UFC fighters, including one former champion, was himself once under criminal investigation regarding a gang-rape case back in 1990. Another recent case, this one from 2014, involved a jiu-jitsu instructor from a suburb of Brasilia who raped his step-son, with the child, who was less than two years old, dying from his injuries. The criminal record of MMA pioneer and failed Hollywood actor Joe Son, mostly known for suffering repeated groin punches back in the days when that was allowed, presents another case of unimaginable cruelty.

The case that spurred the article more than any other was the revelation that Jon Koppenhaver, a former contestant on *TUF* who recorded a single professional fight in the UFC before bouncing around organizations, severely assaulted his on-again-off-again girlfriend, Christy Mack, an adult film actress (Koppenhaver had also performed in a handful of pornographic movies). The 23-year-old Mack posted sickening images to Twitter, showing a face that was so swollen it was practically unrecognizable, with terrible bruising on her thigh. She alleged that Koppenhaver, who had legally changed his name to "War Machine," stopped by her house, uninvited, at 2 a.m. in early August. War Machine proceeded to first beat the man who was Mack's guest, and then turned his vengeance on Mack herself. Mack revealed that she suffered broken bones, including 18 breaks around her eyes, missing and broken teeth, a fractured rib, a ruptured liver, difficulty walking with her damaged leg, and "several lesions" that were inflicted by a knife, which War Machine allegedly used to saw off some of her hair. She described War Machine as forcing her to shower in front of him, and he had threatened to rape her. According to her story, he was prevented from committing the rape by an inability to get an erection. It was only when War Machine went into the kitchen, allegedly to get a larger knife, that Mack was able to escape the house.

War Machine, who owns a clothing line called "Alpha Male Shit," has had a history of violent encounters with people, outside of his professional life as a mixed-martial artist, having been involved in a series of assaults between 2007 and 2010. Before his attack on Mack, he was handed a year-long sentence in 2010 for assaulting a former girlfriend at a party put on by members of the porn industry, a world that he was becoming more involved in. After his release, War Machine became an active poster on Twitter, often using the social media network to express rage at the world, much of it directed at women. In one notable post, cited on his *Wikipedia* page, War Machine ludicrously whined in a delusional post that "the oppression of MEN is worse than oppression of Jews in Nazi Germany, worse than the slavery of Blacks in early America…. I'm not exaggerating either." In another post, this one cited by Clark-Flory, War Machine bragged about how he just raped Mack, and followed that post up with another asserting that "Real men rape. (Their GF's and wives, not strangers, don't get your panties in a bunch)." The fact that War Machine qualifies his statement by sounding as if he thought he was living in Afghanistan, or the U.S. in the 1950s, reveals the kinds of assumptions this man has about women, relationships, and humor, and they are norms that he believes he shares with his Twitter audience.

Clark-Flory suggests that the misogyny found in MMA is patriarchy's reactionary movement against feminism and women's rights. She references Matt Morin, a former lightweight who had an unenviable 4–6 career that stretched between 1999 and 2008. Morin wrote a response essay to the documentary *Fighting Politics*, which featured Mark Driscoll's call for Christians, of all people, to support MMA for its expression of hypermasculinity. Morin's understanding of the outpouring of misogyny is that it is rooted in the desire of men to get "back in the driver's seat of a world that has been careening out of control ever since we allowed our women to remove their head coverings." MMA captures this discontent for some of these men, who, resentful of women, scapegoat feminism as the cause of their inadequacies and failings. MMA is then naturally connected to a man who would change his legal name to War Machine and believes that

## 5. Feminization, Fighting for Recognition and Octagon "Girls"

men today are more oppressed than Black slaves in antebellum America, or the Jewish people who suffered and died during the Holocaust.

These incidents involve fighters who were former UFC fighters, or fighters who were cut from the organization for their actions. There is a tendency in the mainstream media to taint the UFC with the violent actions of its former fighters. When War Machine's abhorrent attacks received public scrutiny, they featured headlines like "UFC Fighter Violently Assaults Porn Star and Friend," even though War Machine was released years before the attacks and was under contract with Bellator at the time. The symbolic power of the UFC is that is has become synonymous with MMA. Legend has it that when Lorenzo Fertitta was advised by his legal counsel against purchasing the UFC, he said that he wasn't buying the organization as much as he was buying those three letters— U-F-C. In North America at least, MMA was UFC, and this is why WME-IMG paid $4 billion for the UFC in 2016, rather than starting a new MMA organization with a fraction of the capital used in the purchase.

However, this does mean that the UFC gets tainted by the criminal actions of fighters and the people who are associated with the sport. The UFC has no control over the actions of sociopaths. All it can do is ban fighters with a history of violence and not tolerate criminal acts of violence. The least it could do is impartially enforce the Code of Conduct that very clearly warns against this kind of behavior. These attacks degrade women, men, and they bring ill-repute to the organization. The sport is not so insecure that it thinks it can only build hype around fights when fighters call each other "pussy," "bitch," and "motherfucker," is it?

The abusive attacks on women and the feminization of opponents, and even people in the media, are symptomatic of the generalized anger and contempt of MMA. It represents part of the underworld of MMA culture. These are men who train themselves to be comfortable with violence. Maybe most of them already are pretty comfortable with violence, with men like Dan Severn, a highly decorated wrestler who became a pioneer of MMA despite his uneasiness about punching men in the face, acting as outliers in the sport. It is presumably quite difficult for a lot of these guys to separate MMA from the responsibilities you have toward society and your family. To be successful in MMA, you are training daily, sometimes even multiple times a day. It is likely naïve to think that guys caught up in this violent world are capable of keeping it professional. I have trouble separating my public life as "Professor Williams" from my personal

## Mixed Martial Arts and the Quest for Legitimacy

life as "Mark." Perhaps a lot of men can't easily live and train in such a cruel culture, one where you are obsessed with dishing out violence, and not have it influence your norms about life. This is ultimately a contempt that rots away at the credibility of the sport, alienating society that is not entertained by professional athletes calling each other bitches.

In 2011, White again made headlines when he blustered to *TMZ* that women were never going to fight in the UFC. How quickly did White change his tune after coming across Ronda Rousey.

> Ronda Rousey. Watching her, meeting her, knowing her. From the outside, she's this beautiful girl who won a bronze medal in the Olympics and everything else, but when you talk to Ronda Rousey, and you get to know her, she's a Diaz brother, inside. She's a real fighter, and that's what I look for in anybody, whether you're a male or a female. She's nasty. She's mean. She likes to fight, and she likes to finish people. Those are the kind of people I like, whether you're a male or a female.

WMMA came to the UFC because of Ronda Rousey. She is tough, determined, an Olympic medalist, and was the face of WMMA during its transition to the UFC. The Olympic bronze medalist in judo won the Strikeforce bantamweight title back when most of the top female bantamweights fought in that organization. Rather than win gold in the octagon, Rousey was first handed her UFC championship in recognition of her achievements in Strikeforce and the aura of invincibility that was forming around her. The decision to award her a belt was clearly justified when she went on to defend that title six times in devastating fashion, with only one of these defenses going beyond the first round. The English language seemed to lack superlatives to describe her dominance. In 2015, Rousey was selected by respondents in an online poll conducted by ESPN as the "best female athlete ever." The UFC's Joe Rogan famously boasted that with Rousey "once in a lifetime" did not adequately describe her performances as a mixed-martial artist. Rousey represented, to the loquacious UFC personality, a "once EVER in human history." She headlined in two of the top-ten best-selling PPVs in UFC history—both of which, however, happened to feature her two defeats, each loss as devastating as her victories were.

Ronda Rousey has both been loved by fans of MMA and hated by fans of MMA. Her polarizing personality largely stemmed from her hardness and her pride. She was an angry competitor, the face of a woman who wasn't interested in making you a damn sandwich, and because of this, she was often labeled a "bitch" by those who despised her.

## 5. Feminization, Fighting for Recognition and Octagon "Girls"

In an article posted to *Fightland*, L.A. Jennings provides a thoughtful defense of Rousey[2]:

> The term "bitch" is a pejorative used to describe women who do not fulfill the social obligations specific to idealized femininity. A woman who is a bitch does not "play nice," whatever that entails. But the qualities that make a woman a bitch are the same qualities of a woman in power. And many feminists, including me, not only welcome the distinction but self-describe as bitches.

Jennings, echoing White, thinks of Rousey as following "the narrative of the bad-boy athlete," in this case, a little bit of Diaz. In Rousey's own words: "It's not just girls playing Miss America like they were before I came along. When everyone was trying to not have any confrontational anything, ever. Not piss anyone off."

Rousey stuck her forehead into the faces of her opponents during the weigh-ins, and she "mean-mugged" about as much as anyone has in MMA. Her confidence, before that brutal head-kick loss to Holly Holm, was unreal, boasting that she could defeat male mixed-martial artists, maybe even heavyweights. She even bragged about beating one of the most technically brilliant boxers ever to practice the sweet science.

It is probably a little unfair to characterize Rousey as a Diaz brother, since she never went around calling people "fag" or "bitch," but her rivalry with Cristiane "Cyborg" Justino, as dominant at women's featherweight as Rousey was at bantamweight, became one of the defining rivalries in WMMA, despite the fact that they have never even fought, and the signs of 2017 point to this fight probably never happening.

Throughout 2005–2011, Cyborg Justino crushed her opposition. Known for pushing a relentless pace and for having a discernible strength advantage over her opponents, she beat down all contenders in the featherweight division, including fan favorite Gina Carano in Strikeforce. Carano had her moments against Cyborg early in the fight, including a full-mount position, but wisely decided to go after some easier paydays in Hollywood and parlay her likeability into acting rather than face a monster like Cyborg again.

Having Gina Carano in Hollywood, a woman who looks tough and is tough, is a refreshing change from the norm of casting the ultra-feminine, petite-body type in action moves. I think that Gina Carano in Hollywood is fantastic for the industry. Of course, no one is expecting a depth and complexity to her acting on the scale of a Meryl Streep, but her presence in movies like *Deadpool* make a statement about what a powerful woman really looks like.

## Mixed Martial Arts and the Quest for Legitimacy

With Gina Carano after big paychecks in Hollywood, WMMA was defined by the Brazilian wrecking-ball. However, all the success Cyborg achieved came into question after a post-fight drug test administered by CSAC came back positive for stanozolol back in 2011. Cyborg's career entered into a hiatus that lasted a year and a half, while Rousey was in the process of carving out her legacy. Still, Cyborg remained the benchmark as the most dangerous female fighter, and her entry into the UFC as a 140-lb fighter first looked like a wolf being introduced into a forested area rich with elk.

I think one reason why the rivalry has become such a fierce one is that Cyborg represented what kept Rousey from achieving universal recognition as the greatest female mixed-martial artist before her defeat to Holm. People who watched Cyborg's reign of destruction wanted to know if Rousey could beat a clean Cyborg.

I think it was the fierce competitor in Ronda Rousey that made her so hostile to Cyborg back in her prime. According to Rousey:

> I've said before, I don't care if she's injecting horse semen into her eyeballs, I'll fight her, but that's just my personal decision. But I can't make a decision for the whole division. I can't say it's the right thing. This girl has been on steroids for so long and [has been] injecting herself for so long that she's not even a woman anymore. She's an "it." It's not good for the women's division. It's not good at all.

A hypothetical Ronda Rousey-Cyborg fight was further complicated by weight-class. Rousey started out as a featherweight, the weight-class Cyborg has traditionally fought at, but has made bantamweight her home during her UFC tenure. I don't know how Cyborg ever made 145 lbs, and she has supposedly been warned by medical professionals not to attempt to cut weight to fight at bantamweight (135 lbs). Before the UFC grudgingly accepted a featherweight division, the organization booked a handful of fights at 140 lbs, seemingly to showcase Cyborg to the UFC fan-base. Back during Rousey's reign atop the bantamweight division, any possible meeting between the two kingpins of WMMA seemed dependent on Rousey moving up to 140 lbs.

Dana White, shockingly (I know), hasn't been able to hold his tongue over the rivalry, coming down very hard against Cyborg.

> There was a reporter in Canada who said he was going to call GLAAD. First of all, she's not a transgender fighter. She's a woman, OK? What Ronda's saying is, she's taken so many drugs that she's probably not a woman anymore. She's not a transgender fighter. She didn't have a surgery. What a moron.

## 5. Feminization, Fighting for Recognition and Octagon "Girls"

> I think that this is the fight business and people say mean things about each other. Is it not true? She got busted for taken winstrol. The same drug Ben Johnson took and many other athletes took, to do what? To cheat. Ronda called her a fucking cheater...
> I said, when I saw [Cyborg] at the MMA Awards, she looked like Wanderlei Silva in a dress and heels. And she did, did she not? Who wants to dispute that she didn't look like Wanderlei? She was walking up the stairs, jacked up on steroids beyond belief and looked like Wanderlei Silva in a dress and heels.
> When you're a female and you've taken that many drugs for so long—when you've been on steroids for as long as this girl has—it's tough. This isn't the same as a guy who had taken some stuff before and got busted, he comes back and is fighting other men.

Cyborg was caught cheating and deserved to have some serious consequences for her actions. One can't help but notice how much more degrading Cyborg's experiences have been from that failed drug test compared to men who have failed. Cyborg is met with scorn and derision on a whole other level compared to what men like Sonnen have suffered. A lot of people have rightly observed that PED cheats get off too lightly in MMA, but don't tell Cyborg that.

It was quite depressing to learn that Cyborg was notified of a potential doping violation conducted by USADA at the end of 2016. Cyborg had recently signed with the UFC and was off to a spectacular start, showing her trademark heavy hands in her two TKO victories at 140 lbs. The UFC even finally relented and established a 145 lb division. Allegedly, Cyborg turned down what was to be the first title fight, with differing rumors abounding in the MMA community, such as that Cyborg either no longer was able to cut to 145 lbs, or possibly simply wanted more time to make the weight cut. USADA eventually cleared Cyborg of intentional wrongdoing in the positive test result for spironolactone, a banned diuretic. The anti-doping group heard the testimony of the medical doctor who allegedly administered the banned substance out of concerns for Cyborg's health, and USADA granted her a retroactive therapeutic-use exemption (TUE). Despite being cleared of charges of doping, Cyborg's failure to inform USADA of her use of spironolactone in advance has likely done much damage to her brand. She should be recognized as the most dominant woman ever to fight as a featherweight. However, the test that revealed spironolactone also happened to be her first-ever random drug test outside of competition. For many MMA fans, Cyborg's remarkable achievements will be likely be weighed down by a heavy asterisk.

## Mixed Martial Arts and the Quest for Legitimacy

One hopes that the addition of female fighters to the UFC roster will help balance out some of the dynamics of misogyny and patriarchy that circulate throughout sport, but the jury is still out on that one. Conor McGregor, an Irish featherweight who has emerged as a superstar in the UFC, becoming the biggest PPV draw due to his outlandish, Rik Flair-esque preening coupled with his dynamite left hand, was asked on Twitter who he liked better, Miesha Tate or Ronda Rousey. His response was, "One riidin dick, one lickin ma toessssss."

Ronda Rousey is a phenom whose accomplishments were incredible, and it is unfortunate that many in the MMA community, and some members of the media in general, have attempted to discredit her wins. The questioning of Ronda's skills has been much more venomous than the questioning of dominant men who enjoyed lengthy winning streaks before suffering a swift defeat.

Clearly not everyone in Hollywood was a big Rousey fan. After she suffered her second defeat, in her greatly anticipated return to MMA at the end of 2016, to the hard-hitting Amanda Nunes, a panel on Fox Sports 1 that included Michael Rapaport, Shannon Sharpe and Skip Bayless sounded off in characteristic fashion. The comedian, Rapaport, as well as Sharpe, doubted that she was ever that good. Rapaport actually made a very good comment during his opening spiel about how quick the media was to label her as the "best ever." Reminding the audience that she had only 12 professional fights to her name, Rapaport was astute in pointing to a problem with UFC promotional marketing. Hungry for PPV revenue, and likely insecure about the long-term prospects of MMA as a sport, the UFC will market a fighter as something of a legend, a "pound-for-pound" great, and a "Greatest of All Time" (GOAT), far too early in a career. I will return to this issue in the penultimate chapter, but for now, I want to focus on the point made by Rapaport and Sharpe that Rousey's success was that she simply came to the sport "first."

It is true that WMMA was clearly not as established as men's MMA during her reign. However, it is simply false to suggest that she was "first" to mixed-martial arts amongst women. Gina Carano made her professional MMA debut in 2006, five years before Rousey. Cyborg Justino first fought a year earlier than Carano. Rousey's first opponent, Ediane Gomes, had seven fights prior to their meeting, with the sole loss coming against the formidable Amanda Nunes, who had made her pro debut three years before Rousey fought Gomes. Miesha Tate, whose two fights against

## 5. Feminization, Fighting for Recognition and Octagon "Girls"

Rousey will probably most define Rousey's legacy, had competed in 14 fights before their first meeting. These few examples do not even include the true pioneers of MMA, such as Rousey's training partner, Shayna Baszler, who made her pro debut back in 2003, or Marloes Coenen, who had her first pro fight in 2000.

Clearly, Ronda Rousey was successful not because she was the first woman to fight. Her victories came because she was better than her competitors. She had a powerful clinch game, complemented by a nearly unstoppable judo toss, honed by untold hours of practice, and finished with one of sport's most brutal armbars. She was beginning to show some explosive striking, including powerful knees in the clinch. Though her boxing did not look particularly technical, she was hitting girls hard and finishing fights with her fists.

Ronda Rousey simply hit a ceiling. She was breaking into Hollywood and must have had to deal with an array of distractions. Holly Holm was a difficult match-up for her, certainly more problematic on paper than her previous opponents. An accomplished boxer and kick-boxer, Holm's mastery of angles and range of the feet was a serious challenge for Rousey's charging style. Though Holm typically only loaded up on shots against an aggressive opponent, this worked perfectly against Rousey, who was intent on fighting in a phone-booth, but to no avail.

Nunes was another tough fighter for anyone. Highly experienced in the cage and a boxer who wasn't shy about sitting on her punches, Nunes was surely not an appropriate fighter to meet in the octagon for anyone after a quasi-retirement. Nunes put on an electrifying performance, rocking Rousey early in the fight, appearing to shatter the once unassailable confidence of the former champ in what will likely remain her last professional fight. The TKO finish was inexorable. Bizarrely, Michael Rapaport blustered that referee Herb Dean's stoppage was too quick, the result of what Rapaport called "white-girl privilege." I'm not sure how anyone watching that fight thought that Ronda Rousey was anything but finished that night in the cage against Nunes. I think that it was more a case of sensationalistic commentating rather than a sincere questioning of race and gender dynamics in professional sports.

Women have been a part of the UFC for much longer than Ronda Rousey has been competing. It's just that they didn't fight. They walked around the perimeter of the octagon. Holding up a card with the upcoming round number on it. I have felt no small measure of embarrassment

## Mixed Martial Arts and the Quest for Legitimacy

while watching this sport with others as a camera follows an "octagon girl."

I'm sorry, but I can't call them "girl." I'm going to use "octagon woman" instead. If you've seen a lot of UFC pressers and events, you will notice how younger people affiliated with the organization are often infantilized. I've seen UFC events and pressers where Dana White, and others, refer to an athlete in his late 20s as a "kid." These women are women, not girls.

I have felt guilt watching this sport by myself and wondering how I can support a spectacle where female bodies are placed on display for drunk men in an arena, cat-calling, whistling, and shouting out vulgarities. A sport where audiences pay to see violence, bikini tops and booty shorts.

Women who perform these supporting roles in sports are not overlooked, they are downright gawked at, but they are rarely thought of. I have no doubts that the curves of their bodies continue to exist in the minds of countless men, and their names—Arianny Celeste, Brittney Palmer—are remembered for image searches on Google. What are their lives like? Their ambitions? Aspirations? How are they treated by the UFC? And how well are they compensated for those smiles and for the disciplined regimen required to keep themselves in such enviable shape?

I have defended these octagon women to others at times. Sort of. Perhaps you have too. Sitting on the couch. The match is about to begin. A stunning blonde winks and waves to the camera. Goldberg acknowledges "the beautiful Chrissy." Your girlfriend scoffs and is more intent than ever to change the channel away from the grotesque gladiatorial games that are just about to get under way.

> "Well, yes, I agree it is distasteful but, you know, it is basically the same women at these events, so it's not like they are just hiring random girls from local strip clubs and paying them with crack."
>
> "They are the faces of the UFC. When I think of the UFC, I think of Dana White, the fighters, but I also think of them. And not just a faceless, curvy woman in a bikini, but I actually think of actual people. I actually think of Arianny when I think of the UFC."
>
> "Arianny promotes active lifestyles on her website and encouraging men and women to have a positive body image."
>
> "Oh, Brittney is actually a pretty talented painter. I saw some of her work and it's cool."

Perhaps many of you approach this more tactfully than I do, simply nod and agree with your partner's denunciation of misogyny in MMA,

## 5. Feminization, Fighting for Recognition and Octagon "Girls"

and secretly pray that your agreeing with her or him has bought you a match or two before pressure to change the channel starts to increase.

Even if you agree that the octagon women we know have an important, though minor, role in the UFC, this does not change the fact that they are subjects of what has been described in the context of film and television as the male gaze, *par excellence*. Are they the masters of their own sexuality, or is their sexuality what male executives think drunken males dream up in masturbatory fantasies? Are these women expressing their sexuality on their own terms? I honestly wouldn't presume to know. I'd also rather not comment on what women should be wearing, one way or another. I just hope they are treated with dignity by their employers and are paid handsomely for the work they do in promoting the sport.

Of course, it is Chael Sonnen (who else?) who has been a public voice in insulting Arianny Celeste, the octagon woman who is most closely identified with the UFC. "We only had one [ring girl] and that was Chandella. The other was the IQ card girl. Arianny kind of walks around and holds up her latest test score. One time when there was a title fight, she got all the way up to five and we were very proud of her."

Too often, those who criticize their presence in the sport make it personal and attack the women themselves. Getting called stupid (and much, much worse) by people online and by high-profile fighters in the UFC is common.

It is an unfortunate dynamic that Ronda Rousey and Arianny Celeste have traded public barbs with each other, rather than trying to find some solidarity in such a masculine and patriarchal sport. After Celeste and Rousey were both named on one of those absurd *Maxim* "Hot 100" lists, Rousey laughed that: "It would have been really funny if I'd beaten Arianny Celeste, because that would be like a triathlete coming along and beating the runners in a marathon. Like, 'Ha-ha, it's your job to show your tits – I do that better than you!' Maybe next year. She's only getting older, and I'm reaching my prime."

Celeste has said that she thinks Rousey is a "bully" and a bad role model for women, and Rousey has fired back. Brittney Palmer did receive recognition from Rousey for using her work with the UFC to pay for school and advance her art career, although she seemed to compare working as a card woman with working at a *Hooters* restaurant:

> If you're working at Hooters because you're trying to pay your way through medical school, then fuckin' work it girl. I respect the hustle. But don't think you're hot shit

just because you work at Hooters. Use it to further yourself in life; don't think that you're awesome just because you do that. I'm sorry, but I'm not impressed with the job in itself.

Celeste, on the other hand, was viciously insulted by Rousey as a "do-nothing-bitch," supposedly using her body to live some kind of life of luxury.

I sincerely hope that women like Celeste and Palmer were treated with dignity by Zuffa, and I hope they are by WME-IMG. If any rumors about some of them being sexually exploited ever surface, the UFC will receive a serious backlash, and rightfully so. Another point relating to dignity is compensation. What women like Arianny Celeste make from the UFC is shrouded in secrecy. I can only hope that they are paid well. It is a damn travesty that NFL franchises pay their cheerleaders a pittance. These women are recognizable faces of the UFC and act as ambassadors for the brand. The innuendoes surrounding the salaries of the UFC's octagon women hint that they are paid well, such as Rousey shamefully complaining about Celeste's salary.

I'm quite torn about the role of these women. I want to say that they can be a part of the sport, under certain conditions. Sure, they represent the side of ultimate fighting and spectacle, NOT some sort of purist expression of martial arts. Maybe it is just naïve to think that you can't have a healthy dose of spectacle in the entertainment industry. However, the symbolism of their sexualized bodies is too reflective of the patriarchal dominance of the male gaze and the hierarchy of men over women. It evokes the Roman Games, when victorious gladiatorial slaves were given women to rape in their filthy cages. Arianny Celeste spends time helping young girls with having a positive body image. However, critics will still say that it can never undo the negative effects on young and old minds alike who are struck with a sense of sexual inadequacy at the sight of her body in a uniform.

Most dangerously, perhaps the "card girl" plays into similar archetypes of MMA as representing a "state of nature," a primal, animal state ruled by savages. Humanity is stripped of artifice and convention, plunged into a cruel struggle for survival in an amoral realm. Perhaps this is what plays out in arenas and casinos when Palmer and Celeste and their colleagues walk the perimeter of the octagon and are met with a chorus of obscenities and cat-calls. Ultimate fighting represents a primal world where masculinity is the dominant trait and the women, gorgeous models

## 5. *Feminization, Fighting for Recognition and Octagon "Girls"*

who live to be attractive for men, are possessions to be won and dominated. It is a state of nature, a realm without rules, where "the strong do what they will, and the weak suffer what they must." It is a realm that Thomas Hobbes thought was characterized by vicious cycles of injustice and vengeance, a realm where women are raped and men are killed, and perhaps, MMA is a not so subtle wink to this savage place.

# 6

# The Needle and the Locker Room Bonus

The Persian King, Xerxes, ordered that all but 1,000 of the 20,000 Persians who were killed during the catastrophic Battle of Thermopylae be buried. The king ordered this so that the multitudinous Persian remains might be hidden from the view of the fleet. Herodotus, chronicler of *The Histories*, records that the Persians who toured the battlefield, upon seeing 4,000 Greek bodies and only 1,000 Persian, remained unconvinced of the ruse being perpetrated by their king, suspicious of why the Persian bodies were spread out so very far. On the next day, with Persian spirits demoralized, the army came across desperate Arcadian deserters, eager to act as informants in return for food and protection. The Arcadians informed their Persian interrogator that the Greeks were currently preoccupied with the Olympic Games. When asked what was won at the Games, the Arcadians responded that they competed for a "wreath of olive-leaves." Tritantaechmes, a commander of the Persian infantry, and a son of Artabanus, the only high-ranking member of the Persian military command to vote against the invasion of Greece, was deeply concerned. Herodotus observed that "When he learned that the prize was not money but a wreath, he could not help crying out in front of everybody, 'Good heavens, Mardonius [a fellow commander of infantry], what kind of men are these that you have brought us to fight against—men who compete with one another for no material reward, but only for honor!'"[1]

Xerxes, sensing the low state of the Persian forces after Thermopylae and fearful that a sentiment of hopelessness was filling the ranks, curtly derided Tritantaechmes as a coward. Herodotus, who reconstructed the narrative, and with the benefit of having the outcome known to him, reflected that Tritantaechmes offered "a very sound remark."

## 6. The Needle and the Locker Room Bonus

Zuffa sold the UFC to WME-IMG for $4 billion in 2016, an extravagant sum that approximately corresponds to the value of two average NFL teams. However, you would be deceived to think that the rank and file of UFC fighters are compensated at the same level as in other professional sports. You can win fights, but only a handful have ascended the socioeconomic status enjoyed by most professional athletes whose competitions are featured on network television while UFC management practically expects its fighters to think like Spartans and sacrifice their bodies for a pittance. At least it is more than a wreath.

Marc Ratner, the Vice-President of Regulatory Affairs for the UFC, once told the website *Sherdog* that he had a map with all the provinces of Canada shaded in green but only 49 of the U.S. states similarly colored. The one exception on that map was the state of New York, colored red. The green represented all the states and provinces that had legalized professional MMA competition. Both Ratner and Ike Epstein, the UFC's Chief Operating Officer, maintained that the refusal of the state of New York to sanction MMA hinged on one man—the Democratic Speaker of the New York State Assembly for two decades, who has represented lower Manhattan for four decades, Sheldon Silver. The strategy of the New York Speaker had been to use his powers to prevent a vote on the sanctioning of MMA from getting on the Assembly floor, despite motions getting passed in the state Senate by overwhelming majorities.

Thomas Hauser, a prolific historian of boxing who was once nominated for a Pulitzer Prize, told *Sherdog* that Silver's opposition to the sanctioning of MMA in New York was rooted in Silver's relationship to the American culinary unions. By preventing MMA from being sanctioned in New York, Silver was positioning himself in solidarity with Las Vegas Culinary Union, Local 226, which has had a long-running battle with the Fertitta brothers, owners of Stations Casinos, over employee unionization, and of course, Zuffa.

Epstein responded to this tactic by maintaining that the UFC and Stations Casinos are two distinct entities. He has argued the following:

> The UFC is not anti-organized labor in any way, shape or fashion. In addition, every single arena that we do business with in the United States and many around the world are stocked full of trade workers, stage hands, lighting guys, and many times, culinary workers of this exact union that is fighting us, staff the concession stands. Teamsters and all sorts of trades are involved at these facilities.

Public sentiment in the MMA community interpreted Silver's historic resistance as unfairly holding MMA hostage to an ongoing labor battle in another sector. Hauser, for his part, finds Ronda Rousey an intriguing American athlete, but remains opposed to the "concept" of MMA and opposed to sanctioning the sport. Hauser's position is that boxing is so potentially traumatic for the combatants that the New York Athletic Commission has its hands full already dealing with the realities of CTE. It is too much for the athletic commission even to contemplate adding MMA to its list of responsibilities. For him, MMA is a sport that represents the removal of "a number of rules that are designed to protect the health and safety of the fighter in boxing."[2]

In 2015, Silver was arrested and charged with corruption. He had allegedly been accepting big payments from a law firm that he never disclosed. Silver planned on remaining a member of the New York Assembly, but he has resigned as Speaker. Ratner got to make use of that green marker again in 2016 in anticipation of the massive UFC 200 event at Madison Square Garden.

It is another paradox of this sport, born out of the tension between the spectacle of ultimate fighting and the sport of mixed-martial arts, that it would be sociopathic, maybe even masochistic, to compete, under the specter of terrible physical trauma, without financial compensation. And yet, it might also be strikingly sociopathic to be participating in such an inherently violent sport for the sake of money, and not much of it, for that matter. It is due to this dialectic that MMA has a real problem about fairly compensating the majority of its fighters.

Fighters will often identify themselves as people who would be fighting for no financial reward whatsoever. They would be here without the Fox deal, without Spike, and even without Zuffa. There persists a narrative that lambasts those who participate to get paid as inauthentic and weak. They are without honor. They are like decadent Persians, slaughtered on the battlefields of history by the indomitable will of Spartan valor.

Many of us, such as the esteemed economist Robert H. Frank in *The Darwin Economy: Liberty, Competition, and the Common Good*, lament the exorbitant wages earned by so many professional athletes. These are wages that represent a transfer of wealth from working-class fans to a handful of individuals (almost exclusively men) who came to excel in their respective sports during their formative years. Many, perhaps even the majority of them are aided by the biases of scouts, and what Machiavelli has described as *fortuna,* such as the structures surrounding Little Leagues that advantage children born between January and March. The fantastic

## 6. The Needle and the Locker Room Bonus

wages that are earned by professional athletes today had been bitterly resisted by owners and leagues. They were fought for through collective bargaining, and this fight has empowered not just the superstars of an era, but also many of the working-class athletes and the journeymen. A rookie in the NFL in 2014 enjoyed a minimum yearly salary of just over $400,000. Even a place on the practice squad entitles you to $6,300 a week. The NHL minimum for hockey players is around $500,000 a year, a figure that is comparable to the league minimum in the MLB and for a rookie in the NBA.

The UFC has no comparable fighter's union or association, and there are very few fighters who appear to be making obscenely large salaries. The official category of UFC fighters, according to the promoter itself, is that they are "independent contractors," not employees. This puts the UFC in a position very similar to baseball and hockey during the 1960s, keeping its superstars handsomely well-paid, while offering the prospect of bonuses (and secretive locker bonuses) to the rank and file, who commonly enter the organization making $8,000-$10,000 per show, with a win bonus that can double their take. It is a classic example of a corporate divide and conquer strategy against labor.

The website *MMA Manifesto* conducted a study of disclosed salaries of UFC fighters for the year 2012.[3] They included show-money/win bonus, as well as other disclosed bonuses, such as knockout of the night, submission of the night, and fight of the night. They found that 15 percent of its roster made $10,000 or less in 2012. The fighter average for 2012 was $80,904, but 53 percent of the roster earned less than $45,000. Just under a quarter of the roster pulled in a six-figure income in 2012, with UFC light-heavyweight champion Jon Jones earning the highest salary at $865,000, and former light-heavyweight champion Rashad Evans earning the second-highest salary at $710,000. Anderson Silva earned a disclosed salary of $475,000, and GSP had a disclosed payout of $470,000.

Some good news that the study revealed was that the percentage of athletes earning $10,000 or less declined from 21 percent to 15 percent between 2011 and 2012. The bad news is that the average salary declined from $92,017 in 2011 to $80,904 in 2012. The study was unable to include the locker-room bonuses or the pay-per-view bonuses, as they are not in the public domain. The locker-room bonuses in particular are frustratingly opaque. A small number of fighters have publicly revealed their extra earnings, but this is entirely at the discretion of the athletes. Occasionally,

Zuffa has released the salary paid to a fighter, but only to use the revelation as a weapon to discredit them, such as one-time welterweight contender Jon Fitch, so that the UFC could make an argument that Fitch had been grossly overpaid. *Forbes* estimated that GSP earned a combined figure of about $9 million for his 2012 fight against Carlos Condit and his 2013 fight against Nick Diaz. The money made from pay-per-view "points," the basis for calculating the pay-per-view bonus, and any other locker-room bonus is not included in the above study, nor is the estimated $3 million in sponsorship money GSP had been presumably making each year, although the ability of fighters to earn lucrative endorsement deals is severely hampered by the UFC's deal with Reebok.[4]

It is worth mentioning that the proportion of athletes earning pay-per-view points is likely quite small. Pay-per-view bonuses are factored into the contracts of the organization's superstars and champions, but Zuffa has been very public about its unwillingness to offer pay-per-view points to just any event headliner. When the Wanderlei Silva–Chael Sonnen fight was being negotiated, Dana White revealed that the stumbling block was Wanderlei's insistence on earning pay-per-view points and threat to retire rather than accept the contract. Despite the high numbers a Silva-Sonnen clash likely would have drawn, largely due to Sonnen's incendiary remarks about Brazil, the clash between the two on the set of *TUF*, and the video footage of Wanderlei warning Sonnen that his hateful comments were going to result in him having to go to a dentist in the near future, Wanderlei was publicly chided for obstinately holding out for contractual obligations of PPV points.

As a commodities broker on Wall Street, John Cholish is one of the more financially savvy fighters who has fought for the UFC. Entering the UFC with a 7–1 record, the lone loss being his first professional match, Cholish appeared to have some momentum in the ultra-competitive lightweight division. After an auspicious start to his UFC career, a TKO win in round 2, Cholish lost his next two fights, the second loss against Gleison Tibau, a veteran of 18 UFC fights going into the match-up. Cholish then announced his retirement from the sport.

For Cholish, the decision to retire was primarily a financial one. Cholish actually took to Twitter before his fight against Tibau to announce his impending retirement after the fight, regardless of the outcome. Making $8,000 to show, and a bonus of $8,000 to win, is simply not a rationale for a graduate of Cornell, or for anyone, to go through the rigors of a

## 6. The Needle and the Locker Room Bonus

training camp and suffer bodily injury. In fact, for his first UFC fight, Cholish's contract was only for $4,000 to show, and an additional $4,000 for his win.

Speaking on a radio station, Cholish broke down an athlete's expenses for a fight. Firstly, there are training camp expenses. The training camp for a fight, typically lasting six to eight weeks, involves gym expenses, working one-on-one with coaches, nutritional control that does not compromise training, and gear. Cholish estimated his training camp expenses at $4,000–$6,000 a month, an admittedly high figure due to his requirement of living in the New York City area for his day-job.

Secondly, there are travel expenses. The UFC covers the travel expenses for the fighter and for one of the coaches. However, the norm is for a fighter to have three people in the corner. Each additional coach must pay any international visa costs ($500 per person for Brazil), and they must pay for their own flight plus hotel room. Cholish estimated his total costs for his last fight, against Tibau in Brazil, at $4,000.

Thirdly, there are taxes to be paid, both to one's home country, and, if the fight is held in another country, to the government authorities of the host country. For Brazil, it amounted to a 27 percent tax on his $8,000 base salary, a sum of $2,160 that must be paid before leaving the country. What Cholish does not include are his management fees, probably because someone as highly educated and with as much professional experience as he has would have no need of them, but for most fighters they are typically set at ten percent. Great management could help secure lucrative sponsorship contracts, but the days when an undercard fight, or low-placed main card fight, can earn an athlete an extra $5,000 are long gone from the Reebok deal. Incurring expenses of approximately $10,000 for a guaranteed pay of only $8,000, plus whatever your agent can bleed out of some sponsors, maybe $1,500, seems like an unfair sacrifice to make for an organization that is featured on Fox and its affiliated sports stations.

Cholish understands how difficult it is for fighters who are under a UFC contract to speak candidly about fighter pay.

> Zuffa [then the owners of the UFC] is a private company so they don't have to disclose a lot of their information, and again this is my personal opinion, I'm not saying it's for anyone else but I've spoken to a vast array of fighters from top level guys to mid-tier guys to lower level guys and I feel at least the guys I've spoken with kind of have that same feeling of maybe they're not being fully compensated the way that they should be. But guys are scared.

## Mixed Martial Arts and the Quest for Legitimacy

> I think people are scared and fear the repercussions. I'm in a position where I can kind of speak out and I don't need the fighter income.

No fighter wants to incur the wrath of UFC management, and especially not the wrath of Dana White. White's response to Cholish's criticisms involved calling Cholish a "moron" and questioning his aptitude for Wall Street. The UFC focused on Cholish's comments on taxes while skirting the issue of establishing an equitable base pay for fighters.

> What's scary is this guy wasn't good enough to be in the UFC. I wonder if he's good enough to be on Wall Street. I mean this guy has to be the biggest moron I've ever seen in my life. He's talking about taxes? Yes, Wall Street guy you have to pay taxes, so do I. When we go down to Brazil and do a fight I pay taxes in Brazil too, and Sweden, and in all these other countries and states. Every state that we go to takes taxes.
>
> He signed a contract. He got the same opportunity that Georges St-Pierre, that Anderson Silva, that Jon Jones, Cain Velasquez and the list goes on and on. The unfortunate part of this business is some of you are good enough to be here and some of you are not. That's life, Cholish.

The common refrain that is heard from White is that fighters are afforded an incredible opportunity to become stars when admitted to the UFC. Fighting for the UFC counts for very little, though.

At another presser, White sounded off on fighter pay, and John Cholish in particular, with even more vitriol.

> That might sound fucking mean and harsh and [mocking tone of voice] "why should somebody not matter, everybody matters." We're getting to where we are in a society now where, everyone wins a trophy. No, everyone doesn't win a fucking trophy. The guys who stand out and the guys who make it exciting, the guys who raise to the top are the guys who deserve the money.

We are actually living in an era that has been meticulously chronicled by economists, such as Thomas Piketty in *Capital in the Twenty-First Century*, as one characterized by inequality divergence for Western societies not seen in a hundred years. The capital-income ratio has not been so large since the American "Gilded Age" and the French *Belle Époque*, and yet people worth hundreds of millions (billions?) complain about how everyone deserves a "trophy." No, we clearly do not live in a world where everyone gets a trophy. We live in a world that is very difficult for the bottom 60 percent in society.

White's comments largely resonate with some of the angrier defenders of capitalism of the early twenty-first century, though. Larry Summers,

## 6. The Needle and the Locker Room Bonus

a U.S. Secretary of the Treasury during the late Clinton era and Director of the National Economic Council during the early years of the Obama Administration, not to mention a former president of Harvard University, once reflected that "One of the challenges in our society is that the truth is kind of a dis-equalizer. One of the reasons that inequality has probably gone up in our society is that people are being treated closer to the way that they're supposed to be treated."[5]

Here is where the UFC sometimes feels like an allegory for the capitalism of our time. In a Darwinian struggle for the survival of the fittest, most will be deemed unfit and deserving of nothing. Fans themselves, men like me in the sense that they could not honestly fathom competing in MMA beyond the weekly time spent in front of a heavy-bag or in a jiu-jitsu class, deride the idea of bolstering fighter pay. These fans swallow the line that no one is forcing these guys to fight for peanuts, so who cares? The deference to the market that these fans hold is shared by men who have defined capitalism over the last three decades, men like Larry Summers. Just what they are deferring to the market includes issues pertaining to ethics, integrity, and *justice*—inherently political issues, that even the founders of Classical Liberalism, such as Adam Smith, saw as profoundly moral questions. What are such things before the great and terrible ordering principle of the free market? The answer, however, represents the very things that make us human and form the bonds of social order.

The deference to the market above all else represents White's thinking on the matter of fighter's pay. Those who "move the needle" of public attention on the sport, as well as a handful of champions, are appropriately compensated. The rest, the John Cholishes of the sport, are given very little for their trouble. There was a time when a pittance was really all an undercard fighter should have expected. However, the UFC is not the bush-league it once was when Zuffa purchased it from SEG for $2 million. Largely due to the promotional savvy of the Fertitta brothers and White, the UFC has become fantastically wealthy. During a lunch with Lucy Kellaway, a journalist with the *Financial Times*, Kellaway asked White about an estimate the *New York Times* made regarding the worth of the organization, a value of around $1 billion. White hesitantly whispered that it was $3.5 billion, but "some would say more."[6] The sale to WME-IMG confirmed that it was indeed more than $3.5 billion. Almost a billion dollars more.

The sense from people in the MMA community is that the annual profits that ownership receives from the UFC are very impressive, and surely why the price WME-IMG paid for the UFC was north of $4 billion. Social media is awash with stories of White losing a million dollars during a night of gambling and living a life where money that would be life-changing for 99 percent of Americans has lost its value. Surely most people agree that the owners of the UFC deserve to be fantastically compensated for their entrepreneurial success. It is highly likely that MMA would still be a fringe spectacle if it wasn't for the $2 million the Fertittas put into the UFC, and the energy and time that White put into it. Clearly, Dana White's work ethic and his dedication to the organization have been astounding and a big reason for the UFC's marketability and profitability. It is also pretty clear that the sweat, blood, and bodily injury suffered by the athletes competing in the UFC is what has made rich owners much richer. The time is now for fighters to be better compensated.

The UFC is infamously opaque on annual profits, so we have no idea what kind of salary and bonus structures exists for Zuffa. It does seem like there is a dramatic pay imbalance between management salary and bonuses and the financial compensation awarded to the fighters, especially after a sale of $4 billion. Revenue sharing for major North American sports organization is around 45 percent for athletes, somewhat more for the NFL and somewhat less for MLB. Nobody seriously believes that revenue sharing for fighters in the UFC is anywhere near 45 percent. Stories of fighters, such as John Cholish, give the impression that this might be the most inequitable and exploitative sport that appears on network television, maybe only third to college basketball and college football if we are to include collegiate-level amateurs, which UFC fighters are supposedly not.

The MMA-focused website, appropriately named www.bloodyelbow.com, reviewed the commissioned reports on UFC earnings between 2001–2014 that were issued by Standard & Poor, Moody's, and two Deutsche Bank reports.[7] The reports show that the revenue of the UFC grew from $4.5 million in 2001 to $180 million in 2006, and then up to $424 million in 2010 and half a billion dollars in 2014.

The figures for fighter payouts are not reported on directly. Instead, *Bloodyelbow* attempted to estimate the percentage of these payouts based on a revelation once offered to ESPN by Lorenzo Fertitta. According to the Fertitta brother who had the more public association with the UFC, fighter payouts between 2005 and 2011 were "more than $250 million." Assuming this to be approximately accurate, but rounding up to $300

## 6. The Needle and the Locker Room Bonus

million to account for Lorenzo's suggestion that it was more than $250 million, *Bloodyelbow* estimated revenue sharing at just over 16 percent. Truly a pittance if it is indeed close to the actual figure. That $4 billion price tag starts making a lot of sense, though.

The defining characteristic that separates the UFC from the NHL, NBA, MLB, and the NBA is that these other organizations make sure anyone who makes it to "The Show" or "The League" gets at least a few big paydays. The average career length for an NFL player is just under three-and-a-half seasons (*Not For Long*), and minor league players in baseball and other sports are notoriously underpaid. But making it to the NFL or MLB for a season or two actually means something to your bank account. Sure, a lot of these guys who play for a few years file for bankruptcy, but that is on them to manage their money prudently. People may turn on a NFL game to watch Peyton Manning and Tom Brady, but without the Von Millers and Akeem Ayerses you simply don't have a football game.

The UFC is in the exact same position, even though they are reluctant to acknowledge this truth. Strip away the undercard and the first half of the main card, and then see what happens to ratings and pay-per-view numbers. Granted, UFC on Fox 1 had only broadcast the heavyweight championship fight between Cain Velasquez and Junior Dos Santos and it became the most-watched fight in MMA history. But this is the exception rather than the norm. It was the first UFC event ever held on Fox, it was for nothing less than the heavyweight title, and it featured the consensus top two heavyweights since Fedor Emelianenko's decline.

However, the fight was over in about a minute, and many in the MMA community argued that the co-main event, an exciting fight between Benson Henderson and Clay Guida, one that demonstrated slick transitions on the ground, should have been aired to help the Fox audience understand the importance of grappling in the sport. How much money can you make from advertising when a fight lasts a minute? Another thing to keep in mind is that both Velasquez and dos Santos were enduring pretty serious injuries, but the idea of one of them backing out of the fight during the weeks leading up to it would be unthinkable when the entire broadcast was depending on these two titans. You need to have a card of fights to support main events and co-main events, or you don't have enough live sporting content to air. Furthermore, you need a card to test prospects and veterans who are building and rebuilding careers, advancing to contender status and earning a chance in the main event.

## Mixed Martial Arts and the Quest for Legitimacy

Further along in Dana White's admonishment of Cholish to the media via press conference, the president expounded on his position.

> The UFC, every time we do a fight, whether its on pay-per-view or on TV or whatever, people make the decision to stay home on a Saturday night and not do anything else when there's movies, dinners, spending time with families. There's a lot of shit to do on a Saturday night. These people make a decision to stay home on a Saturday night and watch our show.
>
> We get a show with a bunch of guys who want to push against the fucking fence and stand there for 15 fucking minutes and try to squeak out a win? How many people do you think are gonna tune in next Saturday? And if this keeps continuing, this becomes fucking boxing, where guys keep running around in circles and nobody fights and you walk away going "this fight sucked."

I think this is precisely why a UFC card is more than the headliner. A headliner can sometimes be boring and monotonous. Any fight can be, even for the best fighters. If you have several fights on your card, a full undercard and a full main card, then you diffuse the fights that "fucking suck" with those entertaining fights, both the Diego Sanchez slobber-knockers and the technical contests that move at a lightning pace. Boxing's problem (among others) is that it is too dependent on the main event. If the main event is unsatisfying, people don't find solace in the undercard. They don't even talk about boxing as a card, or a slate of fights. In the public imagination it is only "*the* fight," never the fights. The UFC has a handful of superstars, but they have so much more than that, owing to the dedication of a modest pool of talent to see how truly exciting this sport can be. The men and women of the entire card deserve recognition, because without them, the UFC loses one of the most important comparative advantages it has over boxing.

Later in White's tirade:

> Be the guy who stands out. You're the guy people want to see again. You're the guy people want to spend money for. You're the guy people by tickets, PPV, people stay home on Saturday night. John Cholish is not that fucking guy and never will be. So now John Cholish says "We don't get paid enough money." No, you didn't get paid enough. You know why you didn't get paid enough? Cause you didn't fucking deserve it.

It is in this venomous, hateful rant that a profound truth of the age is expressed. In his "labor theory of value," Marx expressed his argument on the centrality of the workforce, or proletariat, in the creation of profit. Without the laborer, no profit can be made. The worker is so easily exploited, denied fair wages, because a "reserve army of labor" exists,

## 6. The Needle and the Locker Room Bonus

comprised of hungry and desperate would-be workers, eager for a place in the mill and the chance to draw a wage.

For UFC management, and probably for a lot of the fans, the vast majority of fighters are easily replaceable. It is a tactic used by owners since the professionalization of sports in the late nineteenth century. Pay off your top talent and your top draws (not necessarily the same people), and keep everyone else insecure of their place in the organization. Remind them that they are in a precarious situation, with a vast reserve army of hungry athletes chomping at the bit to take their place. This is why Curtis Flood was on his own when he attempted to stand up to the owners of Major League Baseball over the "reserve clause," and why UFC fighter Tim Kennedy, after speaking out about fighter pay, quickly backed down from the debate for a few years.

UFC fighters have a classic collective action problem. It is the incentive of every fighter to coordinate their relations with Zuffa, and now the new owners, and to negotiate higher wages, but there is a fear that the leaders of a labor organization movement will be sniffed out by management and given their walking papers as well as a public dressing-down by the fiery president. Leadership in collective action needs to arise from champions, men like Curtis Flood and the NHL's Ted Lindsay, athletes who are either indispensible to the sport or so well-respected that society will listen to their voices of dissent. The problem is that the fighters who could push contract minimums somewhere above the new standard of $10,000 to show are getting taken care of quite nicely by the UFC, and they are unwilling to disrupt the status quo.

That is not to say that a fighters' association is impossible. These champions train with a host of up-and-comers, has-beens, and dreamers. Surely they are aware of what their sparring partners, languishing between UFC contracts and various regional promotions, are getting paid. All it is going to take is a magnanimous champion with a social conscience and the courage to push the management to let some of those profits trickle down to a minimum pay in the neighborhood of $20,000, and maybe then the UFC might start looking a little more like a major sporting league. It is quite likely that WME-IMG will be more amenable than Zuffa to a fighters' association. WME-IMG has been involved in a host of mainstream sports, and they represent many athletes that are members of associations. The next couple of years look like the ideal time for a fighters' association. However, after ponying up $4 billion, WME-IMG might be looking to receive a very high rate of return on their capital, especially if they are faced with high commitments of service payments on their debt.

Not all fighters are quite as docile on fighter pay. Nick Diaz and Nate Diaz, brothers who grew up in Stockton, California, have become two of the voices of discontent over pay scales. The Diaz brothers represent a fairly serious challenge to the status quo, owing to their high profiles. Nick was a champion in Strikeforce who challenged GSP for the UFC welterweight championship in one of the most anticipated fights in the company's history, and Nate was a challenger for the lightweight title and the man to have temporarily, though not decisively, put the breaks on Conor McGregor's aspirations to be a two-division champion. Not only have these two men come within a fight of UFC gold, they have also been fan favorites, employing a boxing-heavy style and an offensively oriented submission game, and relying on iron chins. They may not have the best takedown defense, nor are they known for their prowess with the leg-kick check, but when they have the right kind of opponent, someone looking to stand in the pocket and trade punches with plodding footwork, they can electrify an audience.

These are two men who encapsulate the tension between sport and spectacle—MMA and ultimate fighting. Nick's honesty about violence as entertainment is particularly striking.

> I'm not in love with fighting. I never was. That's crazy. I don't love to fight; I don't want to fight. I get my ass beat more when I win a fight than when I lose. I know you don't want to get your ass beat. I feel the same way. I feel the exact same way about retirement. I could give a fuck.
>
> I'm not going backwards in this sport ever, especially in pay. Why would I? To get my ass whooped? No. I would rather work at Wal-Mart. I have enough money to buy a nice house, do some gigs, save some money. I feel like this whole popularity thing keeps escalating, too. It's weird. Everywhere I go, I get stopped. If I make eye contact with someone, they're like, Whoa, you're Nick Diaz! So I could do signings for a while.
>
> But I'm not so sure my heart was ever in it. I don't know what that means. If I'm getting paid what I want to get paid, hell yeah I'm into it. I'm not into it if it's not worth it to me. If they want to renegotiate, I like that. But if not, then I don't give a shit. I never loved fighting. I never wanted to fight. That's probably why I come off the way I do. These guys, either they're all a bunch of freaks and weirdos or they put on a front. I do martial arts. They line up a guy to fight, so that's who I fight.
>
> I got my ass kicked in a sandbox by some kid when I was six years old. This Mexican kid whooped my ass. I was so pissed. I was bleeding, sand all over my mouth. I was so pissed. I didn't like it then, and I still don't like it now. It's all fun and games until you get in there and try to fight somebody.

## 6. The Needle and the Locker Room Bonus

Nate has echoed a lot of the same sentiments as Nick. During a period of time when Nate seemed disinterested in continuing to fight for the UFC, he offered some reflections:

> I don't get paid shit, and I'm about to tell the world. I didn't like what my brother and my partners got paid. Now that they got a better contract, which still ain't shit, it blows what I get out of the water. And they deserve triple what they get. I've been in the UFC for eight years and never turned down a fight. It's not like I'm getting paid 20 bucks an hour and they're getting 50 bucks an hour. I'm getting 20 bucks an hour and they're getting paid 15,000 bucks an hour. They blow me out of the water. At this point, I can't even go to lunch with my partners because if we start talking about contracts or our business, I don't have anything but bitter shit to say. We're entertaining entertainers. We get Shaq, Justin Bieber and Lil' Jon at the show. How are we entertaining billionaires and we can't even get shit?

Dana White was publicly unsympathetic to Nate's contestations. "Nate Diaz had his opportunities and he lost to Ben Henderson and he got stopped by Josh Thomson. Those were his opportunities to win that belt, or get back to the belt, and make Justin Beiber money, as he put it. He didn't win. He didn't win." This is the inequality facing UFC fighters. Most of them, even if they put their long-term health on the line and engage in slobber-knockers for the fans, *even if they contend for championship titles*, they are not going to make much money. Definitely not Justin Bieber money. That is reserved for the elite champions, like Anderson Silva and GSP, and above all, Conor McGregor, who will be the subject of an entire chapter himself.

This is a hard truth of the sport that should not be lost on its fans, because it is certainly not lost on class-aware fighters such as Nick Diaz.

> You see this stuff about my brother right now? I gotta watch him go through that bullshit. It's kinda harsh. That's my brother. That's my fault that he's even in this. He doesn't want to fight either, but he's not going to get a job at Wal-Mart, and he didn't make a million dollars his last fight. So he doesn't have a lot of options, and I don't like that. Something needs to be done about that, especially when you have someone as entertaining as my brother.

It is dangerous to lose touch with the human dimension of inequality. To lose touch with that is to lose touch with our own humanity and a sense of an interdependent society.

During the conference call for UFC 183, headlined by Nick Diaz vs. Anderson Silva, Nick returned to his critique of what competing in this sport does to you.

## Mixed Martial Arts and the Quest for Legitimacy

I don't enjoy fighting. I don't use that word [excited] in this sport. I use that word maybe if I'm starving and food is showing up, I'm getting excited now. That's kind of excitement. Or I'm excited to have a couple days. Trying to fight somebody is really, I don't know, people are confused with that term when it comes to fighting.

Sometimes I feel like I'm the only one who's in tune with what's really going on. Everybody's fighting anybody. Like I said, I think the people lie to you and tell you they enjoy doing things that they don't like to do. A lot of it is a front, and they like to put on a good look in front of their family and have a positive effect on people around them and not get in any bad positions, so they keep their mouth shut or they say bullshit like they like to hurt people. I mean, I don't want to hurt anybody. I'm a non-violent person. I don't necessarily enjoy violence. Like that show *Ridiculousness*, the host is a really funny guy. I love that guy. But I hate watching people get hurt over and over again. It's not something I enjoy doing.

And you see these guys come out and say, "I just want to hurt somebody," or, "I just want to go out there, I just love it." Sometimes you say, you know, you're full of shit. I do what I do because I've got to do it, for whatever reasons are behind it. A lot of it has to do with just martial arts and a martial arts background, and I don't think if there was any quit in me that I wouldn't have made it this far anyway. You can call it a curse if you will, or whatever you want. But that's just how I feel.

I can't complain. I can't ask for anything more. I'm happy with the deal that I made. It's hard out there, especially when the rest of these guys aren't getting paid what they should be paid, and they sit around and they can't open their mouths about anything, for the most part, when it comes to what they do. They've invested a lot into being pro MMA fighters and a lot of them have lives on the side, and they've had half the fights I've had, so it's a bit different for a lot of people. It's a really complicated road if you're an MMA fighter.

Maybe the UFC can never really be like MLB, the NHL, or even the NFL, and the idea of journeymen making above $10,000 to show is just not going to happen. Maybe it has to do with the nature of the sport itself. A fighters' association might simply be a contradiction. Men and women paid to fight each other in a cage just aren't going to sit down at the table together and act collectively. If that is true, then is it truly a sport, or is it something else? Do we deceive ourselves in calling it MMA when it is really ultimate fighting and spectacle we are watching?

What is ironic about organized labor for the UFC is that the promoter acts like the fighters are employees, rather than independent contractors, but only when it suits them. I'm no expert on American law, I'm not an American citizen and I don't live in the U.S., but the website of the U.S. Internal Revenue Service has a helpful page on their website called "Independent Contractor (Self-Employed) or Employee?" The IRS lists the three categories from common law that are used to determine whether persons or groups are independent contractors or employees.[8] These categories

## 6. The Needle and the Locker Room Bonus

include: Behavioral, Financial, and the Type of Relationship. For Behavioral, the IRS asks; "Does the company control or have the right to control what the worker does and how the worker does his or her job?" For Financial, the question posed is: "Are the business aspects of the worker's job controlled by the payer? (these include things like how worker is paid, whether expenses are reimbursed, who provides tools/supplies, etc.)." And Type of Relationship is determined by whether "there [are] written contracts or employee type benefits (i.e., pension plan, insurance, vacation pay, etc.)? Will the relationship continue and is the work performed a key aspect of the business?"

The answers to these questions can be murky, a fact that the IRS acknowledges, but accurately classifying your workforce is deemed "critical." It is not at all clear that UFC fighters are independent contractors, based on the categories listed by the IRS. With respect to the Behavioral category, the UFC gives out bonuses, both the official and of the locker-room variety, for what the fighter does and how the fighter does his or her job. Fighters are under a lot of pressure from UFC management to put on exciting fights. The UFC president himself has lamented the so-called "sport-killers" who privilege winning above excitement. An affirmative answer for the Behavioral question is suggestive of an employer-employee relationship.

The Financial category is also suggestive of fighters as employees rather than contractors. Fighters are provided official UFC gear for their bouts, and they could only wear sponsors who have given the UFC money. The UFC and Reebok have signed an agreement where, since mid–2015, UFC fighters and their corners are issued Reebok uniforms, with any failure to wear the uniforms resulting in significant penalties. The positive side of the deal is that they are effectively getting rid of the MMA sponsors who did not honor their contractual agreements with fighters who wore their shirts, or placed their emblem on their trunks. With all due respect to Condom Depot and Dude Wipes, Reebok is a blue-chip company, and its logo and apparel bring a lot of legitimacy to the UFC and MMA in general.

The negative side of the Reebok deal was that the pay structure meant that the vast majority of fighters were getting paid less than they were when they independently sought out sponsorships. The deal, which delivers $70 million over six years directly to the UFC, pays out very small amounts to fighters. Dana White once promised that all Reebok money would go to fighters, but now the reality looks much different. Fighters with the experience of 1–5 UFC fights earn $2,500 per fight, 6–10 fights get you $5,000, 11–15 fights earn you $10,000, 16–20 get $15,000, and above 20 fights will earn a fighter $20,000. Many fighters have become unusually vocal about the loss of income, such as heavyweight Brendan Schaub, who once earned approximately six figures in sponsorship money per fight, and former WMMA champion Miesha Tate, who has talked about losing 80 to 90 percent of what she once made in sponsorships.

By mandating uniforms, the UFC is treating their independent contractors as employees. Another clear piece of evidence regarding the Financial category is that the UFC must cover travel expenses for its fighters. A further example is the Code of Conduct that fighters must adhere to.

The final category posed by the IRS, Type of Relationship, is also suggestive of an employer-employee dynamic. The UFC took the admirable move to extend health insurance to their roster when MMA began to expand and enter the mainstream. Before this, fighters only received health coverage after fights. This meant that a lot of guys (at least American fighters who did not enjoy the benefits of a public health care system) were coming into bouts injured and then acting as if the injuries were caused during the fight so that their treatment would be covered. Extending health insurance was a move that is rightfully applauded, but it reveals how the fighters are more than independent contractors.

Type of Relationship is about more than contracts and benefits. It is also about the ongoing nature of work and whether the work performed is a key aspect of business. UFC fighters, as Dana White likes to remind them, can be cut after any loss. Even middleweight champion Anderson Silva could have potentially been cut in his prime, as we looked at in an earlier chapter. In that sense, UFC fighters are independent contractors. However, what is the UFC but a promoter of MMA bouts? Without the fighters, there is no business. I do not see how one could make a case that MMA is not the key aspect of the UFC and that its fighters are not the most meaningful aspect of the brand.

The UFC gets squeamish about changing the classification of its fighters from independent contractor to employee. If fighters became employees, the new owners will have to start paying taxes on Social Security and Medicare. The more dominant reason why Zuffa never let go of the claim that fighters are independent contractors is that once the UFC recognizes

## 6. The Needle and the Locker Room Bonus

them as employees, then the fighters are one step closer to forming an association to bargain collectively. You can't have the UFC without the men and women who step into the octagon to engage in the dangerous and potentially life-altering sport of MMA, and the UFC needs to come to terms with that.

A new challenge to the status quo is emerging from the U.S. House of Representatives. Markwayne Mullin, a Republican representing Oklahoma, and a former MMA fighter with a 3–0 professional record, introduced a bill in 2016 to extend the Ali Act to MMA. The Ali Act, a federal law enacted by the U.S. Congress in 2000, has the potential to alter the way the UFC does business. An important provision of the Ali Act is that fighters have the right to request that promoters reveal the amount of money that they directly made from the bout. While this is not the same thing as requiring the WME-IMG to open their books and explain the percentage of revenue that goes to their athletes, such as is done in legitimate professional sports leagues in North America, but it is a step in the right direction.

The problem with the Ali Act is that the amount of money earned from any particular bout on a card is entirely subjective, especially for an organization like the UFC where the main card is judged overall, not just the headliner. Also, if a fighter thinks that the promotion is citing a low number, that fighter must take the promotion to court, a nigh impossible task when one is paid $10,000 or $12,000 to show. Still, Mullin's bill is to be applauded, and hopefully it will pass into law.

A second challenge to the status quo was announced just after the applicability of the Ali Act was broached. Georges St-Pierre, the greatest welterweight fighter of all time, flanked by former heavyweight champion Cain Velasquez, former bantamweight champion T.J. Dillashaw, lightweight/welterweight contender Donald Cerrone, and top-ranked middleweight (now retired) Tim Kennedy, announced the formation of a fighters' association—The Mixed-Martial Arts Athletes' Association (MMAAA). The purpose of the association was to institutionalize collective bargaining on behalf of fighters and to increase the percentage of revenue that goes to fighters up to the neighborhood of 50 percent, to align it with mainstream sports organizations. This fighters' association gave an even bleaker estimation of revenue sharing for fighters than *Bloodyelbow*, citing a figure of eight percent.

The prospects of the MMAAA do not look entirely promising as of early 2017. Very few of the UFC's most prominent fighters have publicly joined it, and the biggest superstar right now, Conor McGregor, has plans of his own that have nothing to do with collective bargaining. The MMAAA looks to have some baggage that may make it less than the ideal solution to the shamefully low payouts for fighters.

Firstly, four out of five of the fighters who are backing the association are clients of the Creative Artists Agency, which is a rival talent agency to WME-IMG. Some fighters may be reluctant to become involved in what may be seen as an inter-agency dispute. Secondly, the MMAAA has made public a relationship with Bjorn Rebney, the former Bellator owner and promoter, who ostensibly has an advisory role with the fighters' association. Such a relationship may not be well received by some of the fighters, as Rebney does not have a stellar record of fighter payouts with Bellator. Finally, it is unfortunate that GSP is only now behind a fighters' association. If he had taken a leadership position on this front back when he was an active fighter, he could have made it much more difficult for the UFC to ignore the MMAAA, as they seem to be doing now. GSP has hinted at a return to fighting, but I'm going to hold off on following that click-bait until details start to firm up. The involvement of USADA does seem to correct the initial problem with the sport that caused GSP to walk away, but he has now cited the Reebok deal, and the requirement to be compensated for lost sponsorship revenue, as his chief concern.

Not every MMA fighter is as highly educated as Josh Cholish, but a lot of them are in fact well-educated athletes. They are men and women who wrestled their way to college degrees. People like Josh Koscheck, Phil Davis, Rich Franklin, Demian Maia, Takeya Mizugaki, Sara McMann and so many others in the UFC and organizations like Bellator are college graduates. Along with those who are college educated are the large numbers of UFC fighters who may not have a degree but have a keenly refined sense of human dignity, honed by their martial arts and the training of both their bodies and their minds. Martial arts has imbued these men with a powerful awareness of respect, integrity, and justice. It ultimately comes down to whether this is the realm of sport or spectacle, whether we are watching human cockfighting or athletic competition, and whether we as spectators expect the combatants to sacrifice mind and body for a wreath, like the pre-modern world of life and death the Spartans inhabited, or whether we, like Tritantaechmes, expect something beyond a wreath for those athletes laying it all on the line.

# 7

# "There is no other guy"

In his majestic *History of the Decline and Fall of the Roman Empire*, Edward Gibbon painfully reconstructed the nature of gladiator violence during Rome's inexorable march toward decay and rot.[1] Gibbon described the games as the Empire's most "ignoble pursuit." Gladiatorial contests "polluted the amphitheater of Rome" and "degraded a civilized nation below the condition of savage cannibals. Several hundred, perhaps several thousand, victims were annually slaughtered in the great cities of the empire; and the month of December, more peculiarly devoted to the combat of gladiators, still exhibited to the eyes of the Roman people a grateful spectacle of blood and cruelty." In Gibbon's analysis, it was a "horrid custom which had so long resisted the voice of humanity and religion."

Gibbon recounted the story of Telemachus, a Christian monk who once attempted to separate gladiators in the amphitheater. The monk was killed for his efforts under a hail of stones thrown by a bloodthirsty crowd. The people there were not simply observing the conflict, but had actually crossed the line between spectator and gladiator, making themselves into combatants and cowardly ending the life of one who dared to condemn the horror.

> The citizens who adhered to the manners of their ancestors might insinuate that the last remains of a martial spirit were preserved in this school of fortitude, which accustomed the Romans to the sight of blood and to the contempt of death: a vain and cruel prejudice, so nobly confuted by the valor of ancient Greece and modern Europe.

Gibbon was acutely aware that what a society prizes as its entertainment is not cut off or removed from society itself. Entertainment can transcend itself, marking our consciousness, influencing how we think, and interacting with our cultural norms, ethics, and morality. Gibbon acutely understood that the gladiatorial games had a pernicious effect in Roman

## Mixed Martial Arts and the Quest for Legitimacy

society and politics. When confronted with the immorality of the sport, spectators reacted with ferocity and barbarism. No longer were they spectators in a crowd, they were combatants and murderers.

Zuffa has brought a sizeable measure of integrity to the UFC by strongly endorsing the unified rules. These rules contain the violence into a sport, issuing a clear set of demands on the part of its athletes to reduce the impact of low-skill/high-reward tactics, such as the head-butt, groin strike, and soccer kick to a downed opponent. The rules offer a modest corrective force to the violence, holding to the concept of the contest being a fight, but giving it the possibility of turning the violence into sport.

Expressions of violence, real or acted, are a form of entertainment for many, including myself. I think that the violence of MMA is so particularly disquietful because of what it may represent. Is its attraction partly owing to a fear of the audience that the violence of the cage represents an anarchic world of broken-down social and political institutions? A fear of a return to some primordial "state of nature," particularly the one described by Thomas Hobbes as "solitary, poor, nasty, brutish, and short"? This dynamic of violence as entertainment, but also something that is feared by spectators, probably exists in other forms of popular culture too, such as Zombie graphic novels, movies, and TV shows. We enjoy going along for the ride through Kirkman's *The Walking Dead*, and yes, we fear the zombie, but we also learn to fear the encounters with other groups because that is where the zombie apocalypse narrative cuts into those real fears that exist at the prospect of the disintegration of civilization. It is an anxiety about whether our political institutions are robust enough to endure some future calamity and whether our social customs have only been normalized through the rule of law provided by the institutions that surround us, such as the state and its legal system. Perhaps the same is true for MMA.

One of the most direct fears that your average fighter on the UFC roster harbors is the one where they are seen as a "boring point fighter." It is a fear born out of their perceived inability to inflict enough punishment to opponents and their struggle to finish them. These fighters are successful, so successful that they surely incite fear in their fellow competitors, not because of the brutal levels of violence they can dispense, but because of their ability to fight within the unified rules to cruise to victory, halt contenders in their tracks, and make their opponents look quite mediocre.

## 7. *"There is no other guy"*

Winning isn't everything in the UFC. You can go on a nice win streak, but this is a sport of independent contractors, where anything can happen and you are only ever as good, and as marketable, as your last showing. Unfortunately, a lot of fans think fighters lose because "they suck" and only win because their "opponent sucks." Part of what makes watching the UFC, and other promotions, fun to watch is that the match can be over in a second. One big shot can put someone away or dramatically shift the momentum of a fight. The lesson is a simple one: you can win, you can win a lot, but you are going to lose, and when you do, you want the UFC to want you. It is hard to kick-box defensively in four-ounce gloves. Even if you are still in the middle of a multi-fight contract, the UFC can terminate your employment with them if you: (1) violate the fighter Code of Conduct; or (2) lose a single fight.

The UFC likes to remind fighters that they are independent contractors, not employees of the UFC. Once again, we have a metaphor for capitalism in the early twenty-first century: flexibility is an asset above all others, and workers face an unending insecurity. I'd guess that you have probably been in an insecure job where the line between employment and being out of work felt like it came down to the capricious impressions of an aloof overseer. Maybe, as it is for most UFC fighters, it was work that you wanted to turn into a long-term career because of how much you enjoyed it and what the work meant to you—it felt as if it was what you were meant to do.

I felt this way in graduate school while I was working on my PhD and teaching at three different Canadian universities in southern Ontario. I had no idea what teaching contracts I could procure for myself in any given term. During some terms, work was plentiful, or it could be quite lean another term, but no matter how much work you were able to get, you knew it never paid much to teach on contract. This state of perpetual insecurity caused a significant amount of fear in my own life as I questioned whether I should continue to sacrifice time away from a stable job outside of academia in pursuit of a full-time teaching post. Everything worked out superbly for me in the end. I moved across Canada (4,500km) to the beautiful locale of Vancouver Island and now engage with some of the most hard-working students I have ever met. I also get to know my students quite well, thanks to wonderfully small class sizes. I still have friends and family pursuing PhDs, and even many with their PhDs finished, immensely qualified people trying to find employment beyond that of contract work.

## Mixed Martial Arts and the Quest for Legitimacy

On the subject of fighter's pay, we questioned whether fighting in the UFC is the same as playing in the NHL or the NBA. Arriving in the UFC, even earning a veteran status, is not going to translate into the kind of paychecks typical of mainstream athletes in "stick and ball" sports. As an independent contractor, even a winning fighter, you will have an insecure place on the UFC roster. You can't just win, you have to score knockouts. You can even be regularly earning submissions victories and still be the forgotten man, just ask Demian Maia or Jacare. This is despite submission victories being a particularly difficult proposition in an era where most UFC-caliber fighters have pretty stout submission defense.

Fighters in the top 15, or even the top 10, of their weight divisions were released by the UFC throughout 2013–2017. Jon Fitch, for years, was the consensus top-2 welterweight in the world. He is a fighter who went on a 13–1 tear in the UFC between 2005–2010, his one loss coming against GSP in an exciting title fight. Fitch's pre–UFC career included an impressive diversity in his methods to victory, including various submissions, TKOs, and even a KO. His 8–0 UFC run that carried him to that UFC championship fight included three submission victories and a TKO over a feared future welterweight contender, once dubbed a "Muay Thai Wrecking-Ball," Thiago Alves. After his defeat at the hands of GSP, who was undoubtedly in his prime, Fitch's five subsequent victories all came via decision. The former captain of the Purdue wrestling team returned to his style of wrestling that was punctuated by a grinding battle of attrition, eschewing powerful double-legs for constant pressure, meant to wilt opponents over the duration of three rounds.

Fitch was earning a reputation as a boring point-fighter who lacked finishing ability, or even a will to finish opponents. To be fair, a lot of MMA fans recognized Fitch's grinding style and looked forward to seeing him compete, but many, many others moaned about his upcoming bouts. Capping his 5–0 run that followed his loss to GSP with a second victory over Alves, Fitch finally earned a title eliminator match-up against former lightweight champion B.J. Penn. The fight was an exciting affair that featured as decisive a momentum swing as possible in a fight that went the distance. Penn came on very fast, unexpectedly shooting deep on Fitch and dragging him down. Penn, one of the first American mixed-martial artists to ascend to the heights of Brazilian jiu-jitsu, dominated Fitch on the mat, threatening the wrestler with rear-naked chokes. Fitch survived round 1 and, just as Penn looked to repeat his domination in round 2,

## 7. "There is no other guy"

dragging Fitch to the ground again, Fitch reversed Penn, got on top and started to batter Penn's head and body. Penn, appearing gassed at the beginning of round 3, was jumped on by Fitch, who hammered away at Penn until the final bell. It was an exciting fight to watch, a fight determined as much by technique as it was by grim determination and heart. There was something appropriate about the majority draw the judges scorecards turned in, a round and a half of domination by Penn, followed by a round and a half of domination by Fitch.

The label of Fitch as a boring fighter persisted. Rather than respect Fitch's offensive output in round 3, his inability to TKO a tired and undersized Penn was met with derision by the "JUST BLEED" fans. In his next fight, Fitch was starched in 12 seconds by Johny Hendricks in the defining victory of Hendricks' trip to eventually winning the welterweight title. A 12-second knockout, despite what UFC promos might tell you, is a rare thing to behold in MMA, especially between two top-10 welterweights. The eruption from the fans in Vegas, and the bar I was in, represented an arousal of spirits beyond what one might expect, even from such a quick knockout. Much of the exuberance was the context of *Fitch* being the person who was knocked out. Fitch always gave off a quiet, serious persona of a man who lived martial arts and the dedication and sacrifice required to excel in the grueling sport of wrestling.[2] Fitch may have been a stablemate of Koscheck, but he was no heel. Instead, it was almost as if the crowd was celebrating the destruction of the grinder at the fist of the bearded Texan.

Following a ten-month layoff, Fitch returned to face the surging Brazilian, Erick Silva. Silva was looking like a future contender in late 2012, relaxed and composed in the octagon, with fight-ending striking power and an aggressiveness in hunting for submissions that define the predators of the grappling world. Once again, Fitch started slowly and Silva looked to make him pay. It was round 2, though, where Silva appeared to be on the edge of victory, sinking in a rear-naked choke. Impossibly, Fitch resisted the urge to tap, got on top of Silva and brutalized the Brazilian until the final bell. The fight earned both men the UFC's "fight of the night" honors, and this time earned Fitch the victory. Fitch lost his next fight by decision, a lopsided defeat against former middleweight contender and Abu Dhabi Grappling Champion Demian Maia, in a fight where Fitch was unable to create space against Maia's own grinding style.

Shockingly, the fight against Maia turned out to be Fitch's last in the

## Mixed Martial Arts and the Quest for Legitimacy

UFC, as he was promptly cut in early 2013. Fitch had gone 1–2–1 in his final four fights in the UFC, with both losses coming to top-10 fighters, one of whom would eventually win the welterweight title. Moreover, three of those fights were quite exciting, the one winning "fight of the night." The last fight, against Maia, was not heralded as an entertaining fight by any means, but it was significant, two top grapplers battling it out for the win. You could even credit Fitch for trying to liven the fight up by throwing a few wild haymakers when he could get a moment of respite from the relentless pressure of Maia.

Instead, Fitch was cut due to the perception that he was boring. Boring and *overpaid*. Here was the long-time consensus number 2 welterweight in the world being told that he wasn't worth the pay he received. This is another characteristic of MMA that separates it from mainstream sports organizations like the NHL and the NFL: The object is not to win as much as it is to entertain the fans. It is not enough for Fitch to win, since his UFC record between 2005–2013 was 14–3–1, or even to have a number of entertaining fights. He ground out five consecutive victories throughout 2009–2010 which tainted him in the minds of the UFC and a certain group of fans.

This would be like Richard Sherman being punished by the NFL in 2014, either docked pay or sent to the CFL, for shutting down quarterbacks like Peyton Manning. Could you imagine the NFL lamenting the ability of the Legion of Boom to shut out the excitement of the passing game and reducing yardage totals? Clearly, spectacle exists at the center of MMA. It seems as if this is a point that does much to discredit the notion that fighting is the "true" sport stripped of metaphor. Dana White likes to say that fighting is in our genes and is universal. Most sports have limited regional appeal, but fighting, according to White and others, putatively has an appeal that transcends MMA's core of the U.S. and Brazil, and can be relatable and popular anywhere.

Other sports, according to this logic, are really only metaphors of a fight. If that were true, then fans of MMA wouldn't need to be coddled more than fans of football and hockey, and we wouldn't be so worried about how "boring" fighters are harming the sport. There is a deep insecurity about MMA in the minds of many fans, media commentators, and the UFC itself. It is the fear that the sport may not be all that entertaining after all.

So acrimonious became the fallout between White and Fitch that

## 7. "There is no other guy"

White even released the payouts Fitch received during his tenure with the UFC, figures that the UFC has traditionally shrouded in secrecy. The move was intended to show the working-class UFC fan-base just how much money Fitch was getting paid to "lay on top of guys."

Another 2013 cut that caught UFC fans by surprise was the case of Yushin Okami, a perennial top-10 middleweight who went 3–0 before getting blasted by top-5 middleweight and former Strikeforce champion Jacare and subsequently being given his walking papers after that one loss. Okami's overall UFC record stretched back to 2006, where he went 13–5 in the organization, a record comparable to Fitch's own.

After what is probably going to be remembered as his most impressive victory—defending his Strikeforce middleweight championship against Dan Henderson, after surviving two thunderous blows from Henderson's right hand in the first round—Jake Shields was signed by the UFC with a lot of fanfare. Even while still under contract with Strikeforce, Shields was shown with Dana White at a WEC event. White had his arm wrapped around Shields, mouthing to the camera, "He's mine!"

Shields had spent his career up to this point as one of the most successful journeymen the sport had ever known. Over a span of a decade, Shields fought for an alphabet soup of promotions, earning a few titles along the way. Jon Danaher, a jiu-jitsu instructor at Renzo Gracie's academy in New York and one of GSP's coaches, once described Jake Shields' ability to end a fight as comparable to a heavyweight boxer. Not because of his striking, which has never been powerful, but because of his submission skills. He once guillotined future UFC welterweight champion Robbie Lawler in just over two minutes.

The real strength of Jake Shields was his ability to grind opponents out and earn judges' decisions, like when he defeated both Yushin Okami and a UFC interim champion who came incredibly close on two occasions to becoming an undisputed UFC champ, Carlos Condit, on the same night in Hawaii in 2006. Shields, similar to so many journeymen of MMA who are compelled to take the fights that are offered, competed as a welterweight, a middleweight, and even somewhere in-between. It wasn't initially clear whether he was being signed by the UFC to compete against which UFC title-kingpin—GSP or Anderson Silva. Suggesting that the UFC's middleweights were going to "kill him," even though he had just defeated a top-10 middleweight in Dan Henderson, it was announced that Shields was going to fight at welterweight. His underwhelming performance against Martin Kampmann was still enough to earn Shields a shot at GSP's belt in Toronto, headlining the largest stadium show the UFC has ever put on. Shields came up short against GSP, but proved he was a top-10 welterweight in the aftermath of that fight, going 3–2, with one no-contest. His last three fights came against a "murderer's row" of top-10 fighters. He defeated Tyron Woodley and Demian Maia, both by split decision, and then lost a unanimous decision to Hector Lombard. Despite being 2–1, all against the elite of the division, Shields was given his walking papers. He reflected on the UFC after his release: "I feel like the sport, they're trying to pull it away from being the best in the sport, and just putting it into, oh, you gotta go and slug it out and fight the way they want you to, which is kind of ridiculous. You wouldn't have guys like Floyd Mayweather being the best in the world if [boxing executives] pressured him like that."

Kevin Iole, a thoughtful MMA reporter for *Yahoo Sports*, described the UFC's decision to cut Shields as a move out of the NFL's playbook.[3] Iole's thinking was that NFL teams, such as the Pittsburgh Steelers, typically cut players with excessive contracts more quickly than other guys if their productivity drops off. For instance, White was quoted as saying that Shields was contracted to earn $120,000 for his next fight, and at 35 years old, White dismissed Shields' chances against the "division of animals" in the welterweight division.

The problem is how productivity is measured by the UFC compared to the NFL and other major sports leagues. Winning is what matters in the NFL, and player productivity is measured by how effective individual players are in contributing to wins, and how much they are responsible for losses. Productivity in the UFC is measured not by wins; if that were the case, then Shields would not have been released after a single loss against a top-10 fighter in Hector Lombard. Instead it is measured by the level of entertainment the fighter produces—how much violence a fighter can dish out and, just as importantly, how theatrically they behave leading up to a fight, such as the case of the incredibly successful Conor McGregor. This is where Kevin Iole's analogy is a little off. NFL teams measure productivity by winning, whereas the UFC measures it by "moving the needle."

Other top-10, even top-5, fighters were simply not offered competitive contracts. Phil Davis, a highly ranked fighter who faltered only against the elite of the division, wasn't able to generate enough interest with the UFC brass, despite the dearth of talent in the light-heavyweight division.

## 7. *"There is no other guy"*

Davis still had the potential to one day contend for a title in the UFC, but the wrestler was left for Bellator to pick up. Ryan Bader, another top-5 light-heavyweight, also headed to Bellator due to the lack of interest being shown by the UFC. Even former champion Benson Henderson did not receive a matching offer from the UFC after he fought out the last of his contract. Incredibly, even Lorenz Larkin did not re-sign with the UFC in early 2017, as the number 5-ranked fighter in the welterweight division is no longer ranked by the UFC.

It is at this point where another dynamic of the sport is being undermined by the spectacle of the show. MMA fans were more likely to tune in to see heavyweight *YouTube* back-yard brawler Kimbo Slice (Kevin Ferguson) fight a man named "Dada 5000" (Dhafir Harris), than watch Demetrius "Mighty Mouse" Johnson, one of the greatest fighters in the sport but a soft-spoken and articulate athlete laying waste to the flyweight (125-lb) division. The bout between Kimbo and Harris nearly ended in the most tragic of circumstances, with Harris suffering cardiac arrest and being briefly pronounced dead in a hospital after the fight, and Kimbo leaving us all far too early, dying of heart failure a few months later at the young age of 42. Even Kimbo's victory was overturned after it was revealed that he failed the drug test.

It is ultimately the decision of the UFC to let go top-15 fighters such as Jake Shields and Jon Fitch. But I think it is a little unfair to blame the UFC entirely. They are acting on the basis of what they think the fans want to see and what they are going to spend their time, and their money, to watch. The mentality of the screaming, shirtless, "JUST BLEED" fan is the logic under which Dana White and Zuffa have historically operated. They are the contemporary heirs of the bloodthirsty horde who, at the coliseum, threw rocks at an enemy of the violence of the games.

It is one thing to be signed by the UFC, enjoy a long and fairly successful career in the fight organization, and be dropped unceremoniously. However, it is a whole other thing to pay your dues, become a champion of other organizations, and not even be given the chance. Ben Askren is a highly decorated collegiate wrestler who became the welterweight champion of Bellator. He was at one time known for being a one-dimensional wrestler, something that even Bellator's then-president, Bjorn Rebney, once admitted, but he was ridiculously good at it. He went through Bellator's welterweight ranks, cleaning out the division of his era all the while showing an increasing versatility to his game, such as developing a vicious

## Mixed Martial Arts and the Quest for Legitimacy

"ground and pound." Incomprehensibly, Rebney suggested that Bellator had no interest in re-signing their champion when his contract expired. Seriously, this kind of foolishness only happens in MMA. It was expected that Askren would be signed by the UFC, but White denied having any interest, suggesting that Askren still needed to pay his dues elsewhere, despite being 12–0 in his career up to that point.

Finally, in the summer of 2014, White seemed open to the idea of Askren joining the UFC "one day." Askren was not amused.

> It's kind of like all of us had that time in high school when we were bullied by the cool group of kids. Then we did something, then the cool group said "oh my god, can you be part of our group?" Then some of us who didn't have low self esteem said "well, you didn't want me the first time, I'm all right." Then some other people, they run, "the cool kids want to hang out with me? Yes, please." I think it's kind of one of those things.
>
> Him saying I'm not good enough for the UFC? I've got more skills in my pinky finger than half the damn guys in the UFC. Have you seen some of these guys fighting lately? It's ridiculous. Having the letters UFC behind my name is not the be-all, end-all it is for someone. Some people think once they get into the UFC, that's it. I think with having more large organizations in the word, it's going to be great for the fighters, because the right now the fighters are being underpaid greatly, in my opinion, and I was one who was able to step outside that box and go find a great paycheck somewhere else.

Askren signed with One FC, an MMA organization based out of Singapore, and easily became their welterweight champion. In late 2014, amounting to what must by the most hypocritical decision the UFC has made over the last couple of years, the organization announced that they had signed Phil Brooks, otherwise known as "CM Punk," a 36-year-old entertainer from the WWE who has never had a professional or amateur MMA bout in his life. The man never even competed as a "real" wrestler. He did his training at Roufusport, one of the gyms Askren calls home. Punk was submitted in just over two minutes by the 2–0 Mickey Gall.

The decision to release top-10 and top-15 fighters in the UFC, even after a single loss against another top-10 fighter, and the decision to not sign consensus top-15 fighters, is all meant to create a state of insecurity for fighters. They want their competitors to go into every fight like hungry dogs. It makes you think of Christopher Nolan's epic *The Dark Knight*, when Joker takes over a criminal gang and invites three of the surviving members of the gang to join. He ominously breaks a pool cue but resignedly tells them that there is only an opening for one of them. White

## 7. "There is no other guy"

wants divisions filled with "hungry animals," looking to eat anyone and everyone for a $16,000 payday.

The dilemma that fighters in the UFC have that is quite a bit different from the situation facing athletes in other sports organizations is that if a player, one who deserves to be in the league by any objective measure, does not fit in with the team, or has a fallout with coaching staff or management, that player can be traded to or sign with another team. Player mobility was especially important for the strengthening of the MLBPA, as when Curtis Flood walked away from baseball over the shackles of the reserve clause. The problem for fighters who are let go by the UFC is that their contracts are with the organization, not individual teams. If the UFC doesn't want them, where are they supposed to go?

A roundtable debate featuring David Dudley, an attorney who formerly worked with the U.S. Federal Trade Commission, and Paul Gift, an Associate Professor of Economics with the Graziado School of Business and Management at Pepperdine University, helped to clarify a couple of issues pertaining to the question on whether the UFC has become a monopoly.[4] A point made by Gift is that a firm with monopoly power, bearing in mind that there is almost always a spectrum between competition and monopolization, does not put it in violation of U.S. law. The U.S. Supreme Court links legal offence to behavior. It is only when a firm abuses monopoly power that charges can be made. Furthermore, Gift explains that monopolization is judged on the "output market," or the product the firm puts into the marketplace. Abuse of monopolization is then decided by factors such as increasing the price of the product to hold consumers hostage, or manipulating the quality or the quantity of the product on a dependent or captive consumer.

The fact that the UFC is in the entertainment business makes it very hard to make an argument of monopoly power being abused. If consumers don't like what they are watching on Fox Sports 1, then they can watch something else, read a book, play a video game, or, heaven forbid, spend time with friends and family over a game of *Risk*, *Ticket to Ride*, or a round of *Mario Kart* (perhaps one of the most simultaneously bonding, and divisive, game experiences ever devised). If the UFC decides to start charging more money for a PPV, as they did for UFC 168, then consumers can enjoy their Saturday night on a budget they are more comfortable with.

Though the UFC is not likely to be considered as abusing monopoly power anytime soon, it is possible that they are becoming a "monopsony."

## Mixed Martial Arts and the Quest for Legitimacy

Gift and Dudley explain that monopsony power is based on the "input market," or the labor market that supplies the firm. In the case of sports, the most important input market are the athletes themselves. Here is where the position of the UFC becomes contentious. Do fighters really have options open to them in a competitive market where organizations are bidding for their services? Pride was a supremely important organization for about a decade (1997–2007), certainly more successful in its prime than the UFC was at the same time. It was Pride that hosted a fair share of bouts that had historical significance for the sport, such as the 2005 heavyweight championship match between Fedor Emelianenko and Mirko "Cro Cop" Filipovic, and the Grand Prix light-heavyweight tournament won by Shogun, as well as its fair share of shameful sideshow matchups featuring overmatched bouts.

In 2003, Pride chairman Naoto Morishita was found dead of an apparent suicide after some sort of tension with a mistress.[5] Sometime after his death, the Yakuza allegedly became more involved in the fight organization, trying to fix fights and using it as one of their many fronts. A story that ran in 2005 in the Japanese magazine *Shūkan Gendai* (*Modern Weekly*) detailed the extent to which Pride and the Yakuza were connected to each other. These revelations soured Japanese public opinion of MMA and were enough to push away FujiTV from the fight business, causing Pride to lose its television deal. In 2007, Zuffa bought Pride for $70 million, claiming that they were going to keep the organization alive but create a NFL-AFL type of arrangement between the UFC and Pride.

Zuffa quickly changed its tune after the deal was finalized and decided instead to close up shop in Japan and bring as many elite fighters from Pride into the UFC as they could. The addition of Pride's formidable light-heavyweights, such as Shogun, Dan Henderson, Rampage, Wanderlei Silva, and Lyoto Machida, looked to shake up a division once ruled by Chuck Liddell. The UFC heavyweight division similarly appeared destined to be changed with the arrivals of Mirko Cro Cop and Antônio "Minotauro" Nogueira, but with negotiations between Zuffa and Fedor Emelianenko's representatives at an impasse, Emelianenko, Pride's greatest champion, and arguably the greatest champion in the history of MMA up to that time, was not going to be joining the UFC.

Other notable purchases by Zuffa include World Extreme Cagefighting (WEC) in 2006. Zuffa first folded the WEC weight classes at 170 and above, bringing fighters such as Carlos Condit and Brian Stann into the

## 7. "There is no other guy"

UFC, and then in 2010, folding in the lighter divisions, bringing in fighters like Anthony Pettis, Benson Henderson, Donald Cerrone, Jose Aldo, Uriah Faber, Renan Barao, Dominic Cruz, and Demetrious Johnson, and along with these fighters, new weight classes at 145 lbs, 135 lbs, and eventually 125 lbs.

Strikeforce, which had a presence on CBS and Showtime, was another high-profile purchase by Zuffa. Fedor Emelianenko, the heavyweight champion of Pride who had cultivated an aura of invincibility over a decade of dominance against generally much larger opposition, had migrated to Strikeforce after another promotion, Affliction, collapsed. Though Zuffa was to cut the legendary Russian after three consecutive losses, squashing any lingering hope that he would have a shot against the heavyweight or light-heavyweights of the UFC,[6] the purchase brought in fighters like Nick Diaz, Gilbert Melendez, Luke Rockhold, Jacare, and a host of noteworthy heavyweights, such as Alistair Overeem, Daniel Cormier, Fabricio Werdum, and Antonio Silva. Even smaller, less notable organizations got on the Zuffa radar, such as the International Fight League (IFL), which was purchased in 2008.

Monopoly can sometimes be a good thing in sports for the consumer. The modern NFL treats its fans to a showdown between the NFC and AFC champions, and before Zuffa bought Pride, there were a lot of questions about a showdown between Chuck Liddell and Wanderlei Silva. By having one league that is pre-eminent, you produce the market forces that compel athletes to join that league. To make the most money and to receive the greatest visibility, fighters need to be part of the UFC and match up against the best. The problem is the limited options available to UFC fighters who are winning fights but are cut because they are not viewed as exciting or who have a troubled relationship with UFC management. However, there is surely no shortage of local fight organizations in the U.S., and they are eager to sign UFC castaways with name recognition to serve as headliners. Maybe it is not such a bad thing that the UFC resembles a monopoly. There is a group of former UFC fighters that sees it as a very bad thing indeed for the athletes, and they are committed to pushing the issue through the courts.

In late 2014, Nate Quarry, a retired fighter who once contended for the UFC middleweight championship, Jon Fitch, and Cung Le, a recently retired UFC middleweight, filed a class-action antitrust lawsuit against the UFC for violations of Section 2 of the Sherman Act. The venerable

## Mixed Martial Arts and the Quest for Legitimacy

Sherman Act, passed by the U.S. Congress during the bleak days of the Gilded Age when the robber barons dominated economic and political life in the Republic, states in its Section 2, "Every person who shall monopolize, or attempt to monopolize, or combine or conspire with any other person or persons, to monopolize any part of the trade or commerce among the several States, or with foreign nations, shall be deemed guilty of a felony." The plaintiffs are alleging that the UFC has attempted to "maintain and enhance" both its "monopoly power" in the promotion of MMA (known as the output market), and "monopsony power in the market" for fighter contracts (known as the input market).

> As part of the anticompetitive scheme alleged herein, the UFC has acquired, driven out of business, foreclosed the entry of, and/or substantially impaired the competitiveness of multiple actual and potential MMA Promotion rivals. As a result, the only remaining promoters of MMA bouts are either fringe competitors—which, as a general matter, do not and cannot successfully compete directly with the UFC—or entities that have essentially been conscripted by the UFC, through the scheme alleged herein, into acting as the UFC's "minor leagues," developing talent for the UFC but not competing directly with it.

The lawsuit delves into some of the unbecoming comments made by UFC President Dana White. It reads:

> White publicly proclaimed that, within the sport of MMA: "There is no competition. We're the NFL. You don't see people looking at the NFL and going, 'Yeah, but he's not the best player in the world because there's a guy playing for the Canadian Football League or the Arena League over here.' We're the NFL. *There is no other guy*" [emphasis in lawsuit]. However, unlike the NFL—which has multiple teams vying for player services—within the UFC, there is no competition for Elite Professional MMA Fighter services. Due to the scheme alleged herein, for Elite Professional MMA Fighters, it's the UFC or nothing. To repeat Mr. White's boastful concession: "There is no other guy."

The lawsuit even brings the court's attention to White's voice in social media where he gloats over the death of his competitors.

> For example, in November 2008, following the UFC's acquisition of the assets of MMA Promotion companies International Fight League ("IFL"), Elite Xtreme Combat ("EliteXC"), and Affliction Entertainment ("Affliction"), UFC President Dana White uploaded a pre-bout video blog to YouTube in which he held up the following mock tombstone prominently displaying the letters "RIP" as well as the logos and "dates of death" of the those MMA Promoters—IFL, EliteXC and Affliction. Each promotion had been put out of business by the UFC's anticompetitive conduct.

## 7. *"There is no other guy"*

The lawsuit cites White as taking credit for the collapse of these MMA organizations, sounding more like a gang-banger than a president of a major sports organization by declaring himself as "the grim reaper, motherfuckers," and in a Twitter post where he claims to have killed Pride.

White's boasts to have killed various MMA organizations are certainly misplaced. Pride's shady connections to the Yakuza are what tainted that MMA organization in the minds of Japanese television, ultimately killing it. Strikeforce was dead in the water when its owners, Silicon Valley Sports and Entertainment, Inc., wanted to focus on their assets in the NHL and break from MMA. Modesty and nuance aren't the two things that come to mind when we think of the UFC. The lawsuit even includes a picture, uploaded to Twitter, of Dana White with the Fertitta brothers unveiling their aggressive global expansion plans. High above their heads reads the caption, "WORLD FUCKING DOMINATION." No, modesty is not really part of the fight game. Male narcissism, however...

The lawsuit also suggests that the UFC's behavior has impacted the relationships athletes have with their sponsors. "The UFC refused to contract with any sponsor who agreed to work with an actual or potential rival MMA Promotion company or Fighter under contract with another MMA Promoter, whether an actual or potential rival, and prohibited these sponsors from appearing on UFC Fighters during UFC events." Once again, the UFC is identified as treating its fighters much more like employees than independent contractors.

Another dimension to the lawsuit is that one of the ramifications of monopoly and monopsony power is the "exploitation and expropriation" of the identity of fighters for UFC merchandise and promotions. Fighters are forced to acquiesce to the UFC on licensing of likeness out of fear of being cut, as Jon Fitch, Josh Koscheck, and the American Kickboxing Academy in general, found out a few years ago. Some fighters, such as former light-heavyweight champion Tito Ortiz, who has had one of the most acrimonious relationships with Dana White, have declined participating in the class-action suit, but the number of plaintiffs has continued to swell.

As of early 2017, it is unclear whether this lawsuit is going to be successful, and as someone who is much more a student of law in Canada than the U.S., my thoughts on the viability of the case aren't going to have much meaning. Jeffrey B. Aris, an attorney who is also a contributor to *Sherdog*, is skeptical that the lawsuit will be successful due to the "rule of

## Mixed Martial Arts and the Quest for Legitimacy

reason" that characterizes Section 2 of the Sherman Act. Basically, the legal team will have to show that the monopoly powers over fight promotions and monopsony powers over fighters have directly harmed competitors. The presence of Bellator, and the experience the UFC legal team had with the FTC after the purchase of Strikeforce, are two other factors that tilt the balance in the favor of the UFC. Aris thinks that the class action suit would be groundbreaking if it forces a "discovery phase" where the UFC is required to release information regarding pay and practices—exactly the kind of information that Zuffa kept very close to its chest. Revealing the percentage of revenue paid out to fighters is probably not in WME-IMG's plans, but it would move the UFC, under its new management, firmly in the direction of mainstream sports, such as the NFL, NBA, and NHL.

# 8

# The Epitome of MMA
## *The Sport and the Spectacle of Conor McGregor*

The preliminary bouts (prelims) of a fight card, especially an international fight card held outside of the U.S., are typically to showcase regional talent and test them against similarly developing talent from the U.S. It is also standard practice of the UFC to put together favorable match-ups for the regional talent. Nothing gets an international crowd cheering like a fighter from a home country beating an American. The UFC is in the entertainment business, and what is more entertaining for an arena full of MMA fans outside of the U.S. than watching a fellow countryman kick a Yankee's butt a bit in the octagon?

Prelims rarely draw in many casual viewers. Maybe the curious will tune in to watch the odd prelim bout, but they are generally more appealing to the more hardcore fans. I always watch the prelims, as I am a fan of MMA who is interested in potential prospects, as well as to see how the old warhorses can perform, such as guys who think they've got another run in them, or maybe just another win or two. One international prelim card stands out for me in particular. Well, one fight on the prelims, that is. It first aired on Fuel TV, the News Corp station that struggled to find purpose during its existence, when the UFC was broadcasting MMA from the trendy looking Ericsson Globe Arena in Sweden. The card was populated with an abundance of European fighters I knew only vaguely, or not at all.

Marcus Brimage was set to fight halfway into the prelims. I knew of Brimage from watching some of his season of *TUF*. I knew that he likened his fighting style to a mini-version of Rampage Jackson, who was about as exciting a fighter as you can possibly imagine back in his prime, and I

## Mixed Martial Arts and the Quest for Legitimacy

also unfortunately knew that Brimage liked big women from an interview that he once did with Jackson, with Jackson disapproving of the revelation. I did not know his opponent, the energetic Irishman hailing from Dublin, looking not like a man making his UFC debut, but exuding the presence of a seasoned vet, bursting with confidence and purposeful movements. The match started, and Brimage burst forward, throwing haymakers, imitating a very aggressive version of Jackson. McGregor saw every punch, effortlessly flowing out of range and then punishing Brimage with laser-beam-straight punches, landing practically every shot with devastating precision. Unable to withstand the speed, accuracy, and the facile power of McGregor, Brimage collapsed, handing an exuberant McGregor one of the most spectacular UFC debuts in the history of the organization.

Just over two years later, McGregor captured the interim featherweight title. He unified the UFC's featherweight titles when he won the undisputed featherweight belt five months later, and then became the first man to simultaneously hold two UFC championships when he put away Eddie Alvarez to win the lightweight title just under a year later. With this feat, Conor McGregor has already established himself as a notably great mixed-martial artist. Perhaps, though he has a lot to prove still, he will one day sit along with fighters such as Fedor Emelianenko, Georges St-Pierre, and Anderson Silva as a Greatest Of All Time (GOAT) contender. However, doing so will demand that he defend at least one of those belts multiple times, and consistently face the best his division has to offer.

McGregor may very well be the epitome of his sport, with slick footwork complemented at times by unpredictable head-movement. His mix of pressure striking blended with devastating counters has made standing with the man a very bad idea for opponents. He has cat-like reflexes, confounding striking accuracy, and a brick for a left hand. His defensive wrestling, submission defense, cardio, and his will under heavy pressure remain questionable.

What is not questionable is that the man is the GOAT for the spectacle that characterizes MMA in the myriad ways that we have discussed in previous chapters. Firstly, and most importantly, Conor McGregor has presented himself as a symbol of extravagant wealth. The main thrust of his persona is that of being fantastically wealthy, reveling in the unknown riches that have been bestowed upon him, and constantly mocking the meager earnings of his fellow fighters in the UFC. McGregor's public persona of flaunting his newfound money, what I will discuss as "conspicuous

## 8. The Epitome of MMA

consumption," is the center of a multi-layered persona that he has cultivated since his UFC debut in Sweden. The other aspects of McGregor's identity revolve around his compulsion to denigrate the abilities of his opponents, his incessant performances of masculinity, a tendency to make racial insults at opponents, and even a bizarre infatuation with Mexican narco-traffickers that has manifested a couple of times, such as when McGregor, adorning a shirt very similar to one worn by "El Chapo," told a crowd that he felt like the alleged head of the Sinaloa Cartel "in his prime."

The public has irrefutably been captured by the preening egoism that is the spectacle of Conor McGregor. He represents one of the greatest success stories of MMA. Ever. His fight against Denis Siver, which set up his first title fight, was the highest-viewed program ever on Fox Sports 1 among the young male adult demographic, peaking at over 3,000,000 viewers, earning more than double the average number of viewers on a typical UFC on Fox Sports 1 presentation. Even more impressively, McGregor has headlined in four out of the UFC's five biggest PPV events, including the top spot for his rematch against Nate Diaz, and the second-highest buy-rate for his first fight against Diaz.

Make no mistake, McGregor's undeniable skills in the octagon are a necessary cause of his record-breaking viewership numbers. It is not a sufficient cause, though. There are plenty of fighters who primarily rely on the stand-up side of MMA and hunt for knockouts, and many of them, such as Anthony Johnson, have more crushing power than McGregor, who is known for "TKOing" opponents rather than earning KOs. The drawing power of these other highly ranked and fearsome fighters are pithy when compared to McGregor's numbers, though. No, the reality is that McGregor's popularity is more dependent on the way he hypes a fight.

It is worth mentioning that one need only visit an online MMA forum to appreciate that Conor McGregor has his many detractors amongst some of the more discerning MMA fans who have come to find his antics wearisome and who would rather just see the man compete. However, the majority of the MMA-interested public has come to follow his narcissistic, out-of-cage performances with glee, eager to hear what new crass insults the man has in store for his next opponent.

Conor McGregor is MMA. He is a highly skilled martial artist, perhaps on his way to earning a legendary status in the sport by the time he reaches 30 years of age. He is also the pure spectacle of MMA, all gaudy tattoos and male bravado. He is the spectacle of a sport that is too insecure to imagine itself as capable of being appreciated on its own terms. Instead, it is a sport that continues to try desperately to convince the public to care, to cater to the lowest common denominator of entertainment, so much so that it undermines its own legitimacy and credibility.

Attaining championship status in a regional organization is an accomplishment and makes a fighter, even a fighter making his or her debut in the UFC, a prospect to note. The arriving champion might even emerge in the UFC as an immediate contender. Fans of MMA tend to be highly UFC-centric, but it does make a lot of sense to be primarily focused on the UFC. Lorenzo Fertitta has a great story about a discussion he had with a financial advisor who was totally opposed to the idea of purchasing the Ultimate Fighting Championship from SEG. MMA looked dead in the late 1990s, and even the fire-sale price of $2 million looked like a waste of money. Fertitta famously told his financial advisor that he was buying three letters—"U-F-C."

The UFC has defined the sport, especially over the last decade, so you can forgive a fan for only bothering to follow the UFC. However, there was a time when the best mixed-martial artists in the heavyweight and light-heavyweight divisions fought in Japan under the banner of Pride. The UFC certainly had elite talent in these divisions, such as Frank Mir, Tito Ortiz, and Chuck Liddell, but very little depth. When Chuck Liddell entered the Pride Middleweight (light-heavyweight) Grand Prix, he was finished by Pride's Rampage Jackson in the semis. Zuffa's buyout of Pride added badly needed depth to the heaviest weight classes, even if Fedor Emelianenko, the best heavyweight of the era, would prove more elusive. Rampage, Lyoto Machida, and Shogun, all Pride fighters, quickly won championships in the UFC light-heavyweight division, and Antônio Nogueira became an interim heavyweight champion. Another Pride fighter, Dan Henderson, contended for three UFC titles upon his return to the UFC and went on to win a light-heavyweight title in another organization with respectable talent.

Pride was not the only organization to host champions who would go on to prove themselves as elite fighters. Quite a few of these fighters even went on to become UFC champions. Carlos Condit, Luke Rockhold, "Jacaré" Souza, Daniel Cormier, Eddie Alvarez, Benson Henderson, Anthony Pettis, Gilbert Melendez, Jake Shields, Nick Diaz, Robbie Lawler, and many others fought for extended periods in other organizations, either

## 8. The Epitome of MMA

becoming champion or achieving contender status, and then either won UFC gold or became a top-five ranked fighter in their respective divisions in the UFC. Even Georges St-Pierre and Anderson Silva were champions in other organizations before they made their UFC debuts.

As the Cage Warriors Fighting Championship featherweight AND lightweight champion, keen observers of MMA knew to keep an eye on the Dubliner as a prospect to watch. McGregor had lost a couple of times in his career, but the hype surrounding him was big-time before he even stepped foot in the octagon. When Dana White allegedly first heard the stories about McGregor that were circulating the Irish MMA community, he thought that people must have been talking about a heavyweight because of the look of awe in their eyes.

After McGregor laid waste to Brimage and pocketed an extra $50,000, the man known as "Mystic Mac" and "Notorious" went on to lay waste to his competition. His next fight, against a future featherweight champion, would be his only fight to go to decision over the next three years. McGregor outwrestled the very green Hawaiian, Max Holloway, showing very effecting guard passes, despite a torn anterior cruciate ligament (ACL) in his knee.

A mere two and a half years after making his electrifying debut, McGregor overcame adversity with Chad Mendes, long heralded as the second-best featherweight in the world, but a fighter who was stepping up as a late replacement. McGregor won an interim UFC title after desperately trying to resist Mendes' takedowns, finally staggering a tiring Mendes. The long-overdue fight with José Aldo took place half a year later, with McGregor knocking out the greatest featherweight of all time in a matter of 13 seconds. Just under a year later, he cemented his greatness by winning a technical knockout against Alvarez, becoming the first fighter to win two UFC belts at the same time.

Does this make McGregor the undisputed Greatest of All Time (GOAT)? Outside of tournament winners, only Randy Couture, B.J. Penn, and GSP became UFC champions in different weight classes, but not at the same time. Even with this notable accomplishment, only a handful of die-hard fans of Penn and Couture (mostly Penn) typically identify them on GOAT lists. Dan Henderson accomplished the feat of being a simultaneous champion of two classes in Pride as the middleweight (light-heavyweight) and welterweight (middleweight) champion, and his career is legendary, but not generally regarded as amongst the best ever.

## Mixed Martial Arts and the Quest for Legitimacy

McGregor's victories are impressive, but MMA is a sport defined by what Machiavelli once described as *virtù*, the actions one takes to carry them to success, as well as *fortuna*, or luck. *Fortuna* and UFC matchmaking have often smiled fondly on the prospect of McGregor's successes. In his first five fights, McGregor never faced any wrestling-intensive fighters or grinders, a very unusual slate of match-ups for a division choked with NCAA experience. When he finally faced a wrestler in Chad Mendes, it was very short notice for the Sacramento-based fighter. All of the opponents that McGregor came up against were good fighters and fun to watch, one (Holloway) even evolving over the years to become undeniably elite.

However, the UFC built these opponents into greater threats than the UFC really perceived them to be. For instance, the fight that won McGregor a chance to contend for UFC gold was the Dennis Siver fight. Siver was 1–1 (1) in his previous three fights, serving a suspension for the PED hCG, and was unranked before the booking. Magically, in the lead-up to the McGregor fight, the UFC ranked Siver at #10 in the featherweight division, despite not having victories against top-15 fighters in the division.

The UFC's official rankings were ostensibly introduced to provide legitimacy to the rise of contenders, and to help casual audiences understand which fighters were amongst the best in their respective divisions. The ranking system is completely divorced from the opinions of news media that are independent of the UFC, and the rankings are often manipulated by the UFC to promote a particular fight. The Siver ranking was probably the most shameless manipulation of a ranking, ironically, to promote McGregor rather than Siver and to justify McGregor's title shot.

Conor McGregor proved to the world that he was a champion when he laid out José Aldo. Nobody has won more fights at featherweight than Aldo. He went undefeated for a decade, winning 18 fights, a feat quite comparable to Fedor Emelianenko's historic achievement at heavyweight. Many websites had come to regard Aldo as the pound-for-pound best fighter in the planet after GSP's retirement and Silva's loss to Weidman, and all websites had listed him in the top-10 for years.

When a dominant champion like Aldo is defeated, such as the case with Silva after the Weidman victory, the convention is to book an immediate rematch. It is not to say that the outcome of the first fight is a fluke, as *fortuna* may be unpredictable and sometimes outside of your control, but it is wrong to think of it as accidental. The immediate rematch is about

## 8. The Epitome of MMA

the deference shown to the deposed champion and honoring the belief that the former champ is now the top contender. Conor McGregor balked at any rematch, setting his sights on a legacy-making fight against the lightweight champion.

The fight against Raphael dos Anjos, then-lightweight champion of the UFC, never materialized on account of a broken foot RDA suffered in training camp. Rather than scrapping the fight and attempting to book a rematch with Aldo, the UFC moved to find a lightweight replacement for McGregor to fight. Accepting the fight on only 11 days' notice was the always game Nate Diaz.

Nate Diaz, when motivated, is one of the most exciting fighters on the UFC roster, a pressure boxer with underrated power and a guard game that gives pause to even the best wrestlers. Diaz has fought elite talent and even beaten a couple of them, such as Donald Cerrone. However, the story of Diaz's career has been that of a high-level gatekeeper rather than champion or contender. With a record of 19–11 (as of late 2016), Diaz has experienced both highs[1] and lows. He once put together an impressive three-fight win streak, including the notable win over Cerrone, and fought for the belt. Though he would come up short against Benson Henderson and serve as Henderson's only lopsided title defense, Diaz was a fighter whom you respected if you were a fighter yourself, and a fan-favorite to watch. Diaz was also a fighter with salient flaws that got in the way of becoming a perennial contender, let alone a champion. One couldn't help but notice that in a division more choked with wrestlers than even featherweight, Conor McGregor would fight against the opponent with the weakest wrestling in the top-15.

Despite this context, you would have to be lacking a pulse to be a MMA fan and not be excited about McGregor-Diaz. The bout was contested at 170 lbs to give Diaz a chance to focus on some training rather than simply cutting weight as a late replacement. To give McGregor full credit, rumor has it that this flexibility was suggested by him. Round 1 featured explosive strikes by McGregor, who landed his ramrod straight lefts with thunderous force, though likely overcommitted to errant wheel-kicks that missed their mark, tiring the featherweight champ. Showing signs of fatigue, the iron-chinned Diaz came to life. McGregor, an incessant trash-talker in the cage, despite the very clear rules against in-cage talk in the unified rules of MMA, found his equal in Diaz. While taunting McGregor, even landing his patented "Stockton-slap" to McGregor's face,

## Mixed Martial Arts and the Quest for Legitimacy

Diaz started to connect with some hard one-twos, causing McGregor, who once indignantly mocked what he called "panic wrestling," to shoot for a take-down, only to find himself on the ground, tangled in the long limbs of the Gracie-jiu-jitsu black-belt, who battered McGregor until the champ stuck his neck out, with Diaz happily obliging with the rear-naked choke. Diaz, battered by McGregor's powerful left hand but far from broken, defiantly shouted to the crowd, "I'm not surprised, motherfuckers!"

The expectation was that McGregor, suitably humbled, might now face Aldo once again, and if victorious, still a big "if," fight against Frankie Edgar, a former lightweight champion who had found new life as a contender at featherweight, and employing a wrestler/boxer style that could be very problematic for McGregor. Victory in these two match-ups could then justify a second shot at lightweight, if not against the current champ, then perhaps a shot for lightweight contender status.

McGregor had other plans. When he insisted on a rematch with Nate Diaz, the UFC obliged. McGregor won the rematch in a very exciting and evenly contested five-round majority decision that kept everyone who watched it live on the edge of their seats, either cheering for or against McGregor. You can bet that they were cheering one way or the other.

The decision to book the rematch against Diaz surely infuriated Aldo. The unwillingness to offer a rematch for the most dominant champion in featherweight history contrasted to the eagerness of the UFC to oblige a champ who had not yet defended his title, and then lost to a one-time contender, must have caused Aldo to become disillusioned with the sport. He began to discuss retirement publicly, and he supposedly entered into negotiations with the UFC about the dissolution of his contract.

One has to acknowledge that McGregor is a special talent in the octagon. Aldo returned to form in a fight against Edgar, proving that McGregor knocked out what likely was a still-prime Aldo. He earned a hard-fought majority decision victory against Diaz, and then superbly out-classed a battle-tested lightweight champion in Eddie Alvarez, thereby winning a second championship and proving that he is a superb mixed-martial artist.

With respect to the spectacle of MMA, there is no debating Conor McGregor's elite status. He represents everything that is sublime about MMA, but also much of what I believe to be deeply problematic.

When Conor McGregor started to bluster to the media that he already considered himself champion, after his UFC debut no less, I admired the man's confidence. In fact, I think that there are some positives

## 8. The Epitome of MMA

to take away from McGregor's self-belief. At the very outset of his UFC career, he was telling the MMA media that he was a mental champion. I can't imagine what kind of self-confidence is required to become a professional athlete, let alone a professional athlete who fights in a cage for the viewing public. Let's face it, the story of how a plumber's apprentice became a two-division UFC champion and the biggest PPV draw ever is nothing short of inspiring.

When I started to read the reaction of people on MMA internet forums, especially after his first couple of UFC appearances, I was totally shocked. Fans were aping McGregor's bravado, calling him McGreGOAT, among other hyperboles. I seriously thought that these fans were being ironic, trolling a fighter who was at the time known to defend himself vigorously on public forums, typically with no small measure of wit. Surely, these fans were simply having some fun with the absurdity of what McGregor was telling the media. After a few months, though, it became clear that these fans were mostly sincere. They really came to think that a man who completely discredits the abilities of his opponents, makes jokes about slavery, calls a German fighter a Nazi, and maintains one of the most shamelessly narcissistic social media presences one can imagine, and had yet not even come close to fighting against elite talent, was the MMA GOAT.

It is facetious to think that McGregor's star-power rose entirely from his highlight-reel-filled introduction to the UFC. Plenty of fighters have entered the UFC and strung together big wins against unranked talent, or later put together an impressive win streak which went largely unnoticed by casual audiences, receiving very little promotional push from the UFC. This is especially true of the weight classes below 155 lbs.

Arriving in the UFC shortly after McGregor, Thomas Almeida terrorized the bantamweight division, winning his first four fights, three of them by KO or TKO. Cody Garbrandt, a fellow bantamweight, started his UFC run with a five-fight win streak, with four stoppage victories, including a victory over Almeida, and then captured the title from Dominick Cruz as a heavy underdog. Neither of these two excellent fighters came even remotely close to gaining either the publicity or promotional push that McGregor experienced during his rise. An even more poignant example from the lower weight classes is the case of Aljamain Stirling, who opened his UFC career with a four-fight win streak, with three finishes, and then reached a contract impasse with the UFC. So low was the UFC's proposed contract that Stirling entertained rival offers and even contemplated retirement from MMA to start a new career as a teacher. The difference between those three rising prospects and McGregor was their presence outside of the cage, and the ability to capture the fan-base, and the media, through spectacle.

Garbrandt would eventually show a public persona who wasn't shy about spewing venom at his opponent in the lead-up to his title fight against Cruz, no stranger to quick-witted insults himself. Garbrandt and Cruz let loose with some tirades against each other during a largely blacked-out argument that erupted on a Fox broadcast. Stirling also got pretty personal on social media to promote his fight against Bryan Caraway by insulting Caraway's partner, the former bantamweight champion, Miesha Tate, in a few exchanges that are best forgotten.

None of these fighters, or anyone else, can match the level of McGregor's trash-talk. He is a modern-day P.T. Barnum. Conor McGregor is a poster-boy for the age of the "selfie" and communicating in 140 characters or less. He is the GOAT in front of the microphone, and the epitome of the spectacle that is ultimate fighting.

I've come to balk at comparisons between Conor McGregor and the late, great Muhammad Ali, a comparison that even the UFC shamelessly makes. Sure, they share a quick wit and a sharp tongue. Neither understood boundaries between promoting a fight and the attempt to rob another man of his dignity, such as the infamously racial insults Ali hurled at Joe Frazier. The problem in comparing the two men is that Muhammad Ali also stood up for the racial injustices of American politics and society, and he exercised his rights as an American to question the legitimacy of the carnage that was the Vietnam War.

What does Conor McGregor stand for? There is no cause. There is no injustice that is condemned. The script is always one of his own superiority above everyone else. His opponents all suck, he is the only draw that matters in the UFC, he is fantastically wealthy, and perhaps most striking, he makes even the UFC irrelevant.

Conor McGregor is in many ways more of a Ric Flair, perhaps the greatest WWE heel that spectacle has ever produced, than a Muhammad Ali. The comparison is not lost on Flair either. After McGregor gave an interview where he referred to WWE entertainers as "pussies" and said he would "slap the head off" of wrestlers, a number of WWE wrestlers countered with barbs of their own or responded by issuing challenges.

## 8. The Epitome of MMA

Flair himself tweeted, "Coming from a guy who built a career copying my persona, I expected the type of class we get from Ronda or Anderson." Flair also predicted that Diaz would finish McGregor a second time, encouraged McGregor to test himself against WWE entertainers with a background in NCAA wrestling, such as Brock Lesnar, and even added "Oh you're welcome for your gimmick."

After witnessing the foot movement and precise punching of McGregor in his fight with Brimage, I was instantly curious about this new prospect. At the post-fight presser, however, McGregor opened up with a diatribe that was bizarre, leaving me to try first to empathize with his comments, and then, unable to reconcile what he said with my own ethics on citizenship and the public good, I had an epiphany. We did not have on our plate another GSP, Anderson Silva, or Fedor Emelianenko. McGregor was going to be something else. An ultimate fighting spectacle for an age of spectacle.

With the attention of the international MMA media squarely on him, Conor McGregor took the opportunity to tell his audience how excited he was to get a $60,000 bonus (who wouldn't!), wondering if he was going to buy a car or get some custom-fitted suits. He also explained how just a week earlier, he was collecting social welfare. A touching revelation and one that reminds us all of how many of these athletes we watch compete in this violent and grueling sport come from very humble circumstances. It is also a story that is intimately relatable for so many of us. I think a very obvious sign of privilege in the twenty-first century is to try and make it in this world without having to rely on social assistance, in one form or another, or at least to know a family member or friend who hasn't had to make that difficult decision to apply to the government for help to cover basic needs in the absence of full-time employment.

However, what Conor McGregor then said was that he was now going to the social welfare offices to "tell them to fuck off!" For some reason, this jarring comment was met with laughter from the MMA media in Stockholm. I'd like to think that one can earn advanced degrees in social sciences and retain a sense of humor. Smiling while you broadcast a comment does not a joke make. The modern welfare state was born out of a period of tremendous anxiety and fear during the Great Depression. The idea that the state should intervene in market relations to offer temporary protection to society has transformed sovereignty itself and the relationship between markets and the state. This once-venerable institution of social assistance is now derided more than ever by many influential groups in Western countries, and it faces an uneasy future. McGregor even attracted the attention of an "alt-right" media group with his comments. *Breitbart* interviewed McGregor a short time after that presser, hoping for a few extra sound bites of scorn they could use in their campaign to convince the American public that social assistance does more harm than good. McGregor didn't give the sensationalistic media group much to work with, though. Instead of further bashing the institution, he instead talked to the bellicose media outlet of his time as a dependent on social assistance and how the frugal life it required made him appreciate the value of money and to be grateful for what he had been able to achieve.

McGregor's comments about what he was planning to say to the social assistance office came around again in the build-up to his fight for the lightweight title with Eddie Alvarez. During another typically heated exchange during a media show, Alvarez took a verbal shot at McGregor that must have hit him at his core. The thing you have to realize about McGregor is that he has created a persona of the fighter-playboy, living a plutocratic lifestyle of outrageously expensive shirts, boots, watches, and cars.

Thorstein Veblen was a Norwegian sociologist who embarked on a trip across the United States approximately a century ago. Veblen toured America during the worst of the Gilded Age's crushing inequality and reflected on the behavior of the fantastically wealthy "leisure class." One of Veblen's most insightful observations from his fieldwork was what he described as "conspicuous consumption." The leisure class, especially the bourgeois *nouveau riche*, spent extravagantly for the purpose of ostentatiously displaying their class and status to society. Conspicuous consumption theatrically projected power relations to the lower classes, but was itself the actions of a social class that harbored deep insecurities about its self-worth.

Conor McGregor's online and media persona is defined by conspicuous consumption. He obsessively posts photographs of himself with outrageously expensive sports cars, watches whose values are presumably justifiable by allowing the wearer to be immune from time itself, boots that were made from the butchering of rare and exotic animals that children aren't even taught about in school, and of course, the obligatory pictures of stacks of money, just in case we didn't get it.

To Conor McGregor, every other fighter on the roster is a "broke

## 8. The Epitome of MMA

bum." He incessantly scoffs at the disclosed pay of his opponents, such as Nate Diaz, gleefully shouting to the cameras that his opponents should be "blessed" that Conor McGregor chose them to fight and that the money earned will "change his bum life." While laughing at one of Diaz's disclosed payouts, $20,000 to show and $20,000 to fight, McGregor exclaimed that he "wipe[s] my ass with that money." At the UFC's "Go Big" presser, he introduced to the world the "red panty night." So excited are the wives of his opponents that their husbands will be fighting him, and therefore earning a paycheck unlike anything they have seen before, they celebrate by putting on the nice lingerie.

Clothes are a particular obsession with his conspicuous consumption. Nate Diaz, known for wearing simple black t-shirts and work-boots, was a predictable target of the vain Irishman. Claiming that his socks are worth more than Diaz's suit, and pompously shouting, as he so often does, about being able to buy and sell Diaz "a hundred times over."

It is important to note that with Conor McGregor, it is rarely the playful banter of a member of the *nouveau riche* reveling in his hard-earned cash. There is always a subtext of cruelty, such as buying and selling Nate Diaz as a slave, or using the value of someone else's hard-earned cash as toilet paper. It is an ugly and cruel mocking that characterizes the spectacle of Conor McGregor. Calling it "trash-talk" doesn't quite capture his venomous verbal onslaughts. He cackles like a sadist to announce that elephants died to make his ivory suit, or that men died for his gold watch. Incredibly, he has even modified the "billionaire strut" of the WWE's Vince McMahon, where he walks with his shoulders slouched, swinging his dangling arms. We wouldn't want to forget, even for a moment, how rich Conor McGregor is.

The carnival to promote the stacked UFC 205 event did not disappoint those who desperately need to feed out of the trough of negativity and indignation to get excited for MMA. However, it was actually a comment made by Eddie Alvarez during a heated exchange with McGregor on Fox Sports that cut through the noise to sting the featherweight champ. Recalling that early post-fight presser that introduced McGregor to the UFC dominated MMA-media, Alvarez went on the offensive, "You were on welfare, bra. You ain't no man, you took welfare." Bristling at the conspicuous consumption that characterizes McGregor's persona, Alvarez pressed his advantage. "Don't you talk about money. You took money from single moms. Single moms go on welfare." Not content to drop it quite yet, Alvarez further admonished McGregor, "Don't talk about money. Keep your mouth shut when you talk about money." If McGregor's stunned silence was any indication, Eddie's remarks likely cut to the core of Conor McGregor.

As I mentioned before, I'm sure that graduate school has done much to undermine my sense of humor, at least to an extent, but I don't understand the appeal of the litany of insults. I think that maybe we have a generation that is more susceptible to a hedonistic philosophy of #YOLO, and maybe McGregor is tapping into that sentiment. The difference between the old conspicuous consumption identified by Veblen and the version of it expressed by McGregor is the direct animosity. Perhaps there existed a latent animosity toward the working classes in the conspicuous consumption of the late-Gilded Age, but there is nothing latent about McGregor. It is bold, direct, and as he notes himself, totally unapologetic.

McGregor's keen awareness of the meager pay of his fellow fighters hasn't translated into him actually caring about revenue sharing in the UFC, at least not revenue sharing aside from his own revenue. I don't imagine that the ethics of fighter pay have caused the man any sleepless nights. After his history-making performance against Alvarez, McGregor announced that he was going to take time off as he transitioned to fatherhood, a sensible decision. He said he would return to the UFC, but on a certain condition—a stake in the ownership of the company. During the post-fight presser, McGregor announced in no uncertain terms the following:

> Where's my equity? If I'm the one that's bringing this, they've got to come talk to me now. That's all I know. I've got both belts. A chunk of money. A family on the way. You want me to stick around? You want me to keep doing what I'm doing, let's talk. But I want ownership now. I want equal share. I want what I deserve. What I've earned.

Calling the disclosed profit earnings of the UFC his "gospel," McGregor has laid out a bold plan to change the nature of fighter-organization relations.

Surely coveting the jaw-dropping earnings of boxers, Floyd Mayweather above all else, McGregor is hoping to remake the UFC into boxing. He hopes to blur the lines between the fighter and the organization, just as he has already largely erased the line between fighter and promoter. He is trying to turn himself into the MMA equivalent of Floyd Mayweather, an ironic twist considering McGregor's incessant needling of Mayweather

## 8. The Epitome of MMA

actually induced the legend to come out of retirement and fight McGregor in perhaps the most lucrative boxing spectacle of all time.

This hardline approach makes a lot of sense for McGregor. He has dominated the list of the top pay-per-view events, became a two-division champ, and is not even 30 years old yet. Based on earned revenue and projected future revenues, McGregor has done more to earn such an accommodation than anyone.

In my opinion, it is unfortunate that Conor McGregor is pushing the UFC into a restructuring that more closely resembles boxing, rather than one of the established sports leagues. Imagine if, instead of selfless men like Ted Lindsay in the NHL or Curt Flood in MLB, hockey and baseball were shaped by the Floyd Mayweathers and Conor McGregors of their respective sports? Rather than collective bargaining to increase pay for everyone, superstar athletes would be offered shares. I shudder to think how low the minimum wage would look in sports leagues of an alternate universe where superstars did not take the side of collective bargaining and instead selfishly fought for individual earnings. In such a world, the minimum wage of the NFL, NHL, and NBA might be even as low as UFC payouts.

Deeply connected to McGregor's gimmick of calling his opponents "bums" and laughing at their disclosed payouts is the endless denial of their abilities. When he was just climbing the ranks in the UFC's featherweight division, McGregor was a regular on sports talk shows, calling out everyone in his division by name as a "midget," a "pea-head," or a "weathered fighter." It is an interesting tactic and one that always confuses me. If you genuinely think that your division poses no challenges to you, then what are you doing fighting in that weight class, especially with what was unquestionably a brutal weight-cut for McGregor? It seems like a real tough guy, one who regularly invites fighters to "suck his Irish balls," would want fights against men his own size. Why should anyone care about your victories against people who you have already heinously dismissed as "midgets"?

When McGregor finally did move up to lightweight to fight men his own size, we never heard the end of it. His two fights against Nate Diaz that were contested at welterweight are illustrative of McGregor's attempt to mythologize the importance of the bouts. For the first fight, Diaz was a late replacement. McGregor, in an act of sportsmanship, suggested the bout be contested at welterweight rather than lightweight, giving Diaz the opportunity to use the short time he had before the contest to focus on training, rather than weight-cutting.

Nate Diaz has failed to make the 155 lb weight limit of the lightweight division on more than one occasion. He even attempted a run in the UFC's welterweight class of 170 lbs. With a six-foot frame and a 76-inch reach, nobody would claim that Diaz is a small lightweight. However, he is not a large lightweight and is most certainly not a physically strong lightweight. As a lithe and modestly muscled volume puncher, Diaz was driven out of the welterweight class by Dong Hyun Kim and a green Rory MacDonald, who forced Diaz to acknowledge that he was at a notable size disadvantage at 170 lbs. McGregor himself even mocked Diaz as "skinny-fat" on multiple occasions, including one televised interview where he attempted to goad Diaz into taking off his shirt for the audience so that the public could bask in the glow of his weak frame. Diaz has historically struggled against elite lightweights who have employed a wrestling-centric approach to the fight, such as Rafael dos Anjos and Benson Henderson. In such match-ups, the strength disparity between Diaz and his opponent has been quite obvious.

In McGregor's delusional narrative, he went up against an opponent that was "three times the size of me" in the younger Diaz brother. At 5-foot-9, the lanky Diaz had a three-inch height advantage on McGregor. Diaz also held a reach advantage over McGregor, but a more modest two inches. To compare, McGregor enjoyed a three-inch height advantage over Chad Mendes, whom he defeated to capture his first UFC belt, and a staggering eight-inch reach advantage against him. Unlike boxing, MMA is generally uninterested in gathering other physical stats, even a particularly bizarre omission of leg length. If such information were gathered, I am convinced that McGregor would be shown to be much thicker than Diaz, especially in the chest and shoulders. If Nate Diaz was three times the size of Conor McGregor, how much bigger was McGregor than Mendes?

As difficult as it is to believe, there is an even more shameless instance of Conor McGregor attempting to mythologize his feats. In 2015, he uploaded video footage of a light sparring session with Hafthor Julius Bjornsson, the actor widely known as "the Mountain" from the HBO blockbuster hit *Game of Thrones*. At almost seven feet tall and 400 lbs, the densely muscled Icelander is about as imposing a figure as has ever gone into acting. Bjornsson has even been a long-time frontrunner in "World's Strongest Man" competitions in Europe and around the world.

## 8. The Epitome of MMA

During a media lunch before his fight with Aldo, McGregor provided a ridiculously hyperbolic description of the encounter with the Mountain. He claimed that the actor was "trying to hit me," "grab me," and that he "tried to pull my head off." Supposedly, McGregor's body shots "folded him [Bjornsson] up," because "I was like, this motherfucker is so big, I have to start smacking him to the body.... But I sunk him good. Not even a 'Mountain' can take these shots from me."

Anyone watching the "sparring session" with a remotely critical eye would raise some eyebrows at such a narrative. The two men were just having some fun. The Mountain's advances on McGregor were hardly intended to pull his head off. If the session was meant to serve any technical purpose, it was to be a session focused on controlling range and creating angles. The occasional swipe the Mountain threw was obviously never intended to land, and there were no real attempts by the Mountain to get his hands on McGregor, let alone any attempt at a takedown. Of course, such a move would have been extraordinarily unfair to the undersized Irishman, as a takedown attempt would carry an unforgivably high probability of causing serious injury. The dance was simply a publicity stunt that McGregor turned around into claiming was an actual fight. The self-promotion never ends.

Conor McGregor, much like Chael Sonnen before him, has developed a tendency of injecting racial attacks into his vitriolic rants. To promote his number one contender's fight against the German, Denis Siver, a man who was not even close to being a contender in the division, McGregor took to Twitter. Imploring Siver to "Kiss them feet, Nazi," McGregor revealed to the public an even uglier side of his persona. After receiving backlash over the comment, perhaps even from the UFC itself, he then tweeted, "Ich bin ein sowwy. Now about them feet...," providing about as disingenuous an apology as possible.

Perhaps McGregor learned that there are some serious boundaries of class and basic decency that should not be crossed. He certainly never abandoned the use of race in the spectacle that was his self-promotion, as evident during his media scrums for the Diaz fights. Calling Diaz a "cholo" and his team a group of "esés," seem to reveal McGregor's perusal of the *Urban Dictionary* in the search for derogatory insults. I have much better things to do with my life than to follow the poisonous sub-cultures of racial slurs, but the top entry of the *Urban Dictionary's* definition of esé is notable, suggesting that it is a phrase that should only be used by

Hispanics, "Otherwise it's like saying nigga when your [sic] white." The only lesson McGregor likely learned from the incident was the ability of racial attacks to generate media controversy and therefore to hype fights.

Much like Sonnen, McGregor's race-baiting attempts have been mostly directed at Brazilian fighters. I find these attacks on Brazilian fighters are particularly distasteful because, just like Sonnen, they combine racial attacks with the dire poverty that afflicts so much of the Brazilian population. While on a whirlwind of a tour to promote the Aldo fight, McGregor launched into attacks against both his opponent and Brazil. "I own this town, I own Rio de Janeiro, so for him to say that he is the king and I am the joker, if this was a different time, I would invade his favela on horseback, and would kill anyone who wasn't fit to work, but we're in a new time, so I'll whoop his ass instead."

His infatuation with the poverty of the favela came to the surface another time, when he disgracefully boasted to the crowd that he would turn "his [Aldo's] favela into a reebok sweatshop and churn out merchandise straight from Brazil." This is the spectacle that MMA has become under Conor McGregor. It is a realm where the martial-arts virtues of respect, modesty and humility find no expression. In place of basic decency is the shameless self-promotion of racist jokes about slavery, sweatshop labor, poverty, and mass killing. Welcome to a place far removed from the ideals of the Enlightenment.

McGregor's racial attacks are not only classless attacks that degrade public discourse, they might also be placing a ceiling on his appeal in Ireland. His popularity amongst the Irish, and especially with self-identified Irish Americans, cannot be denied. The man has fostered a strong sense of nationalistic pride for many Irish, and for Americans who maintain a cultural affinity toward Ireland in their personal identities, such as in New England and New York.

However, it is a pretty big stretch to argue that Conor McGregor represents to the Irish what GSP represents to Canadians. GSP has been one of the greatest ambassadors the sport could have ever hoped for. St-Pierre's Canadian detractors must be a very small group, consisting of people who doggedly oppose the sport on ethical grounds of humanitarian standards for sport, and a handful of "JUST BLEED" fans who only tune in to watch a "slobber-knocker" of a fight featuring swinging haymakers thrown with reckless abandon. As Tom Rooney explained in a *MMAJunkie* from 2015, McGregor's stardom is soaring, but he remains "a polarizing figure" who

## 8. The Epitome of MMA

is "either loved or disdained" in Ireland for his unsportsmanlike antics.[2] Support for McGregor in Ireland is a little more complicated than the outpouring of respect and admiration that men like GSP elicit from Canadians, or Big Nog does with Brazilians.

What would the spectacle of Conor McGregor be without the tired and predictable gendered insults that seek to feminize his opponents? When the world tour to promote the Aldo fight came to Dublin, McGregor took the opportunity to seize Aldo's belt, to the riotous applause of the Irish fans in attendance at the media event, proclaiming to Aldo that "I'm the champion, you bitch!" When Aldo complained of McGregor's unprofessionalism while on tour, particularly McGregor's constant groping of Aldo, McGregor continued to pursue Aldo's neck, laughing, "what are you going to do, little bitch?"

Aside from the constant litany of calling fellow fighters "bitch" and "pussy," and referring to himself as a "pimp," McGregor also attempted to expand his shtick with more novel insults intended to feminize his opponents. Aldo, the consummate professional who ruled the featherweight division since before the UFC opened up a 145 lb class, was the recipient of the majority of the immature bullying. At Fox Sports Live, McGregor insisted on being called Aldo's father, saying, "I am your daddy. I want you to sit on my lap."

No observation of the manipulation of gender in the persona of McGregor would be complete without noting his obsession with his genitalia, demanding that other fighters "suck my balls" and promising to "rest my balls" on the forehead of any fighter who tries to wrestle with him. The most classless exchange occurred at the massive presser for the title fight between Eddie Alvarez and Conor McGregor. Alvarez, foolishly, insisted that McGregor apologize for bringing Alvarez's wife and kids into his classless personal attacks. McGregor refused to allow Alvarez the opportunity to air his grievance, screaming instead for Alvarez to "suck these big Irish balls," with the crowd, and the MMA media, predictably cackling their riotous approval.

Social media certainly allow people to be instantaneously connected with each other around the world like at no other time. Space and time no longer represent much of an obstacle to interpersonal communication and dialogue. However, social media are usually used by people to scream into the echo-chamber of those who share similar ideological viewpoints and are therefore not even remotely interested in dialogue. This is potentially making politics even more polarizing than before. Apparently, another purpose of social media is to indulge narcissistic tendencies by uploading selfies to show off bling, beauty, butts, biceps, boobs, and bulges. I'd guess that cage-fighting is an outlet that is particularly attractive to someone with such tendencies in the first place, but Conor McGregor is on a whole other level. I am convinced that he has a member of his entourage whose sole job is to photograph his conspicuous consumption and to photograph him as often as possible with his shirt off, preferably in underwear and standing so that his crotch is overexposed. McGregor is almost always flexing menacingly, or posing as if he was fighting, often with chest out and fists clenched. If there are others in the photograph, McGregor usually looks as if he has moved into the foreground to give the illusion that the five-foot-nine McGregor eclipses the frame of the other people. In these photographs, as well as in the media press conferences, McGregor's shoulders are rolled forward, with his arms flaring out at his sides, as a textbook example of what the internet has christened "imaginary lats syndrome."

The media presence of McGregor reeks of insecurities. I'm just a professor. I hope to live the rest of my life throwing punches only into the heavy bag of my university gym and into my brother's mitts. At five-foot-11 and 180 lbs, I'm certainly not some big, hulking guy, and I'm not going to talk about anyone suffering from a "Napoleon complex." McGregor's behavior of feminizing his opponents and dismissing their talents is surely connected to an abiding need to come across as a fearsome tough guy. To be fair, though, I attribute McGregor's projected insecurities more to the insecurities of the sport itself, rather than his person. It is an insecurity born out of the perceived need to promote savage warriors from a forgotten era, unable to cope with the modern world. The UFC and other organizations doubt that the mild-mannered professional, reasonably at ease with the conventions of our modern world, can put "butts in seats." Either Conor McGregor really is a vicious bully who, if he weren't a cage-fighter, would be at the local pub encouraging his fellow patrons to "suck his balls," which I don't believe for a minute, or it is all an act. McGregor appears to be insecure about letting his unbelievable talent as a martial artist speak for itself. He doesn't seem to think that people care enough to tune into a Conor McGregor fight without the spectacle. I know I'll buy his PPVs just to watch him fight, but do my best to ignore what he says.

A common trend to be found in the sub-culture of MMA is the eagerness of promoters and fans to pronounce a fighter as the "pound-for-pound"

## 8. The Epitome of MMA

(p4p) best, and to debate the GOAT. Other professional sports, with the exception of boxing, don't talk about a p4p best because there are no separate weight classes. Everyone competes against everyone else, though certain body types and weights certainly dominate particular positions or roles. Discussion of whether an athlete is a GOAT candidate doesn't typically start until the twilight of a career, such as Peyton Manning's relative status as a GOAT quarterback as his career advanced into his late 30s.

MMA doesn't work this way. Fighters get promoted as a p4p great quite early in their careers, usually as they blossom from prospect to contender, or after they win or defend a title. Promoters have a shameless tendency to pronounce this, as if they can simply will a young champion into being perceived as an all-time great, an instant legend, and a PPV must-buy. MMA fans will forever mock Joe Rogan's pronouncement welcoming us all to the Machida era, after Machida blasted Rashad Evans to win the light-heavyweight title, but before he ever defended it. Another favorite was the supremely hyperbolic statement that Ronda Rousey was not just a once in a lifetime fighter, but a "once ever" fighter in "human history." Whether McGregor is a GOAT is a whole other matter, one best left to consider over the *longue durée*, or at least a few years, if he chooses to compete for that long.

Dana White certainly attempted this feat of alchemy with Anthony Pettis after his brilliant submission of Benson Henderson to capture the UFC lightweight title in 2013. Pettis had a great run to earn that title shot, winning a competitive split decision against the featherweight-bound Jeremy Stephens, a brutal head-kick finish of a bonus winning machine and gatekeeper, Joe Lauzon, and then a body-kick finish of perennial contender Donald Cerrone. Never mind that Pettis was a replacement for Canadian T.J. Grant, whose career came to a heartbreaking end due to a concussion he suffered in training, Pettis had earned the shot. The fight against Benson Henderson was also significant because Pettis handed Henderson his last loss, in the last fight of the WEC. At the end of a close, back-and-forth contest where Pettis seemed to have a slight edge, Pettis leapt off the cage and delivered an incredible head-kick, forever remembered as the "Showtime Kick." Henderson was dropped but would make it to the end of the round, unable to prevent the inevitable decision victory for Pettis and unable to realize his goal of being the last WEC lightweight champion.

Pettis had proven himself as an outstanding fighter in the shark-tank that is the lightweight division in MMA. He was fast, had punishing head and body kicks, and was an aggressive grappler, even dangerous off of his back. Furthermore, it was not simply that he had an effective style that helped him win fights, but he had a flashy style that could not be missed. Who doesn't want to see another Showtime Kick? Pettis wasn't the kind of guy to hold a fighter against the cage or shoot for takedowns for the sole purpose of top-control and point-fighting. No, Pettis was in the cage to hunt for big-time knockouts and submissions.

In addition to his fighting style, the man also had the look that the UFC seems to love to promote. Naturally handsome, but also the kind of handsome you achieve from always having a recent haircut and cutting your facial hair strategically. Tattooed, not ripped, but strong and slim. The kind of guy who looks like a million bucks in a custom-fitted suit. You know what? I'm sure Pettis would look good in one of my own cheap suits! And he was young, only 26 years old when he won UFC gold against Henderson. This guy was the p4p best, according to Dana White.

It was too much, too soon. Pettis was a champ, and he was awesome. I don't mean to put him down. In his title defense, he submitted the very durable Gilbert Melendez in the second round with a guillotine. Pettis, however, was then, and is today, also a flawed fighter. Before his tough win over Stephens, Pettis got beaten by lightweight gatekeeper Clay Guida when Pettis couldn't handle Guida's wrestling. When Pettis went up against another pressure fighter, this time Rafael dos Anjos, a former gatekeeper who reinvented himself into an athletic powerhouse who expertly mixed wrestling with powerful punches, Pettis was dominated. This was followed by a very close loss against another wrestler-boxer pressure fighter, Eddie Alvarez, and then a punishing loss to the powerful and creative kickboxing of Edson Barboza sent Pettis to the featherweight division to redefine himself. Pettis at featherweight desperately struggled to make the 145 lb limit and was TKO'd by Max Holloway in an interim title fight.

I think Pettis is a great fighter. I'm certainly not going to miss an opportunity to see him compete, and I don't root against the man. I'm also a Machida fan, for what it is worth. What I have trouble with is this tendency in MMA to act like an emerging talent or a newly crowned champion is the greatest phenom we have ever witnessed. I believe that this tendency emerges out of the insecurity of the sport and this need to attach hyperboles to young talent. Organizations like the UFC attempt to transmute a young, handsome champion who hunts for the finish into legend

## 8. The Epitome of MMA

before the weight of his accomplishments forces us, as fans, to reflect on the meaningfulness of his accomplishments compared to those trailblazers who came before him. So focused is the UFC on the present, and the desperate hustling of PPV buys, that it feels compelled to tell us who the new GSP is or announce the next Anderson Silva, or simply an emerging "monster."

It is an insecurity that drives the sport into spectacle. When Russell Wilson led the Seattle Seahawks to a Super Bowl in his second season in the NFL, nobody was talking about Wilson as an all-time great quarterback, just a great QB with a ton of potential. Wilson proved that you don't have to be a 6'5" behemoth to win games as a quarterback in the NFL, and he showed fans how a quarterback can successfully run the ball. He also earned the respect of fans everywhere, outside of California's Bay Area anyway. But there was no pressing need to overhype Wilson out of fear that if we don't have the making of a new legend, people will turn off and tune out the NFL. The UFC does have this insecurity, fearful of what the decline of legends like Anderson Silva and the quasi-retirement of others; like George St-Pierre, will mean for PPV buy-rates.

There are flaws to all of the traditional GOAT front-runners. GSP certainly has his share of detractors. Nerves got the better of him in his first shot at the title against Matt Hughes, once regarded as the welterweight GOAT, who put St-Pierre away with an armbar. In what should have been his prime, GSP tapped to strikes against the heavy-hitting Matt Serra in the most shocking upset in MMA history. Once known for fast-paced attacks that could TKO opponents or rock them enough to open them up for a submission, GSP's explosive style earned him the moniker of "Rush." However, GSP abandoned his frenetic approach to ending fights quickly and replaced it with meticulous game-planning that became quite conservative. GSP changed after the Serra loss. Gone were the aggressive assaults, and in their place arose a wrestling-centric fight style, capped with a double-leg takedown that seemed improbable coming from a Canadian fighter who never wrestled at the collegiate level.

GSP never fully abandoned his traditional karate roots, electing to stand against some of his opponents, such as guillotine ace Jake Shields. Instead of power shots at a retreating foe, GSP hid behind a crisp jab. It was a brilliant tactic, though. For a long time, commentators, especially those from a boxing background, lamented the ineffective use of the jab in MMA competition. GSP showed that a quick jab can be a highly effective tool to the modern mixed-martial artist, especially combined with a takedown threat. It was a fairly powerful jab, too, breaking Koschek's orbital bone.

What became frustrating for GSP's detractors, and even some of his fans, was his reluctance to push for a finish, even against a beaten and over-matched opponent. One can't help but think that a hungrier GSP would have finished Koscheck during their fight in Montreal, or taken Dan Hardy's arm home with him. The fight against Nick Diaz was such a one-sided affair, resembling a big brother style man-handling. However, GSP finished Hughes twice in rematches, once with an armbar of his own and the other with a head-kick. GSP beat Matt Serra so convincingly in the rematch that talk of a trilogy never even materialized, and he went on to have one of the most impressive championship reigns in MMA.

The UFC announced in early 2017 that GSP would return from his quasi-retirement. Rather than compete in his native welterweight division, GSP fought against Michael Bisping for the middleweight title, finishing Bisping with a RNC. It was a controversial move. On the one hand, GSP captured a UFC championship in a second weight class, an accomplishment that further cements his already exceptional legacy. The decision to move up a weight class, even though it has long been rumored that he could probably make the weight cut down to lightweight, only adds to the greatness of his career. However, Michael Bisping had a murderer's row of legitimate contenders to face in the middleweight division. GSP cut the line and got ahead of Yoel Romero and Jacare, two contenders that Bisping would probably be a heavy underdog against. The prospect of a Bisping-GSP headliner was simply the big money PPV fight to book, especially during a year where it was unknown if McGregor would be fighting in the UFC. It is ironic that GSP, the epitome of martial arts and class in the sport, is getting a title shot at middleweight for the spectacle of the fight business.

Anderson Silva also had his share of skeptics. The middleweight division that he once ruled was regarded as comparatively thin, though Silva did always seem to bring his "A" game against the highly regarded competition, such as Dan Henderson, Rich Franklin, and Vitor Belfort. Silva didn't always look sharp, though. He lost a few times during the first decade of his career, including one of the most mind-blowing flying scissor heel hook submissions that has ever been seen in MMA. During his title reign, he lost rounds or at least struggled at times against middleweight

## 8. The Epitome of MMA

gatekeepers fortunate enough to have put together enough wins to justify a title shot, such as Travis Lutter, Patrick Côté, Thales Leites, and Demian Maia. In these fights, Silva even looked indifferent, or perhaps disaffected, in the cage.

Though Silva's takedown defense looked immaculate on paper, it was inflated by all the jiu-jitsu fighters he encountered, when he was nearly impossible to take to the mat. Ever since the Dan Henderson fight, where Henderson dragged Silva down and lightly punched him in the temple a few dozen times in the first round, a lot of people thought that he might have a lot of trouble against a tenacious wrestler unaffected by the mystique of Silva. Silva would be tested by Sonnen in those two legendary fights, but Silva came out on top. Silva couldn't outrun time and was eventually betrayed by the slowing of his reflexes and the deterioration of his once-mighty chin at the age of 38 against Chris Weidman. Silva's drug test failure might prove to have done more to undermine his legendary status than any performance in the cage.

Fedor Emelianenko is traditionally cited amongst the trinity of fighters vying for GOAT status in the sport. Unlike GSP and Silva, Emelianenko never fought in the UFC. There is a story circulating in the MMA world that Dana White has told about the attempt to sign Emelianenko for a fight with Brock Lesnar. Supposedly, White flew to an isolated part of Russia and attempted to negotiate with Emelianenko's entourage. According to White, "We had to build a fucking stadium in Russia, and we had to do all this stupid shit, stuff that no normal fucking human being would do." The biggest obstacle identified by White was the insistence of Emelianenko's managers that the fight be a cross-promotion between the UFC and M-1 Global, the Russian MMA promoter that is partly owned by Emelianenko and whose president, Vadim Finkelchstein, has been closely connected to Emelianenko's career. Cross-promotion, for sensible reasons, is not part of the UFC's wheelhouse, and the negotiations collapsed.

Emelianenko's legend was built inside the roped ring of Pride. As an undersized heavyweight, surely better suited to fight in the light-heavyweight division (known as the middleweight division in Pride), he proved to be a sensation, defeating all challengers to the heavyweight title and going undefeated for ten years. He beat the top two heavyweight fighters of his era, Antônio Rodrigo Nogueira and Mirko "Cro Cop" Filipovic, the latter in a highly publicized "fight of the decade." What was mind-blowing about Emelianenko's run at the top was that he always seemed to beat opponents at their strengths. GSP elected to expose weakness, but Emelianenko attacked against the best of what his opponent had to offer. The fights against Nogueira involved ground fighting, and he fought standing up against Cro Cop. There are not enough superlatives to describe the accomplishment of staying undefeated for so long in the heavyweight division.

However, there are reasonable qualifications that one can make regarding Emelianenko's career. He fought the two best heavyweights of his era, but there were a number of high-level heavyweights of his time whom he did not fight, such as Frank Mir, Josh Barnett (his fight with Barnett was scrapped due to Barnett's own follies), Randy Couture, or Brock Lesnar. That is not to say that I would bet against Emelianenko in any of these counter-factual match-ups, but anything can happen when elite fighters clash, and perhaps *fortuna* is felt more acutely in the heavyweight class than elsewhere. Emelianenko also fought a lot of men beneath him, inexperienced fighters who had no business being in the ring against a champion like him at the stage of their careers when their paths crossed. He fought overblown middleweights and freak-show fights against massive giants with very little training. Furthermore, the vast majority of his fights occurred in Japan, where there was zero drug testing, even on fight night.

Emelianenko experienced a rapid decline when he joined the organization Strikeforce on Showtime. Gone was the fluid, strategic fighter who ruled the Saitama Super Arena. In his place was a reckless brawler, fearlessly swinging his anvil of a right hand. Though he was able to achieve one more come-from-behind victory against Brett Rogers, he would not be so lucky against Werdum's crafty armbar-triangle, Antônio Silva's boulder-sized fists, or most catastrophically, in a wild scramble with Dan Henderson. Though it is an overstatement, White has also recounted his ominous, and what proved to be prescient, warning to Emelianenko's people. "You're one punch away from being worth fucking zero."

A fourth fighter now deserves mention in this pantheon on GOAT contenders. Jon Jones became the youngest UFC champion ever, excluding tournament champions, when he forced Shogun to tap to strikes at the end of a dominating and brutal performance. He went on to defend his light-heavyweight title eight times. His only career loss was a disqualification in his fourth UFC fight, when he rained illegal 12-to-6 elbows from top position on Matt Hamill, who was basically already finished from a shoulder injury that occurred when Jones tossed the NCAA wrestler to

## 8. The Epitome of MMA

the mat. Jon Jones' UFC run included some devastating strikes, typically involving sweeping elbows on the ground or spinning elbows on the feet, and methodical submissions. Jon Jones only rarely faced adversity, such as when Vitor Belfort nearly submitted him or when he disfigured his toe against Chael Sonnen. The former Olympian and Strikeforce heavyweight tournament champion Daniel Cormier had some good moments against Jones, and Machida landed one good punch, but the only fight that was genuinely close was against Alexander Gustafsson, who appeared to be on the brink of victory when a spinning elbow hit the Swede with the force of a helicopter blade.

What has hindered, and possibly derailed, Jones' career has been his private life, such as a self-described former marijuana dependency, too much partying right before a bout, testing positive for cocaine, and most frighteningly, a hit-and-run involving a pregnant woman, an event which Jones seemed to express only a modest measure of remorse for during an interview on the *Joe Rogan Experience* in late 2016.

Jones' USADA anti-doping violation represents another unfortunate mark on his career. A panel eventually ruled that Jones did not intentionally use clomiphene, but it was still deemed as irresponsible of Jones to be taking erectile dysfunction pills, what Jones crassly called "dick pills," he was given by a casual acquaintance. Many in the MMA community have found the excuse feeble, especially when the invoice for the ED drugs produced by this friend also listed clomiphene as a product that was purchased.

These are the four fighters most commonly identified with GOAT status, but there are others who hold claims to this non-existent honor. Demetrious "Mighty Mouse" Johnson has quietly, but decisively, defended his flyweight title nine times as of December 2016, one win away from tying Silva's record and only two wins away from matching GSP's record of most championship fights won (including interim fights). Based on Mighty Mouse's previous performances and his competition in the flyweight division, these records look like they will inevitably fall.

Conor McGregor is a long way from being the greatest mixed-martial artist that has ever competed, but all the greats had their flaws. These flaws become especially pronounced as fighters age. Though this is true of other sports, MMA seems to be particularly unforgiving to aging legends. Peyton Manning's 2015 campaign with the Denver Broncos was a pale reflection of his record-breaking season in 2013, and he received his share of criticism, but he still won the Super Bowl in that final season, carried by Von Miller and the defense, but delivering at crucial moments. MMA is a sport where you are only as good as your last performance, and you only win because your opponent "sucks."

MMA rarely allows for an aged veteran to win a final championship and bask in glorious triumph one last time. Perhaps the only good example of a wily vet pulling off the championship victory was Michael Bisping. The Brit alternated in status between contender and gatekeeper for the eight years he fought in the UFC's middleweight division. Bisping made use of his call to serve as a late replacement against the seemingly invincible Luke Rockhold, flattening Rockhold in the first round and becoming champ at 37 years old. A more representative final hurrah is something much less significant, such as when Mark Coleman won a unanimous decision against a flat Stephan Bonnar on the prelims of the historic UFC 100, proving that even the grandfather of ground-and-pound still deserved respect, or when an aged Tito Ortiz choked out an aged Chael Sonnen in Bellator.

All of the aging greats seem to stay for at least one fight too many, often a few too many. Emelianenko, Coleman, Couture, both Nogueiras, Cro Cop, Liddell, Ortiz, Hughes, Penn … the names go on. It is also true that many fighters, gatekeepers, one-time contenders or almost-contenders, often stay too long, take disturbing levels of punishment, but they don't garner the same amount of sympathy. Mike Pyle was a WEC welterweight champion and a stalwart of that division in the UFC. His fight career lasted 17 years and over 40 professional bouts. Pyle started his career fighting against Rampage Jackson, where he was officially outweighed by Jackson by 30 pounds, but unofficially much more. Pyle continued to fight at a high level of competition into his 40s, suffering a spectacular knockout loss to Alex Garcia to close out 2016. As incredible as Garcia's victory was, it was also upsetting to see a vet knocked out so cleanly. Gabriel Gonzaga is another fighter who stayed longer than was prudent, but without much fanfare. One of the greatest jiu-jitsu heavyweights ever to transition into MMA, Gonzaga once knocked out Cro Cop with a head-kick of his own, and fought a losing battle against Couture for the UFC heavyweight belt. Gonzaga's career never recovered well after that title shot, losing about as often as he won, with nine of his 11 career losses coming by way of KO or TKO.

Conor McGregor is surely in the midst of the prime of his fighting

## 8. The Epitome of MMA

career and has looked sensational in the octagon. We shouldn't get ahead of ourselves, though, and be too naïve about the hype. He has won four fights against independently ranked top-10 fighters for their weight classes, and this includes Nate Diaz (which is questionable). This is an outstanding achievement, but let's see if he is able to defend his lightweight strap. McGregor does look to be untested in some ways, and he has his flaws, but as noted above, all of the greats have had their flaws. What made them great were their title defenses and their commitment to consistently fight the best fighters they could within the boundaries of their existing contracts. Will Conor McGregor be able to achieve this? I'm not sure, but I will tune in to find out.

There is an uncomfortable question that comes to mind when one reflects on the spectacle that has been Conor McGregor's rise. Could he have achieved this financial success if he were a black fighter? In between Conor McGregor's victory over Nate Diaz and his capturing of the lightweight championship, Tyron Woodley flattened Robbie Lawler in the first round, becoming the new welterweight champion of the UFC. Woodley has asked some difficult questions about persistent biases in the patterns of the UFC's promotional work, as well as possible biases found in the UFC's fan-base.

More specifically, Woodley has questioned whether there are racial biases at play. Woodley has pointed to the way in which the UFC appears to give only a marginal promotional push to Demetrious "Mighty Mouse" Johnson, despite his being a dominate champ, as we noted, well on his way to possibly breaking Anderson Silva's and Georges St-Pierre's records. When Conor McGregor is about to fight, it is practically treated as the most important event in the history of the sport. When "Mighty Mouse" is about to defend his title for the fifth, sixth, or seventh time, it goes on with barely any notice outside of the dedicated fans who will stay up until any hour of the night to watch a "fight night" from the other side of the world.

Woodley has also expressed concerns about the backlash he has received from the UFC fan-base. After his dramatic victory over Lawler, Woodley started asking for "money fights," suggesting Nick Diaz and GSP as potential match-ups. The MMA community generally snubbed its collective nose at Woodley's requests, and the champ has felt slighted. At least one important voice in the MMA media, *MMAFighting*'s Luke Thomas, has expressed sympathy toward Woodley's criticisms and has asked tough questions about racism in the sport.

## Mixed Martial Arts and the Quest for Legitimacy

One can't help but appreciate a double-standard on the part of the MMA community and the lack of fairness in the promotional efforts in the UFC. "Mighty Mouse" really does seem to be treated as the poor champion, largely neglected by the vast promotional machine that the UFC deploys to hustle its events. The lack of promotional effort behind Mighty Mouse speaks to the general insecurities of MMA. Demetrious Johnson is the consummate professional, the soft-spoken competitor who lets his hands, and his submissions, speak for him. "Mighty Mouse" isn't interested in pandering to the "JUST BLEED" crowd who depend on depraved insults and expressions of cruelty to get hyped for an event. Johnson certainly isn't interested in feminizing his opponents or insulting their class status or country of origin. He is the professional athlete stuck in a sport that is shaped by spectacle. He isn't going to laugh at childhood poverty. The UFC, for its part, seems unable to know how to promote a professional like Johnson. For all of its vaunted money and influence, the UFC is still dependent on the crude sound-bite and the bravado of male narcissism.

What I find disturbing is whether the case of Johnson actually reveals to us the need of spectacle within MMA. Perhaps the sport alone is not enough to attract viewers. There appears to be a fundamental requirement of spectacle for the success of the sport, and this should give us pause. If spectacle is required for the success of the sport, then can it ever enter into the mainstream?

I'm not entirely convinced that the case of Demetrious "Mighty Mouse" Johnson ought to convince us of the limitations of MMA without spectacle. Another factor to consider is the division Johnson rules. The flyweight division is the lightest weight class in the UFC, and the most recent addition. At 125 lbs, the pool of potential fighters to fill out the division is pretty small. Johnson hasn't simply defeated all challengers to his title—he's also fought a ridiculously high percentage of the roster at 125 lbs. For the flyweight division to find success, it needs to see MMA talent develop in countries where a greater percentage of the population of athletes might be closer to that weight than it is in the U.S. Perhaps, as MMA continues to develop in China, India, Thailand and elsewhere, the flyweight division will realize a depth that has eluded it until now.

Another limitation of flyweight is that it is the lightest division, and it might not be viable beyond hardcore MMA fans. A lot of "JUST BLEED" fans just want to see hyper-roided goliaths throw brick-crushing haymakers

## 8. The Epitome of MMA

and don't care to watch a division filled with what the online community has ignominiously referred to as "manlets." One can't help but wonder about the athletic prowess of those keyboard warriors who scoff at the so-called "manlets" of the flyweight division, and how long they would last in the octagon against Johnson or John Dodson. Flyweight contests tend to be fast-paced and exciting. A heavier weight class fight that follows a flyweight contest generally feels like it is moving in slow motion with the fighters wearing ankle weights. There was a time when the lightweight division (155 lbs) never got the respect that it deserved in the UFC, and it is hard to find a MMA fan who isn't intensely invested in that division. Norms will change, and the flyweights will eventually get the respect they deserve. I can only hope that this begins to happen before Johnson walks away from the sport.

As noted above, I'm not convinced that Johnson's lack of popularity with the fan-base or the UFC brass is because the man is black. On this point, I'm inclined to disagree with Woodley. However, when you think about the rise of Conor McGregor through a racial lens, I think that you do come around to accepting that there are some racial double standards at work.

Could Conor McGregor have achieved the same phenomenal economic success if he were black? I think not. The spectacle that is the Conor McGregor hype machine would likely not have generated this much support in the sport. His conspicuous consumption, obsession with money, and constant way of insulting his opponents would likely have been met with derision by the MMA fan-base. There have been a few black mixed-martial artists who have attempted to promote themselves in a similar manner to Conor McGregor, such as Bobby Green, and they were either met with animosity from fans or, more likely, mostly unnoticed. McGregor's spectacle does not appear to work for black athletes because someone who is black would be hated for being "cocky," "uppity," and as "someone who doesn't know his place." McGregor's shtick works in part because he is white. "White privilege" is a phrase that gets bandied about too often in questionable context, but I think that McGregor is relying on white privilege with his routine. Boxing may have its Floyd Mayweather, and though there is some overlap between fans of boxing and fans of MMA, the sport of MMA has not accepted the loud, brash, and wealthy black heel that boxing has, even if as many people were watching Mayweather to see him lose as to see him win. On this issue, I do think that Tyron

Woodley is making a socially important point on the racial prejudice that boils just under the surface of MMA.

The greatest irony of Conor McGregor is that the man with the greatest self-belief in himself as a fighter has continued to rely on spectacle to sell his fights. One can't help but wonder if he is insecure about fan interest in his talents and fighting ability and relies on the heel routine as a crutch. It is an irony born of a sport desperate for recognition from mainstream audiences, often promoting the kind of behavior that will prevent MMA from ever being genuinely accepted by polite society.

There is a second irony to Conor McGregor and the UFC that started to emerge during the build-up to UFC 200, the final card delivered under Zuffa management. The UFC's second massive anniversary event was a staked event from prelims to the main card, with just about any fight on that card capable of headlining a "Fight Night" card, and a few of the main card fights capable of headlining a PPV. The main card suffered a huge blow when Jon Jones was notified of the USADA anti-doping violation. Jones was replaced by none other than Anderson Silva, but the card became severely handicapped when it lost its original main attraction.

Originally, UFC 200 was going to be headlined by the Conor McGregor–Nate Diaz rematch. The decision to schedule this fight as the headliner represented nothing more than cynical self-interest on the part of Zuffa, as it was placed above legitimate title fights. The fight with Diaz had to be postponed, however. Conor McGregor issued a cryptic tweet claiming that he was retiring (while reminding us all of the money he has made). It was revealed that he refused to attend a press conference for the event stateside, on account of his training camp in Iceland. In an incredible reversal, the man who has thrived in front of the camera more than any fighter before him had now shunned the spotlight to focus on his training. Dana White dropped the fight from UFC 200, requiring the Diaz fight to be rescheduled for UFC 202, an event that would become the highest-grossing UFC event ever.

One can't help but wonder if the decision to remove Conor McGregor from UFC 200, and an allegedly guaranteed $10 million paycheck, was an act meant to reestablish the power relations of promoter and contractor. McGregor even offered to conduct a press conference in New York state to make up for the one that he skipped, but White was not interested. Surely, the UFC was trying to remind their ambitious champ that this was not a partnership and that his place was do what the company told him.

## 8. The Epitome of MMA

Furthermore, after McGregor won the lightweight championship and announced that he was taking a short break, the UFC unilaterally stripped him of the featherweight title, though he once threatened to the media that the UFC would need an army to take that belt from him.

The message was not lost on McGregor, but rather than show acquiescence, he appears to have responded with defiance. After his historic victory over Alvarez, as we noted earlier, McGregor demanded an equity share in the company. McGregor has been increasingly focused on Floyd Mayweather, directing vindictive tweets at him in an ultimately successful effort to instigate the unbeaten, all-time great into accepting a boxing match.

While the UFC was broadcasting a live event on Fox, Conor McGregor was hosting an interview with Ariel Helwani, actually charging admission to the live Q&A session and even charging a PPV rate to watch it online! Immediately before the interview took place, McGregor unleashed one of his most audacious tweets. "I'm so mad! Heading to do a Q and A in front of 5000 fans! You read that right. That's more than UFC attendance tonight. And it's on PPV.... Fuck the UFC. Fuck Floyd. Fuck boxing. Fuck the WWE. Fuck Hollywood. And fuck you too pay me." Once again, I don't claim to have retained the greatest sense of humor, but I don't think this counts as the "playful banter" of a "good lad."

Does this portend a split with the UFC? Will McGregor attempt to repeat the strategy of his nemesis, Floyd Mayweather, and promote his own events that feature himself as the headliner? Will fans continue to adore his endless barrage of negativity and vanity, even when they are the targets of his immature insults? All these questions persist regarding the man who christens himself as "Mystic Mac." It is not even obvious in early 2017 whether the man who thinks of himself as the Greatest Of All Time will even defend his 155 lb strap in MMA, despite the presence of two very strong contenders.

# Conclusion

I think that there is something of America that surfaces in the arenas and casinos of MMA, and also something of Brazil, Canada, Sweden, Japan, and other countries that have opened up their laws to sanctioned MMA events. What is surfacing is the realization that it is not just the athletes who are fighting. It is also the audience. Our struggles, our personal victories, and our crushing defeats. The drama that is our lives. This is one of the things that makes MMA so relatable and one of the reasons why Greg Jackson compared MMA competition to a morality play. Sam Sheridan once quoted the Brazilian jiu-jitsu legend, Renzo Gracie, saying "Everybody is fighting something."[1]

Perhaps the great metaphor of MMA is one of struggle in a hostile environment. In an age when globalization and special interests have eroded the gains once made by the middle-class during the first three post-war decades, MMA has ascended to the mainstream. It makes sense in a world with so much personal insecurity surrounding work and the future. It is also a metaphor that undermines the legitimacy of MMA and threatens to turn it away from sport and back into spectacle. Sheridan has offered the following reflection:

> Fighting plays to the instinctual nihilism in some men, the part that when faced with impossible odds, or certain destruction, says "Fuck it" and charges. It's not something easily understood, and here I think the sexes often diverge—not many women can be satisfied with "fuck it" as a real reason, but most men will understand it.[2]

Sheridan believes that this is why UFC fighters are often bristling with machismo, claiming that they will fight "anyone" and even making horrific comments about how they would accept death in the octagon. It is this primal, animalistic place in all of us that convinces Dana White that "fighting is in our genes."

## Conclusion

MMA taps into the discontent and the fears that permeate society. It is a vain realm that is self-destructive and evokes a perverse longing for a Hobbesian state of nature where life is poor, solitary, nasty, brutish and short. This is a place of desperation and reflects the insecurities of a desperate society, fearful that they might never measure up, never find a meaningful career, and have little hope for a secure future. Ultimate fighting is a realm devoid of ethics and the pursuit of justice. It is a place where millionaires and billionaires earn a rate of return on their capital from the physical and emotional sacrifices of the men and women courageous enough to fight each other in front of cameras and a live audience.

I maintain that MMA can represent more than crass spectacle. The realm of spectacle and ultimate fighting is but one-half of the dialectic that is MMA. It will always have elements of ultimate fighting, but there are powerful forces pushing the sport away from spectacle and into the mainstream, and the new ownership of WME-IMG has the potential to continue this trend. Under Zuffa, the UFC brought legitimacy to MMA, transforming it from barely legal strongman contests to a sport populated by athletes with health insurance who compete at different weight classes. The unified rules have given an ethical clarity on the boundaries of violence, and the UFC's own Code of Conduct for fighters is, at the very least, a symbolic statement on the responsibilities that fighters have as ambassadors of a professional sport. TRT has been banned, and out-of-competition drug testing will do much to clean up the sport. The UFC has even unwittingly brought itself very close to identifying its fighters as employees, rather than independent contractors. Women have joined the ranks as fighters, once led by a veritable superstar in Ronda Rousey, but now with a talent pool that is deepening very quickly. The sport has even turned a handful of fighters into millionaires who have positively inspired national communities around the world. Surely some, the Meryl Streeps of this world for instance, will scoff at MMA as a cultural wasteland, but you know that progress has been made when the sport is compared to football. At least she didn't call it human cockfighting.

There will continue to be forces that will challenge the very idea of the virtues of martial arts and pull it into ultimate fighting, and how effectively WME-IMG engages with these pressures will do much to determine whether the UFC will become a fully mainstream sport. Baseline fighter pay in the top organizations is shamefully low. Guys in the top-15 of their weight class are cut after a single loss if they are perceived as

## Conclusion

boring point-fighters. Violence against women, both the symbolic kind that is performed through language, but especially the direct physical kind, needs to be confronted decisively by all promotions. Severe head trauma is likely going to loom ominously over the sport over the coming years. Fans and fighters alike will have to ask themselves difficult questions about the cruelty of the fight business. This last point might represent the most serious challenge to the concept of MMA, as the more positive characteristics of mixed-martial arts will be forever inadequate as arguments for the sport's legitimacy when weighed against the traumatic brain damage suffered by fighters.

A major study that was published in 2008 attempted to understand what factors motivate people to go see a live MMA show. The researchers sought to gauge fan interest by distributing questionnaires at a local cage-fighting show in a Midwestern city in the U.S.[3] The possible responses listed on the questionnaire to account for why respondents attend a MMA event were based on previous research done on fan motivation in other sports, as well as a couple of other responses thought to be particularly germane to MMA. The ten motivations that were listed included: a general interest in the sport; the drama of the experience; the aesthetics of the sport; partaking in a social event; being entertained by violence; vicariously experiencing the achievements of fighters; hero adoration; an escape; national pride; or the attraction of gambling.

The results of the longitudinal analysis revealed that general interest in the sport was the most important motivation for attending the cage-fighting event, followed very closely by the drama of the sport and then an aesthetic appreciation for strategy and technique. Entertainment derived from violence was in the middle of the pack, along with socializing, vicarious achievement, and hero adoration, with escapism, national pride, and gambling at the bottom.

While revealing, the study seems to have a few limitations, making it tough to generalize the results too far beyond what motivates fight fans to attend a show. The event was a small local show where all the fighters on the card were American. If the same question were asked on a questionnaire for a UFC card in Brazil, where every fight typically features one Brazilian against another nationality (with the exception of *TUF Brazil* Finales), the results could look very different. Living vicariously through the action and hero adoration could score much higher at a UFC event that features a main draw, such as Conor McGregor or Ronda Rousey.

## Conclusion

It is also interesting, as the authors of the study note, that violence was surprisingly low on the list. Direct violence between individuals is perhaps the key comparative advantage that MMA holds over other contact sports, such as hockey, football, and rugby, and the sport is largely defined by gratuitous violence. I do think this says something very positive about the crowds who go out and support a small cage-fighting show. It dispels a myth about crowds being bloodthirsty sociopaths, losing touch with human empathy and basic decency, almost expecting a ritual of human sacrifice to the "JUST BLEED" gods. However, out of the 275 questionnaires distributed at the event, the authors point out that only 208 were returned. Does a bloodthirsty patron really take the time to read a questionnaire and thoughtfully reflect on his reasons for being there? He probably just gets drunk with his friends and catcalls the card-girls. And of course, as political pollsters were reminded on Tuesday, November 8, people lie on surveys.

General interest in the sport as the most important motivation for attending a regional show reveals how important the UFC truly is and its potential to achieve the status of a mainstream sporting organization. Almost 18 percent of respondents in the above study identified *TUF* as their first exposure to MMA, and over 80 percent cited the UFC as their favorite organization (I'm guessing just about everybody else are diehard Pride fans who never came to grips with its end). The UFC is so important to the sport that it almost subsumes it. Just as Lorenzo Fertitta told his attorney that he was paying $2 million for three letters, Zuffa earned over $4 billion for the sale of those same three letters. WME-IMG could start a MMA league of their own for less than $4 billion, but missing those three letters, it is hard to think it could compete against whoever owned the UFC.

Perhaps a majority of the people who attend a local show, hosted by an organization that isn't even close to the UFC's radar, are there because of the dominance of the UFC. It is a dominance of market-share, but something more than that. It is also a dominance of the imagination for so many MMA fans. It therefore remains the organization on which the tension between spectacle and sport will define the politics of MMA, the livelihood of its athletes, and its presence in society.

# Chapter Notes

## Preface

1. Clifford Geertz, *The Interpretation of Cultures* (New York: Basic Books, 1973), 444.
2. *Ibid.*, 446.
3. To be fair to the guy, it's not entirely obvious that he's drinking alcohol.

## Chapter 1

1. The wonderful Ken Burns documentary *Baseball* is a testament to the meaning and importance of America's pastime.
2. Liam Stockdale, "More Than Just Games: The Global Politics of the Olympic Movement," *Sport in Society: Cultures, Commerce, Media, Politics* 15, no. 6 (2012): 839–854.
3. Clifford Geertz, *The Interpretation of Cultures* (New York: Basic Books, 1973), 443.
4. The graphic novel contains a critique of violence, which the Zach Snyder film certainly lacks. The Snyder film does a lot of things quite well, such as utilizing Dr. Manhattan more in the climactic finale, but the violence seems more meant to entertain you than the violence in Moore's graphic novel, which is more of a commentary on the violence of superhero comics.
5. However, most of the goombas, koopa troopas, and other enemies in the early Mario games did just seem to be going about their business, mostly indifferent to the plumbers. Mario games on Nintendo's later consoles featured goombas that charged directly at you, making the actions of our protagonist more defensive in nature.
6. Though I could rarely get the button mashing right for most of the finishing moves.
7. Readers under 18 years old should consult your parents or grandparents for the definition of "video rental stores."
8. Gwynne Dyer, *War: The New Edition* (Toronto: Random House, 2004), 11.
9. Kenneth N. Waltz, *Man, the State, and War: A Theoretical Analysis* (New York: Columbia University Press, 1954).
10. The passages are from 1253a1 and a29 of Aristotle's *Politics*.
11. Harold Lasswell, *Politics: Who Gets What, When, How* (New York: Whittlesey House, 1936).

## Chapter 2

1. For a superb analysis of the way in which professional wrestling plays on the anxieties of Americans, I recommend the first chapter of Christopher Hedges, *Empire of Illusion: The End of Literacy and the Triumph of Spectacle* (Toronto: Vintage Canada, 2009).
2. One of his challengers, Travis Lutter, failed to make the 185-pound weight limit required for title fights, rendering this a victory but not a defense.
3. Lyoto Machida is known to drink a glass of his morning urine.
4. One of the odder stories to emerge

## Chapter Notes

during the transition of the UFC into mainstream sports has been the friendship between B-movie action star Steven Seagal and the Brazilian gym "Blackhouse."

5. Santino DeFranco, "What It's Like Auditioning for 'The Ultimate Fighter,'" *Vice.com*, http://fightland.vice.com/blog/what-its-like-auditioning-for-the-ultimate-fighter.

6. Dave Meltzer, "Chael Sonnen Credits Paul Heyman for Saving *TUF III Brazil*," *MMAFighting.com*, http://www.mmafighting.com/2014/5/3/5670532/chael-sonnen-credits-paul-heyman-for-saving-tuf-brazil-3.

## Chapter 3

1. The first UFC fighter to test positive for PEDs was Josh Barnett for boldenone, nandrolone, and fluoxymesterone, after he lay waste to Randy Couture and captured the UFC heavyweight belt in April 2002. According to Mike Sloan, a journalist with *Sherdog.com*, Barnett actually tested positive in November 2001 for two other steroids. The NAC issued a private warning to Barnett after the 2001 offense. It was only after Barnett tested positive again, just a few months later, that the NAC decided that it was going to disclose failed tests publicly and not give warnings for breaking the rules.

2. Stephie Haynes, "Teammate who gave Jon Jones 'd**k pills' also bought clomiphene," *BloodyElbow.com*, http://www.bloodyelbow.com/2016/11/9/13577682/ufc-news-teammate-who-gave-jon-jones-dick-pills-also-bought-clomiphene-usada-ped-ban.

## Chapter 4

1. Josh Tucker, "If MMA Doesn't Change, Someone is Going to Die," *Deadspin.com*, http://deadspin.com/if-mma-doesnt-change-someone-is-going-to-die-1556957162.

2. Michael G. Hutchison, David W. Lawrence, Michael D. Cusimano, and Tom A. Schweizer, "Head Trauma in Mixed Martial Arts," *American Journal of Sports Medicine*. Published online before print (21 March 2014).

3. The video analysis of KOs and TKOs omits the undercard matches.

## Chapter 5

1. Tracy Clark-Flory, "The Horrific Misogyny of Mixed Martial Arts Culture," *Salon.com*, http://www.salon.com/2014/08/12/he_sawed_off_my_hair_with_a_dull_knife_the_horrific_misogyny_of_mixed_martial_arts_culture/.

2. L.A. Jennings, "Ronda Rousey and the Feminism of the Bitch," *Vice.com*, http://fightland.vice.com/blog/ronda-rousey-and-the-feminism-of-the-bitch.

## Chapter 6

1. Herodotus, *The Histories*, 443, 509.

2. Lem Satterfield, "Battle for New York: Fighting Resistance," *Sherdog.com*, http://www.sherdog.com/news/articles/Battle-for-New-York-Fighting-Resistance-73499.

3. Jeff Fox, "2012 Year in Review: Fighter Salaries," *MMAManifesto.com*, http://mmamanifesto.com/root/ufc-fighter-salary-database-root/2012-year-in-review-ufc-fighter-salaries.html.

4. Kurt Badenhausen, "UFC 167: How Georges St. Pierre Makes $12 Million a Year," *Forbes.com*, http://www.forbes.com/sites/kurtbadenhausen/2013/11/16/how-georges-st-pierre-makes-12-million-a-year/.

5. Ron Suskind, *Confidence Men: Wall Street, Washington, and the Education of a President* (Toronto: HarperCollins, 2011), 197.

6. Lucy Kellaway, "Lunch with the FT: Dana White," *Financial Times*, http://www.ft.com/intl/cms/s/2/03ccce22-aebf-11e3-aaa6–00144feab7de.html#axzz3Tq8XFK51.

7. John S. Nash, "What investors are

*Chapter Notes*

being told about UFC revenues," *Bloodyelbow.com,* http://www.bloodyelbow.com/2015/10/20/9547333/what-deutsche-bank-moodys-and-standard-poors-tell-us-about-the-ufc.

8. IRS, "Independent Contractor (Self-Employed) or Employee?" http://www.irs.gov/Businesses/Small-Businesses-&-Self-Employed/Independent-Contractor-Self-Employed-or-Employee.

## Chapter 7

1. The following passages are from Vol. 5 of the 1906 edition, between pages 150–165.

2. Fitch has probably lost most of the goodwill he enjoyed from people who respected what he brought to MMA when it was revealed by CSAC that he failed a pre-fight drug test leading up to his WSOF title fight with Rousimar Palhares.

3. Kevin Iole, "In Cutting Jake Shields, UFC Takes a Page out of NFL's Playbook," *Yahoo.com,* http://sports.yahoo.com/news/in-cutting-jake-shields—ufc-takes-a-page-out-of-nfl-s-playbook-203152661-mma.html.

4. John S. Nash, "Panel Discussion: Is the UFC a Monopoly?" *Bloodyelbow.com,* http://www.bloodyelbow.com/2014/6/30/5846330/ufc-monopoly-panel-discussion-paul-gift-david-dudley.

5. Jake Rossen, "Pride Before the Fall," *Sherdog.com,* http://www.sherdog.com/blog/Pride-Before-the-Fall-25249.

6. Fedor Emelianenko always looked like he could have cut down to 205.

## Chapter 8

1. Forgive the pun!

2. Tom Rooney, "Is Conor McGregor really such a big deal in Ireland? A fellow Irishman explains," *MMAJunkie.com,* http://mmajunkie.com/2015/07/is-conor-mcgregor-really-such-a-big-deal-in-ireland-a-fellow-irishman-explains.

## Conclusion

1. Sam Sheridan, *The Fighter's Mind: Inside the Mental Game* (New York: Grove Press, 2010), xi.

2. *Ibid.,* 278.

3. Seungmo Kim, T. Christopher Greenwell, Damon P. S. Andrew, Janghyuk Lee, and Daniel F. Mahoney, "An Analysis of Spectator Motives in an Individual Combat Sport: A Study of Mixed Martial Arts Fans," *Sport Marketing Quarterly* 17 (2008): 109–119.

# Bibliography

Aristotle. *The Politics*. Peter L. Phillips Simpson, trans. Chapel Hill: University of North Carolina Press, 1997.

Badenhausen, Kurt. "UFC 167: How Georges St. Pierre Makes $12 Million a Year." *Forbes.com*. http://www.forbes.com/sites/kurtbadenhausen/2013/11/16/how-georges-st-pierre-makes-12-million-a-year/.

Clark-Flory, Tracy. "The Horrific Misogyny of Mixed Martial Arts Culture." *Salon.com*. http://www.salon.com/2014/08/12/he_sawed_off_my_hair_with_a_dull_knife_the_horrific_misogyny_of_mixed_martial_arts_culture/.

DeFranco, Santino. "What It's Like Auditioning for *The Ultimate Fighter*." *Vice.com*. http://fightland.vice.com/blog/what-its-like-auditioning-for-the-ultimate-fighter.

Dyer, Gwynne. *War: The New Edition*. Toronto: Random House, 2004.

Fox, Jeff. "2012 Year in Review: Fighter Salaries." *MMAManifesto.com*. http://mma-manifesto.com/root/ufc-fighter-salary-database-root/2012-year-in-review-ufc-fighter-salaries.html.

Geertz, Clifford. *The Interpretation of Cultures*. New York: Basic Books, 1973.

Gibbon, Edward. *The Decline and Fall of the Roman Empire, Vol. 5*. Cambridge, MA: Harvard University Press, 1977.

Haynes, Stephie. "Teammate who gave Jon Jones 'd**k pills' also bought clomiphene." *BloodyElbow.com*. http://www.bloodyelbow.com/2016/11/9/13577682/ufc-news-teammate-who-gave-jon-jones-dick-pills-also-bought-clomiphene-usada-ped-ban.

Hedges, Christopher. *Empire of Illusion: The End of Literacy and the Triumph of Spectacle*. Toronto: Vintage Canada, 2009.

Herodotus. *The Histories*. Aubrey De Sélincourt, trans. New York: Penguin Books, 1954.

Hutchison, Michael G., David W. Lawrence, Michael D. Cusimano, and Tom A. Schweizer. "Head Trauma in Mixed Martial Arts." *American Journal of Sports Medicine*. Published online before print (21 March 2014).

Internal Revenue Service (IRS). "Independent Contractor (Self-Employed) or Employee?" http://www.irs.gov/Businesses/Small-Businesses-&-Self-Employed/Independent-Contractor-Self-Employed-or-Employee.

Iole, Kevin. "In Cutting Jake Shields, UFC Takes a Page out of NFL's Playbook." *Yahoo.com*. http://sports.yahoo.com/news/in-cutting-jake-shields—ufc-takes-a-page-out-of-nfl-s-playbook-203152661-mma.html.

Jennings, L.A. "Ronda Rousey and the Feminism of the Bitch." *Vice.com*. http://fightland.vice.com/blog/ronda-rousey-and-the-feminism-of-the-bitch.

Kellaway, Lucy. "Lunch with the FT: Dana White." *Financial Times*. www.ft.com/content/03ccce22-aebf-11e3-aaa6-00144feab7de.

Kyte, E. Spencer. "Josh Koscheck: A Picture of Evolution," *The Province*. http://theprovince.com/sports/mma/josh-koscheck-a-picture-of-evolution/comment-page-1.

# Bibliography

Lasswell, Harold. *Politics: Who Gets What, When, How.* New York: Whittlesey House, 1936.

Meltzer, Dave. "Chael Sonnen Credits Paul Heyman for Saving *TUF III Brazil*." *MMAFighting.com.* http://www.mmasfighting.com/2014/5/3/5670532/chael-sonnen-credits-paul-heyman-for-saving-tuf-brazil-3.

Nash, John S. "Panel Discussion: Is the UFC a Monopoly?" *Bloodyelbow.com.* http://www.bloodyelbow.com/2014/6/30/5846330/ufc-monopoly-panel-discussion-paul-gift-david-dudley.

_____. "What investors are being told about UFC revenues." *Bloodyelbow.com.* http://www.bloodyelbow.com/2015/10/20/9547333/what-deutsche-bank-moodys-and-standard-poors-tell-us-about-the-ufc.

Palmquist, Chris. "Chael Sonnen Blasts Brazil, Makes National News There." *The Underground.* http://www.mixedmartialarts.com/news/chael-sonnen-blasts-brazil-makes-national-news-there.

Rooney, Tom. "Is Conor McGregor really such a big deal in Ireland? A fellow Irishman explains." *MMAJunkie.com.* http://mmajunkie.com/2015/07/is-conor-mcgregor-really-such-a-big-deal-in-ireland-a-fellow-irishman-explains.

Rossen, Jake. "Pride Before the Fall." *Sherdog.com.* http://www.sherdog.com/blog/Pride-Before-the-Fall-25249.

Satterfield, Lem. "Battle for New York: Fighting Resistance." *Sherdog.com.* http://www.sherdog.com/news/articles/Battle-for-New-York-Fighting-Resistance-73499.

Seungmo, Kim, T. Christopher Greenwell, Damon P.S. Andrew, Janghyuk Lee and Daniel F. Mahoney. "An Analysis of Spectator Motives in an Individual Combat Sport: A Study of Mixed Martial Arts Fans." *Sport Marketing Quarterly* 17 (2008): 109–119.

Sheridan, Sam. *The Fighter's Mind: Inside the Mental Game.* New York: Grove Press, 2010.

Stockdale, Liam. "More Than Just Games: The Global Politics of the Olympic Movement." *Sport in Society: Cultures, Commerce, Media, Politics.* Vol. 15: 6 (2012): 839–854.

Suskind, Ron. *Confidence Men: Wall Street, Washington, and the Education of a President.* Toronto: HarperCollins, 2011.

Tucker, Josh. "If MMA Doesn't Change, Someone is Going to Die." *Deadspin.com.* http://deadspin.com/if-mma-doesnt-change-someone-is-going-to-die-1556957162.

Waltz, Kenneth N. *Man, the State, and War: A Theoretical Analysis.* New York: Columbia University Press, 1954.

# Index

Affliction 145–6
Aldo, José 27, 100, 145, 153–6, 165–7
Ali, Muhammad 77, 148
Ali Act 131–2
Alvarez, Eddie 32, 150, 152–3, 156, 160–2, 170, 181
Aris, Jeffrey 147–8
Aristotle 29, 187
Askren, Ben 141–2

baseball 8, 11, 13, 30, 45, 91, 117, 123, 125, 145, 163, 187
Bayless, Skip 46, 108
Belfort, Vitor 27, 44, 47, 63–7, 69, 88, 172, 175
Bellator 1, 52–4, 64, 99, 103, 132, 141–2, 148, 176
Bisping, Michael 43, 65, 68–9, 172, 176
Bocek, Mark 60–1, 75
bonuses 58, 73–9, 92, 95, 117–8, 122, 129, 159, 169
boxing 13, 15, 24, 30, 44–5, 68, 76–7, 86, 105, 115–6, 124–6, 140, 155–6, 162, 164, 169–71, 179–81
Brazil 8, 21, 35–6, 39–42, 45, 47–53, 65–6, 73, 85, 118–20, 138, 166–7, 182, 184
Breitbart 160

CABMMA (Brazilian Mixed Martial Arts Commission) 58
California State Athletic Commission (CSAC) 43, 55, 58, 106, 181, 189
Canada 8, 11–2, 19, 35–6, 82, 115, 135, 182
Carano, Gina 105–8
Celeste, Arianny 110–21
championships 7, 21–2, 33, 53, 55, 63, 78, 104, 123, 126, 136, 139, 144–5, 150, 152–3, 156, 172, 175–7, 181
Cholish, John 118–24, 132
Clark-Flory, Tracy 100–2
cockfighting 1–5, 14, 17, 76, 132, 183
code of conduct (UFC) 52, 99, 103, 133, 135, 183
comic books 18–22, 28, 187
compensation 1, 110–2, 114–23, 125–6, 132, 136, 138–9, 161–2, 180–1
concussions 30–1, 76, 80–1, 83, 92–5
conspicuous consumption 150–1, 160–2, 168, 179
Cormier, Daniel 59, 64, 69–70, 86, 97–8, 145, 152, 175
CTE *see* concussions
Cyborg (Cristiane Justino) 105–8

Denis, Nick 73–5
Diaz, Nate 95–7, 126–7, 151–2, 155–6, 159–61, 163–5, 177, 180
Diaz, Nick 31, 70, 77, 80, 86–7, 104–5, 118, 126, 145, 152, 172
Dos Santos, Junior 7, 17, 57, 123
Driscoll, Mark 102

Emelianenko, Fedor 44, 64, 144–5, 150–4, 159, 173, 189
Endeavor *see* WME-IMG

Fertitta brothers (Lorenzo and Frank) 23, 26, 31, 103, 115, 121–2, 147, 152, 185
Fitch, Jon 61, 90, 118, 136–9, 141, 145, 147, 189
Flair, Ric 108, 158–9
Fox 5, 17, 28, 32, 47, 53, 80, 108, 116, 119, 123, 143, 151, 158, 161, 167, 181
Frazier, Joe 77, 158

193

# Index

Geertz, Clifford 3–6, 13–5, 22, 26
gender 30, 41, 52, 93–4, 97–100, 106–7, 109, 167
Gibbon, Edward 133
gladiatorial games 22, 52–3, 86, 110–2, 133–4
GOAT (Greatest of All Time) 7, 37, 44, 70, 108, 150–8, 169–75
Gracie, Royce 21–3, 27, 89

Hauser, Thomas 115–6
heel 33–6, 40, 50–3, 137, 158–9, 179–80
Henderson, Dan 37, 43–4, 48, 63–6, 69, 78–9, 139, 144–5, 152–5, 172–4
Herodotus 114
Hobbes, Thomas 4, 93, 113, 134, 183
hockey 8, 11–3, 17–20, 30, 45, 52, 80–6, 94, 117, 138, 163, 185
human nature 14, 23–9, 75, 83, 93, 138, 182; see also Hobbes, Thomas
Hunt, Loretta 94–5

Jackson, Greg 14–5, 44–5, 182
Japan 8, 17, 34, 36, 48, 58, 144, 147, 152, 174, 182
Jennings, L.A. 105
jiu-jitsu 15, 21–2, 36, 39, 99, 101, 136, 139, 156, 173, 176
Jones, Jon 27, 44–7, 50, 59, 64, 67, 70–1, 86, 88, 97–8, 117, 120, 174–5, 180

Kellaway, Lucy 121
kickboxing 57, 80, 98, 170
Koscheck, Josh 33–5, 53, 61, 147, 172

Las Vegas, Nevada 7, 26, 39, 42, 44–5, 48–9, 66, 115, 137
Lesnar, Brock 27, 34, 66, 71, 78, 159, 173–4
Liddell, Chuck 23, 52–3, 144–5, 152

Machiavelli 15–6, 116, 154
Machida, Lyoto "The Dragon" 41, 44, 47, 80, 85, 99–100, 144, 152, 169–70, 175, 187
Mack, Christy 101–2
male gaze 111–2
masculinity 14, 30, 41, 93, 99, 102, 111–3, 151–2, 157, 168, 178
Mayweather, Floyd 140, 162–3, 179, 181

McCain, John 1, 3, 14, 26, 76
McGregor, Conor 2, 30, 32, 108, 126–7, 132, 140, 149–69, 172, 175–81, 184
McKee, Ann 92
Mighty Mouse (Demetrius Johnson) 141, 175–8
Mixed-Martial Arts Athletes' Association (MMAAA) 131–2
MLB (Major League Baseball) 91, 117, 122–3, 128, 143, 163
monopoly 30, 143–8
monopsony 30, 143–8
Montreal, Quebec 33–5, 48, 60, 74, 172
Morin, Matt 102
Mullin, Markwayne 131
Musashi, Miyamoto 75, 78

nationalism 29–30, 36, 41, 46
Nevada Athletic Commission (NAC) 29, 56–68, 71, 77, 188
NFL (National Football League) 5, 23, 30–1, 68, 76, 79, 85, 91–2, 94–5, 112, 115, 117, 122–3, 128, 138, 140, 144–8, 163, 171
NHL (National Hockey League) 11–3, 17–20, 52, 79–80, 85–6, 91–2, 117, 123, 125, 128, 136, 138, 147–8, 163
Nogueira, Antônio "Minotauro" (Big Nog) 36, 39, 41, 47, 55, 99, 144, 152, 167, 173–4, 176

octagon girls/women 109–13
Olympic games 12–3, 17, 30, 41, 61, 68–9, 104, 114

Palmer, Brittney 110–2
pay see compensation
PEDs (performance enhancing drugs) 16, 52, 59–61, 65, 72, 75, 188; see also TRT
Pettis, Anthony 80, 145, 152, 1690–70
Pride Fighting Championship 22–3, 36–7, 39, 42, 44, 63–4, 69, 88–9, 144–7, 152–3, 173, 185
professional wrestling see WWE
Punk, C.M. (Phil Brooks) 34, 142

Quarry, Nate 22, 145

racism 13, 45–6, 177
Ratner, Marc 58, 115–6

## Index

Rebney, Bjorn  132, 141–2
Reebok  118–9, 129, 132, 166
revenue sharing  122–3, 131–2, 148
Rogan, Joe  37, 60, 63, 78, 87, 104, 169, 175
Rousey, Ronda  104–11, 116, 159, 169, 183–4

St-Pierre, Georges (GSP)  27–8, 31, 33–6, 44, 60–3, 117–8, 126–7, 132, 136, 140, 154, 159, 166–7, 171–7
SEG (Semaphore Entertainment Group)  26, 121, 152
Sherdog  7, 89, 94, 115, 147, 188
Sheridan, Sam  5, 182
Sherman Act  145–8
Shields, Jake  90, 139–41, 152, 171
Silva, Anderson "The Spider"  7, 37–9, 41–2, 45–8, 52–4, 55, 65, 70, 98–9, 117, 120, 127, 130, 139, 150, 153, 159, 171–2, 177, 180
Silva, Wanderlei  40–2, 47–8, 50–2, 56, 59–60, 63, 68–9, 99, 107, 118, 144–5
Silver, Sheldon  115–6
social media  10, 19, 36, 39–40, 52, 58, 95, 101–2, 108, 118, 122, 146–7, 157–8, 165, 167–8
Son, Joe  101
Sonnen, Chael  36–54, 55–60, 64, 70, 85–6, 99, 107, 111, 118, 165–6, 173, 175–6
state of nature  *see*  Hobbes, Thomas
steroids  *see*  PEDS
Streep, Meryl  2–3, 8, 14, 76, 105, 183
Strikeforce  44, 64, 69, 78, 86, 98, 104–5, 126, 139, 145–8, 174–5

Telemachus  133
tournaments  17, 20–3, 63–4, 69, 153, 174–5

TRT (testosterone replacement therapy)  29–30, 43, 56–9, 63–70, 183
TUF (The Ultimate Fighter)  17, 22, 33–4, 43, 45, 47–50, 60, 90, 101, 118, 149, 184–5

unified rules  8, 25–6, 34, 76, 87–92, 98, 134, 155, 183
United States  23, 42, 48, 115, 121, 131, 146, 149
USADA (U.S. Anti-Doping Agency)  63, 70–1, 107, 132, 175, 180

Velasquez, Cain  7, 17, 28, 69, 91, 120, 123, 131
video games  18–21
the void  *see*  Musashi

War Machine (Jon Koppenhaver)  101–3
White, Dana  23, 26, 31, 37–8, 49–50, 58, 62, 66, 67, 70, 76, 79, 82–3, 90, 94–5, 97, 106, 110, 118, 120, 122, 124, 127, 129–30, 138–9, 141, 146–7, 153, 169–70, 172, 180, 182
WME-IMG (William Morris Endeavor-International Management Group)  5, 8–9, 26, 28, 31–2, 70–1, 88, 103, 112, 115, 121–2, 125–6, 131–2, 148, 183
World Extreme Cagefighting (WEC)  100, 139, 144, 169, 176
wrestling  55, 80, 98, 136–7, 150, 154–6, 159, 164, 170–1
WWE (World Wrestling Entertainment)  34, 53, 71, 142, 158–9, 161, 181

Xerxes  114

Zuffa  2, 5, 8, 26, 37, 70–1, 112, 115–6, 118–9, 121–2, 130, 134, 141, 144–5, 148, 152, 180, 183, 185

**195**

www.ingramcontent.com/pod-product-compliance
Ingram Content Group UK Ltd.
Pitfield, Milton Keynes, MK11 3LW, UK
UKHW042010140426
5217IPUK00015B/1096